FALKLANDS GUNNER

A DAY-BY-DAY PERSONAL ACCOUNT OF THE
ROYAL ARTILLERY IN THE FALKLANDS WAR

FALKLANDS GUNNER

A DAY-BY-DAY PERSONAL ACCOUNT OF THE ROYAL ARTILLERY IN THE FALKLANDS WAR

TOM MARTIN

Foreword by
Major General Julian Thompson, CB, OBE

FRONTLINE
BOOKS

FALKLANDS GUNNER
A Day-by-Day Personal Account of the Royal Artillery in the Falklands War

First published in 2017 by Frontline Books,
an imprint of Pen & Sword Books Ltd,
47 Church Street, Barnsley, S. Yorkshire, S70 2AS.

ISBN: 978-1-47388-121-1

Printed and bound in India by Replika Press Pvt. Ltd.
Typeset in 10/12 point Palatino

For more information on our books, please email: info@frontline-books.com,
write to us at the above address, or visit:
www.frontline-books.com

CONTENTS

Foreword

THE DESCRIPTION ON the dust jacket of Tom Martin's book *Falklands Gunner* says that 'The Royal Artillery played an absolutely vital, although often forgotten, part in the British armed forces' successful operation to re-capture the Falkland Islands in 1982'. It may have been forgotten by the media and the public, but not by those who took part. We know that without the gunners we would not have won – however bravely and skillfully the Marines, Paras, and other soldiers fought. Only devastatingly accurate and powerful fire missions on the enemy defensive positions enabled the infantry to close with, and overcome, well-sited Argentine soldiers among rocks and crags on the formidable objectives.

In many cases we were attacking positions held by units in equal, or greater, numbers than us, the attackers. Unlike air support, which is often not available, or impossible to employ because of darkness, rain or snowstorm, the artillery can provide support whatever the weather or time of day. Properly handled, as was the British artillery in the Falklands, it is on tap 24/7. It can be rapidly switched to engage new targets, and provided the ammunition supply is maintained, can sustain the support through the long hours of a battle.

This is a very personal story told by Tom Martin, a Command Post Officer of 29 (Corunna) Field Battery Royal Artillery. The battery was not part of the 3rd Commando Brigade, which I commanded, but joined us with 2nd Battalion The Parachute Regiment at Ascension in time to sail south with us – and very glad we were to see them too; we knew we were going to need all the artillery support we could get. The battery quickly fitted into the Commando Brigade, and after the landing at San Carlos on 21 May 1982, fired the first fire mission of the land campaign.

As a Command Post Officer, Second Lieutenant Tom Martin was with the guns throughout. Those unfamiliar with how the artillery in the British Army operates might be surprised that the most junior officers in the battery are in charge of the guns, their positioning, and their movement from gun position to gun position. This is because the battery commander is always with the commanding officer of the supported unit, or should be, providing artillery advice and working out the fire plan to assist that unit in achieving its mission. The other officers in the battery are employed as forward observation officers (FOOs), registering and adjusting targets, bringing down the fire where it is required.

To do this they must be well forward, where they can see the ground, and alongside the commander of the sub-unit they are supporting. This is contrary to the practice in many other armies, or was when I was serving. In these armies, the battery commander is with the guns, and the junior officers are forward. This can lead to confusion because the battery commander is not in direct touch with those he is supporting and is unable to make speedy and correct judgements on the priorities for fire missions and so forth.

One of the themes that runs through this excellent account is the uncertainty that surrounds war. Someone once described war as 'an exercise where the umpires don't turn up, and no one knows when it is going to end'. Hand-in-hand with this uncertainty is the discovery that routines that have been good enough on exercises may not prove to be adequate in war. Peacetime financial restraints may result in units being short of the requisite number of key people, so on exercise there may be only one person to do a job that requires three running a watch-keeping routine, which allows time for sleep, meals etc. Whereas on exercise, that one individual survives on bars of chocolate and no sleep; fine for about 48 hours, but over a protracted period the descent into a zombie-like state means that he can no longer do his job properly. He only gets away with it because the exercise has a known end date, and so muddles through by pacing himself and thus survives. Furthermore, without live ammunition on both sides including an enemy who shoots back, exercises lack the sharpness of war, and mistakes can be 'air brushed' out – no one gets killed. The uncertainty of war in contrast with an exercise also raises other unknowns, for example: 'When are we going home'.

The chaos of war is well described in Tom Martin's book. I am reminded of the words of a Second World War brigade commander addressing his brigade on the eve of the invasion of Normandy in June 1944: 'Gentlemen, do not be dismayed if chaos reigns; it undoubtedly will reign.'

The well-trained gunners of 29 (Corunna) Battery Royal Artillery worked through the chaos time and again to achieve their mission. They, along with their gunner comrades in the other batteries down south, were a major ingredient in the recipe for British success in the Falklands War of 1982. A well-known picture by the artists 'Snaffles' of guns dashing forward to support the infantry in the First World War is captioned: 'The guns, thank God, the guns.' That is what we thought too.

Major General Julian Thompson, CB, OBE
June 2017

Acknowledgements

I HAVE TRIED to write this book as a personal account; however, it became very clear to me from the outset that it is very much more than that, drawing on the collective memories of others that I served with, in order that as accurate record as possible of our experiences can be told.

Special mention must go to Bill Moore, who has very patiently and diligently helped me piece together both the narrative and the technical details. Bill's encouragement to chronicle my account for others, has spurred me to write and record events and memories before they are lost to posterity. I am also greatly indebted to David Gibbins, who has also given much of his time, particularly in helping to piece together the build up to our departure, as well as providing a critical overview. A fortuitous meeting between Bill and one of our number, brought a late addition to the team, in the name of Joe Walker. Joe was able to provide both colour and candour in helping to bring out the narrative. Through Joe's contacts, George Kirvell has contributed from a Gunner's perspective, which has helped to bring balance to my account.

I must thank Tony Rice, our Battery Commander, whose leadership and direction guided us through those hard days, as well as providing me with an overview of the bigger picture. I would also like to acknowledge Mike Seear, a Gurkha Officer, who was close by but never met, who both witnessed and wrote what we went through in our last position, of which I have drawn upon. I would like to thank the Young Officer's Wing of the Royal School of Artillery, Larkhill, along with the staff of 'Firepower – The Royal Artillery Museum' for their help in confirming some of the finer technical areas of Gunnery. I would like to thank Mark Khan, of Command Post Media, along with Martin Mace, publisher, and John Grehan, editor, both from Frontline Books, for their guidance and help to make this project a reality. Special thanks must go to the Falklands Veterans' Foundation and Karen Cole, who were instrumental in securing our small returning party's travel arrangements.

I am deeply indebted to my wife Jill, who has patiently allowed me the time and, not least for the endless cups of tea, to write this book and knowing how important it was for me to tell of our endeavours. Under normal circumstances, she would be the last to thank; however, I think it fitting to reserve that acknowledgement to all those members of the Battery not mentioned, for their hard won fighting spirit which was my inspiration, which saw us go off to war as individuals, but return as one.

Introduction

THE GUNNERS WERE involved in some way in almost every aspect of the Falklands War; however, little has been written regarding life at the gun-end. This is more of a personal account, which tells of my time as a very junior officer during the Falklands War, which I hope is an honest one. It is based on my diaries and notes taken at the time, which reflects events as they happened, not only from my recollection, but also of some of those that I served alongside. I did not do anything worthy of note, save only trying to do my job to the best of my ability. What I can claim, is that when a call for fire came in, that when I was on duty in the Command Post, that the Battery 'won the adjustment' in the overwhelming majority of fire missions and that all rounds landed where requested.

I kept two diaries of my time in the Falklands. The first was an office desk diary which I completed daily during the voyage south; the second was a war diary, again filled out daily both during the war, as well as the immediate aftermath, which included the return journey home. This was supplemented by my operational notebook which recorded details such as the gun positions and various orders.

As the Battery's junior officer, I was responsible for the Battery history and thought to keep various documents and papers for potential posterity, which have proved invaluable in the writing of this account.

What has not been covered here are the lessons learnt from our collective experiences during the War, from a post-operational stance, which were in the main hard fought. We learnt so much both as individuals and as a fighting Gun Battery, that it warrants a project in its own right; however, my intention was to record the events of my fellow Gunners and give them the recognition that they rightly deserve.

With hindsight, my journey into the Royal Artillery was rather circuitous and more of a means to an end and is outlined as follows.

After leaving Wrekin College in 1977, after what can only be described as disastrous 'A' Level results, something I was to rectify much later in life, I declared that I was going to embark on a military flying career, much to the surprise of my parents. I sought to find a career that offered 'professional' status, without any hope of gaining a university qualification and to make good the sacrifices that my parents had made towards my education. I was, up until that time, destined to carry on and follow my father as a Veterinary Surgeon and be the fourth generation to do so, spanning a period of some 100 years.

In November 1977 I attended the Officer and Aircrew Selection Centre, at RAF Biggin Hill, in order to sit the three-day aptitude tests and be medically assessed, on a Fleet Air Arm ticket. That reason being threefold. The first of these was, at that time, that the Army Air Corps did not recruit officer pilots directly into Sandhurst, save one per year. The second was that the shortest engagement in the RAF was twelve years and lastly it was just eight for the Fleet Air Arm. The concept of signing up for eight years, let alone twelve as an 18-year-old was almost beyond comprehension!

The selection process was, to say the least, attritional, with numbers falling at every turn. Having passed both the aptitude tests and medical, I finally went in front of the board to be told my fate. In the opinion of the board I'd done well at the tests; however, they saw me at that time as lacking in life experiences. The head of the board went onto say that I was in an incredibly competitive competition for places and that they were judging me against my peers at selection. The truth was that they were all to a man some three to four years older than me, all with degrees and all had spent their time at university in the University's Air Squadron. They had by default an existing track record with the RAF's recruiting process and were deemed a safe bet, compared to a callow youth, straight from school. The advice from the Group Captain was that I should go away, get a really dirty job, experience life and come back in two years, when they would almost certainly take me in.

Far from being too disheartened, I went away and soon found myself a job fitting the specification, working in a grain store, a few miles from home. The work was physically hard, handling thousands of tons of grain, drying and storing it in equal measures, mainly to be turned into animal feed of some description. I also soon learnt to be self-sufficient, teaching myself such skills as driving fork lifts, an 8-ton lorry and a JCB, as well a learning to weld. My two-year plan was almost at an end, when in the autumn of 1979, I had a change of direction and saw myself more as an aspiring helicopter pilot in the Army Air Corps (AAC); however, the reality was that at that time, as I was soon to find out, was that the AAC still didn't directly recruit their officers.

The AAC's policy was that they relied on officers coming into their fold after Sandhurst and having completed a three-year tour of duty first, before applying for the year-long Army Pilot's Course. The issue was that I was applying to join the Army on a three-year Short Service Commission (SSC), which would only see me to the end of my first tour; with that on the huge presumption was would get into Sandhurst in the first instance. The conundrum was addressed when the Recruiting Officer assured me that the SSC, whilst requiring a three-year return of service on commissioning, could be extended incrementally, to a maximum of eight years.

On hearing that news I asked the question, that if the AAC didn't recruit directly, who or what cap badge provided the most pilots? The Recruiting Officer took my question and promised to get back with an answer within the week. True to his word, I was called back into his office, where he told me that it was the Royal Artillery by cap badge, that provided the majority of Army pilots. I declared that 'if it's the Royal Artillery that provided the most, then get me into the Royal Artillery!'

In order to increase my chances at the Army Officer Selection Board in Westbury, Wiltshire, I joined the Royal Artillery as a Potential Officer in November 1979 at Woolwich, London. Passing both the course and selection at Westbury in early 1980, I went on to Sandhurst in May 1980 and was commissioned as a Second Lieutenant that December into the Royal Artillery. Royal Artillery Young Officer training followed and I was posted to 4th Field Regiment Royal Artillery, based in Aldershot, that Easter. On arrival, I was immediately dispatched to join 29 (Corunna) Field Battery Royal Artillery in Northern Ireland, which was two thirds of the way through its tour.

After leaving 4th Field, I achieved my goal of gaining my pilot's wings in the late spring of 1985 and was posted to the British Army of the Rhine, in Germany. In 1988 I transferred to the AAC, became a helicopter flying instructor, flew with the Royal Air Force, Royal Marines and Fleet Air Arm and retired from the Army in late 1997.

Whilst my journey to gain my pilot's wings took me via the Gunners, I feel very fortunate that my path took me via 4th Field Regiment and in particular 29 Battery. I cannot emphasise the debt of gratitude I have to those I served with during my time there, in particular to those in 'Corunna'; as the benchmarks and standards that were set, helped underpin my life and the values I retain.

I'm still flying today as an emergency services pilot, based in Southern England; it's a different coloured flying suit, but I'm still flying over the same areas as I served in and talking to the next batch of Air Traffic Controllers, as from my first days in aviation.

Tom Martin,
Somerset, 2017.

GLOSSARY AND ABBREVIATIONS

A–E	Guns 1-6
AA(A/A)	Anti-Aircraft
AAC	Army Air Corps
ACC	Army Catering Corps
Accom	Accommodation
Ack	Assistant
AD	Air Defence
ADAT	Army insurance scheme
Adjt	Adjutant
Adv	Advance
Ammo	Ammunition
Arg(ie)	Argentine
A/T	Anti-Tank
Avgas	Aviation Fuel
BC	Battery Commander/Battery Centre
Bde	Brigade
Bdr	Bombardier
Bivvie	Small low profile canvas tent
BK	Battery Captain, Battery Second in Command
Blowpipe	British shoulder launched AA missile
BMA	Brigade Maintenance Area
Bn	Battalion
Bofors	Anti-Aircraft Gun (40 mm)
BOS	Battalion Orderly Sergeant
BQMS	Battery Quartermaster Sergeant
BSM	Battery Sergeant Major
Bty	Battery
Buckshee	Free
C130	Hercules Transport Aircraft
Cabby	Free ride
Cam	Camouflage
CAP	Combat Air Patrol
Capt	Captain
Carts	Shell cases
CASEVAC	Casualty evacuation
C/A	Centre of Arc
CB	Counter Battery
Cdo	Commando
CEI	Communications Electronic Instruction
Cfn	Craftsman (REME)
Ch	Charge
Chalk	Flight detail
Cmb	Combat
CO	Commanding Officer
Coy	Company
Comd/Cmd	Command
Comms	Communications
Conv	Converge (concentrated fire)
Covers	Gun detachment member normally Bdr or L/Bdr
CP	Command Post
Cpl	Corporal
CPO	Command Post Officer
CPX	Command Post Exercise
C/S	Call sign
Cymbeline	High angle shell radar
Danger Close	Own shellfire within 50m

Def	Defence
Dets	Detachments
DF	Defensive Fire (target)
Dhobi	Laundry
Don 10	Communications cable
Ech/ech	Echelon
En	Enemy
ETA	Estimated Time of Arrival
Ex	Exercise
FAC	Forward Air Controller
FACE	Field Artillery Computer Equipment
FAME	Field Artillery Manual Equipment
Fd	Field
FDC	Fire Direction Centre
FFE	Fire For Effect
FFR	Fitted For Radio
FGA	Fighter Ground Attack
FM	Fire Mission
FN	Folding Butt 7.62mm similar to British issue SLR rifle
FOO	Forward Observation Officer
FPF	Final Protective Fire
Fwd	Forward
FUP	Forming Up Point
G1098	Miscellaneous stores
Gd(s)	Guard(s), Grid(s)
Gen	General
GLC	Gun Line Commander
Gleaming	Very Clean
Gnr	Gunner
GPMG	General Purpose Machine Gun
GP	Gun Position
GPO	Gun Position Officer
GR	(1/7) Gurkha Rifles
H1/2	Command Post 1/2
Harry Black	Strong masking tape
HE/He	High Explosive
Heads	Toilets (Navy slang)
Heli/Helo	Helicopter
Herc	C130
Hexi	Hexamine – Solid fuel blocks
HF	High Frequency
HQ	Headquarters
Illum	Illumination (round)
II-MM	Example of password
Inc	Include(d)
Inf	Infantry
Int	Intelligence
Jkt	Jacket
Kip(ping)	Sleep(ing)
Kip Sheet	Plastic/fabric sheet
L2	Type of grenade
L27	MT HE fuse
L32	Standard HE fuse
L/Bdr	Lance Bombardier
L/Cpl	Lance Corporal
L/R(LR)	Land Rover
LAD	Light Aid Detachment (REME)
LCU	Landing Craft Utility
LMG	Light Machine Gun (7.62mm)
LOG REP	Logistical Report
LOG REQ	Logistical Request
LSL	Landing Ship Logistic

Lt	Lieutenant
2Lt	Second Lieutenant
Maj	Major
MAPCO	Secure Code
Met	Weather
MFC	Mortar Fire Controller (Inf)
MG(g)	Machine-gun
Mils	17.77 Mils = 1 deg 6400 Mils = 360 deg
Mor(s)	Mortar(s)
MT	Mechanical Time (HE) [see VT]
NAAFI	Navy Army Air Force Institution (canteen/shop)
Nav	Navigator
NBC	Nuclear Chemical Biological (Warfare)
NCO	Non Commissioned Officer
Net	Radio Call sign grouping
NGF	Naval Gun Fire
NGFO	Naval Gun Fire Officer
Nirex	Stationary folder with plastic insert sheets
NGFS/NGS	Naval Gunfire Support
Nos	Numbers
NOK(in)	Next of Kin
No 1 Burner	Cooker
Obj	Objective
OC	Officer Commanding
Offr(s)	Officer(s)
O Gp	Orders Group
OP	Observation Point
OPDEM	Operational Demand
OPS	Operations
ORBAT	Order of Battle, i.e. Operation listing - persons/equipment
Pack How	Pack Howitzer (105mm)
PADS	Position and Azimuth Determination System
PARA	Parachute Regiment (Bn)
Pax	Personnel
Penthouse	9'x9' canvas frame tent for CP
Phos	Phosphorous (round)
Pinger	Anti-Submarine warfare (pilot)
Pipe	Ship's announcement
Pkt	Flight detail
Posn	Position
POW/PW	Prisoner of War
Priority Call	Dedicated First Response Fire Support to 'C/S'
Prox	Proximity (radar detonated HE round, explodes 10m above the ground)
PT	Physical Training
Pte	Private
Ptl	Patrol
Puritabs	Water purification tablets
P/word	Password
Q	See BQMS
QM	Quartermaster
QM(MAINT)	Quartermaster Maintenance
RA	Royal Artillery
RAP	Regimental Aid post
Rapier	RA Anti-Aircraft Missile
RAS	Replenishment at Sea
RATS/Rats	Rations (24 hour Arctic packs)
Rd(s)	Rounds
Recce/Recon	Reconnaissance
Ref	Reference
Regt	Regiment
REME	Royal Electrical and Mechanical Engineers

Replen	Replenish(ment)
Res	Reserve
Rg	Range
RHA	Royal Horse Artillery
RHQ	Regimental Headquarters
RM	Royal Marine(s)
RN	Royal Navy
RSA	Royal School of Artillery
RSM	Regimental Sergeant Major
RV	Rendezvous point
S	Super (Ch S = Charge Super)
SA	Small Arms
SAS	Special Air Service
Schermuly	2-inch parachute flare (Handheld)
Serial	Helicopter flight
SG	Scots Guards
Sgt	Sergeant
SSgt	Staff Sergeant
Sigs	Signals
SITREP	Situational Report
SLR	Self Loading Rifle (7.62mm)
Smk	Smoke (round)
SNCO	Senior Non Commissioned Officer
SMG	Sub-machine gun (9mm)
SMIG	Sergeant Major Instructor Gunnery
SOP	Standard Operating Procedure
Sp	Support
Spoiler	Ring placed on 105mm round
Stag	Period of duty
Stick	Passenger list
SUB	Gun Detachment (Guns 1-6)
Tab	Cross Country March (PARA)
TARA	Technical Assistant Royal Artillery
TAC(P)	Tactical Air Control (Party)
Tgt	Target
Tom	Parachute Regiment soldier (Private)
Tps	Troops
Trg	Training
TSM	Troop Sergeant Major
UCM	Under Command
UEO	Unit Enplanement Officer
Veh	Vehicle
Victor	Air to air refuelling tanker
Vulcan	'V' Force bomber
VT	Variable Time (HE) [as MT]
Weapons Tight	Air Defence State
WG	Welsh Guards
WO	Warrant Officer
Wpn(s)	Weapons
XPD	Expend
1/7 GR	1/7 Bn Gurkha Rifles
2IC	Second in Command
7.62mm	Small arms ammunition
40mm	Bofors ammunition
66mm	Light Anti-Tank Weapon
81mm	Mortar
84mm	Carl Gustav - Anti-Tank Weapon
105(mm)	Light Gun
155(mm)	Medium Howitzer
320	Clansman HF Radio
344	Clansman backpack radio
349	Clansman handheld radio

29 Battery - *Norland*

(All left to right)

Bow Rear (4) Bdr Imisson, Bdr McGovern, Gnr Jardine, L/Cpl Bailey
Front (4) L/Cpl Robinson, Pte Lee, Gnr Brown, Cfn Bracegirdle

Mid Rail Right (3) Gnr Porter, Gnr Simpson, Gnr Truswell
Lower Rail Right Rear (2) Sgt Bullock, Gnr Muir
Front (3) Bdr Phillips, Gnr Usher, Gnr Oliver
Mid Rail Left (4) Bdr Marsh, L/Bdr Woodgate, Gnr Horn, Gnr Kemp
Left Of Bell (2) Gnr Mackey, LBdr Powell
Rear (4) Gnr Love, Gnr Bell, Gnr Botterill, Bdr Armstrong K
Continued Right of Black Capstan (10) Bdr Hagan, Gnr Grierson, Gnr Oteh, Gnr Seed, L/Bdr McGoldrick, Gnr Martin, Gnr Hunter,
Gnr Darby, Gnr Frame, Gnr Muir F
Left From Rail (10) Gnr Haughton, Gnr Ramsey, Gnr Comlay, L/Bdr Dowden, Gnr Forbes, Gnr Crompton, Gnr McKenzie,
L/Bdr Owen, Bdr Armstrong P, Gnr Williams
Front (4) L/Bdr Handley, Gnr Ell, Gnr Finlay, Gnr Hadjicostas

Forward Left Corner Rear (4) Gnr Baxter, Gnr George, Gnr Kirvell, Gnr Morris
Middle (6) Gnr Earp, Gnr Cowley, Gnr Hughes, Gnr Wilkinson, Gnr Tottle, L/Bdr Murphy
Front Kneeling (4) Gnr Allen, Gnr Morris, L/Bdr Wyke, Gnr Straughan

Forward Right Corner Group   Rear (1) Gnr Darwin
Rear Standing (5) Gnr Rowe, Gnr Chilton, Gnr Gower, Gnr Herron, L/Bdr Butler
Front Standing (5) Gnr Miller, Gnr Armour, Gnr Wall, Bdr Armstrong G, Gnr Cleverly
Front Row Kneeling (2) Bdr Schofield, Gnr Shaw

Front Second Row Standing (7)
SSgt Mutter, Lt Moore, Capt Watson, WO2 Winch, Capt Ash, 2Lt Martin, WO2 Banton

Front Row Sitting (9)
Sgt Scott , Sgt Irvine, Sgt Dobson, Sgt Walker, SSgt McQueenie, Sgt Maxwell, Sgt Morgan, Sgt Taylor, Sgt Pelling

Battery History

TRADITION HAS IT that the most junior officer in the Battery, is to recite the Battery History on the anniversary of the battle wherever they be at that time. Being the junior officer that task fell to me and as such, I had copied it down into the back of my note book for possible future reference in Aldershot just prior to departure. This is the transcript:

The Battery was originally formed as Hislop's Company in 1755. After being stationed in Canterbury in 1802 the Company landed at Corunna in 1808, under Truscott's command (1805-1814), and joined the army advancing towards Salamanca. Napoleon's victories forced the army into withdrawal during which the Company formed part of the rear guard. Sir John Moore brought this army to Corunna and on the evening of 14 January began the embarkation onto the waiting transport ships.

The next day the French pushed back the rear guard and occupied the heights overlooking the British positions. Throughout the 15th the sick and wounded, along with most of the cavalry and all but a few of the artillery pieces, were embarked without interference by the French.

On the 16th the French attacked and met with some success, however the British infantry, with Truscott's guns in support, held firm and began to outflank the French. The latter, finding themselves under fire from both the front and the flank, started to withdraw, but the retreat soon turned into a rout. During the battle, Sir John Moore was killed. No pursuit was attempted and during the night and the following morning the remainder of the exhausted British army was embarked.

For this action as well as heroic efforts during the retreat, the descendants of the Company were, in 1936, allowed to assume the Battle Honour 'Corunna'.

Battery Composition

THE STANDARD FIELD artillery regiment is commanded by a Lieutenant Colonel, the 'CO'. He is supported by his senior non-commissioned officer, the Regimental Sergeant Major (RSM). Each regiment is made up of three Gun Batteries, with each Battery commanded by a Major, who is known as the Battery Commander, or 'BC' for short. The senior enlisted soldier in the Battery is the Battery Sergeant Major, which again is shortened to 'BSM'. The relationship between the BC and the BSM is exactly the same as that between the CO and the RSM, but one level down. The Battery's second in command is the Battery Captain, which in this case is shortened to that of 'BK', to avoid any confusion. Each gun battery is made up of six guns, split into two 'Troops' of three, which are also referred to as 'Sections' within artillery circles. These six guns (usually referred to as the Guns) are grouped together to form a Gun Position, which is commanded by a Lieutenant, known as the Gun Position Officer, or 'GPO' for short. On each Gun Position the command and control is provided by one of two Command Posts, each commanded by a Second Lieutenant, or Warrant Officer Class 2, both of which are referred to as Command Post Officers, or again – 'CPOs' for short.

The role of the artillery is to provide firepower to the battlefield in the form of fire support. In order to do this, the 'rule of three' is a way of understanding how this artillery support is provided. Ideally, each brigade has its own dedicated artillery regiment in direct support, with each battalion assigned its own Gun Battery. In terms of that support, the artillery regiment's Commanding Officer, provides artillery advice and support to the Brigade Commander. Similarly, at the next level down, the Battery Commander provides that same level of support to the Battalion's Commanding Officer.

In order to do that at Company level the battery 'splits', with the Battery providing three embedded Observation Parties, each commanded by a Captain, who is known as a Forward Observation Officer – or 'FOO'. The Battery has now split along operational lines, with the BC and his FOOs forward and embedded within the infantry, with their calls for fire support met by the Gun Position, towards their rear.

29 (Corunna) Field /Battery Royal Artillery
Officers and Warrant Officers

BC	Major Tony Rice RA (Tactical Headquarters, 2 Para)
BK	Captain David Gibbins RA (Battle Replacement, FAC 5 Brigade)
FOO	Captain James Watson RA (A Company, 2 Para)
FOO	Captain Bob Ash RA (B Company, 2 Para)
GPO	Lieutenant Bill Moore RA
CPO	Second Lieutenant Tom Martin RA

CPO   Warrant Officer 2 (Technical Sergeant Major) Trevor Banton
BSM   Warrant Officer 2 (Battery Sergeant Major) Bernie Winch

29 (Corunna) Field Battery Royal Artillery ORBAT

X	R3	R1	R5
Maj Rice	Capt Ash	Capt Watson	Sgt Bullock
Sgt Pelling	LBdr Dowden	Bdr Armstrong P	Bdr Phillips
LBdr McGoldrick	Gnr Comlay	Gnr Love	Gnr Muir
Gnr Seed	Gnr Haughton	Gnr Williams	Gnr Oliver
Gnr Oteh	Gnr Ramsey	Gnr Bell	Gnr Usher
Gnr Martin			

K	H1	G	J1
Capt Gibbins	2Lt Martin	Lt Moore	WO2 (BSM) Winch
	Bdr Marsh	Sgt Taylor	Sgt Irvine
	LBdr Woodgate	Gnr Hadjicostas	Bdr Imisson
	LBdr Powell	Gnr Horn	Gnr Hunter
	Gnr Finlay		
	Gnr Botterill		

H2	SVY	M	Q1
WO2 (TSM)Banton	LBdr Saxby	Sgt Maxwell	SSgt (BQMS)
Bdr Armstrong K	Gnr Mackey	Bdr Hagan	McQueenie BEM
LBdr Handley	Gnr Ell	Gnr Kemp	Gnr Jardine
Gnr Porter			
Gnr Brown			
Gnr Truswell			
Gnr Simpson			

	Q2	Q3	Q4
	Gnr Armour	Bdr Elsby	Bdr McGovern
		Sgt McGlinchey	Gnr Earp

A	B	C	D
Sgt Morgan	Sgt Walker	Sgt Sprotson	Bdr Armstrong
LBdr Wyke	Gnr Cowley	LBdr Murphy	LBdr Owen
Gnr Fowler	Gnr Kirvell	Gnr Baxter	Gnr Cowburn
Gnr Allen	Gnr Morris	Gnr Gowland	Gnr Frame
Gnr Grierson	Gnr Foster	Gnr Thompson	Gnr Rowe
Gnr Norris	Gnr Hughes	Gnr Tottle	Gnr Darwin
Gnr George	Gnr Rose	Gnr Straughan	Gnr Wall
		Gnr Wilkinson	

E	F	J2	PAY
LBdr Butler	Bdr Schofield	SSgt Mutter	LCpl Robinson

Gnr Forbes	LBdr Knight	Sgt Dobson	
Gnr Mckenzie	Gnr Darby		
Gnr Miller	Gnr Shaw	COOKS	REME
Gnr Crompton	Gnr Chilton	Sgt Scott	Sgt Jones
Gnr Herron	Gnr Wight	LCpl Bailey	Cpl Hildabrando
LBdr Dixon	Gnr Cleverly	Pte Lee	LCpl Giles
	Gnr Gower		Cfn Bracegirdle

The above list is a transcript, taken from the Battery's after-action report, detailing the Battery personnel as they deployed by sub-detachment. One individual, Gunner Frank Muir, is not listed, but was a member of C Sub. The ranks shown in the ORBAT are military abbreviations, which can be found in the Glossary. The sub-detachments were:

X	Battery Commander's Party
R1/3/5	Forward Observation Officers (FOO) Parties
K	Battery Second in Command
J1	Battery Sergeant Major's Party
H1/2	Command Post
G	Gun Position Officer's Party
SVY	Survey Party
M	Signals Party
Q1/2/3/4	Quartermaster's Parties
A to F	Gun Detachments
J2	Battery Guides
PAY/COOKS/REME	Support Parties.

The Battery strength on deployment was 111 all ranks, consisting of:

Officers	6
Warrant Officers	2
Staff Sergeants	2
Sergeants	12
Bombardiers	11
Lance Bombardiers	15
Other Ranks	63

The Battery was split down during the initial deployment as follows:

2 Para's Advance Reconnaissance Party	1
Norland	93
Europic	17

Once ashore, the Battery deployed into its operational groupings:

Forward Observation Parties	21
Gun Position	90

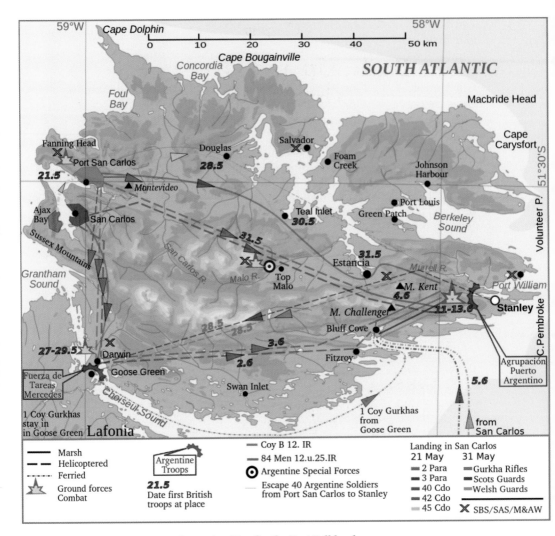

Campaign Map for the East Falkland

Chapter 1

The Build Up and Deployment to The Falklands

DAILY NOTES WERE taken throughout the day, rather than as a single entry, hence their staccato format, and recorded in my 'desk' diary, of which the transcript for each day is shown below. Additional diary entries were also made, but may not have been written on that particular day, but were, nevertheless, contemporaneous. All these diary entries are shown in italics. Normal text provides either clarification, explanation or relevant anecdotes.

March 1982
9–11 March, Regt CPX
These few days were taken with training, by means of a Regimental Command Post Exercise, on the Regiment's parade square at our barracks in Aldershot, in order to reinforce and sharpen our drills prior to live firing.

15 March, Regt Ex & Live Firing, Bde Ex
The Regiment then departed to Salisbury Pain to put the whole Regiment through its paces with a Regimental Exercise, which led on to conducting artillery live firing for the Guns. This was immediately followed by a Brigade Exercise.
19 Mar – Argentine 'scrap merchants' land on South Georgia - raise Argentine Flag.

22/3 March – Start support to RSA
4th Field Regiment's support to the Royal School of Artillery (RSA) at Larkhill was due to the change-over of the School's dedicated support unit. Whilst this change went ahead, the School's training program continued, with the full range of courses being run. As a Light Gun Regiment, we were an obvious choice, being relatively close by in Aldershot; however, the deployment could not be run from there on a daily basis and we set up at Tilshead's transit/training establishment in Westdown Camp, right in the middle of Salisbury Plain.

Westdown Camp is both isolated and Spartan and in late winter and early spring offers a bleak existence. Little did we appreciate at that time, as to the importance of this deployment and how we were to draw upon it in the months to come. There's an old Army adage which simply says 'train hard – fight easy', of which the first element of it was certainly tested.

April 1982
2 April – Argentinian forces invade Falklands, British Marines surrender in Stanley.
3 April – South Georgia and Sandwich Islands seized by Argentina.
5 April – British Armada sets sail for Falklands.
8 April – RSA support ends.
9 April – leave starts.

The news of the day was dominated by both the political furnace that was the Argentine invasion of the Falkland Islands and the diplomatic efforts to curry favour on the world stage. Support fell on party lines, with the Spanish speaking world of Central and South America aligning themselves with Argentina and with the Unites States standing beside the United Kingdom. Not least in the news and of most relevance to us, was the monumental military effort, set by the Prime Minister – Margret Thatcher, to deploy a Task Force and retake the islands.

The Task Force's fighting troops were predominately to come from 3 Commando Brigade Royal Marines (3 Cdo Bde RM), consisting of 40, 42 and 45 Commandos; augmented with its dedicated supporting arms and services: 29 Commando Regiment Royal Artillery (29 Cdo Regt RA), 59 Commando Squadron Royal Engineers, 3 Commando Brigade Air Squadron (3 BAS) and various other Brigade assets. It was quickly established that three fighting units was not sufficient for the task and an extra infantry battalion was desperately needed. At that time, and as a legacy from the troubles in Northern Ireland, the Army had one infantry battalion in rotation on standby, which was known as 'Spearhead', with one company at twenty-four hours' notice, with the remainder following on within three days. The Spearhead Battalion at that time was the 3rd Battalion, Parachute Regiment (3 Para), which was based in Bulford, and was added to the Brigade's fighting strength. On 9 April, 3 Para sailed with the Commando Brigade on the SS *Canberra*, following the Task Force that had sailed a few days earlier. Vying for consideration was the 2nd Battalion, Parachute Regiment (2 Para), which was at that time in the role as the Leading Parachute Battalion Group (LPBG). 29 (Corunna) Field Battery Royal Artillery (29 Bty RA) as part of 2 Para's grouping, was in Direct Support and as such was an integral part of the Battalion's fighting strength.

The LPBG was in essence the Government's military 'firefighters', who were on five days standby to deploy to anywhere in the world. We were trained and scaled for operations and ready to go with immediate effect – and being such a balanced force, saw ourselves as strong contenders for deployment. Little did we know of how the minds of our leaders in Whitehall worked, as the explanation of our non-inclusion was that we weren't being sent, just in case we might be needed should a crisis develop!

Robert Fox, in his book *Eyewitness Falklands* throws a different light onto how 2 Para and ourselves were sent to join the Task Force. At that time, Fox was a reporter and was assigned to cover the conflict at short notice, coming therefore into frequent contact with senior officers. He describes 2 Para's inclusion as somewhat of a mystery. He tells of their CO, Lieutenant Colonel 'H' Jones, as being on holiday, deciding to return to England and lobby the Ministry of Defence for 2 Para's inclusion, presumably on the strength that we were the LPBG. He cites that 'H' successfully managed to make his case and unlike the other fighting units already sent, brought with him his own integral artillery and engineering support.

Needless to say, that throughout this period, the talk amongst us all in the Officers Mess, along with the more senior members of the Battery, was of the military build-up and the possible scenarios that could take place, in the weeks to come. Every newspaper article and news bulletin were avidly digested, as we tried to reason amongst ourselves what might happen. There was one thing that was not disputed and that was the fact that most had absolutely no idea where the Falkland Islands were and if they did, had no idea of what they looked like. I was one of the few who had any inkling of what or where these islands were, solely down to the fact that my father's brother, Nib, had emigrated out to Argentina in the late 1950s. He went out to work on a very large estancia (farm) for an international British based food company, predominantly rearing beef; and worked his way up to managing one of these vast farmsteads, of approximately 100,000 acres. Having settled, he married a local girl and raised two sons. The irony was not lost on the whole family that had Nib and his wife Yolanda had children a few years earlier, that their eldest would have been of conscription age and could easily have been 'playing for the other side'. Nib recounted after the war that the substantial English ex-pat community, whilst left in relative peace out in the countryside, felt that their mail was being intercepted by the military Junta and were being watched from afar.

Lieutenant Colonel Tony Holt RA, the Commanding Officer (CO) of 4th Field Regiment Royal Artillery (4 Fd Regt RA), held a Regimental Parade on the main parade square. Whilst it's traditional for a CO to address his Regiment at the 'end of term', this was different, as the unfolding events, were far from normal. He was to brief all pre-leave on the situation and assure the Regiment that 'this is purely a Commando operation and that we will not be involved. Go away, enjoy your leave and I'll see you all when we get back after Easter'. Major Tony Rice, 29 Battery's Battery Commander (BC), on the other hand, firmly believed that the Battery would be involved in proceedings before too long and before the men were dismissed he ordered a Battery Parade at Corunna's lines.

Tony Rice joined the Battery soon after we returned from Northern Ireland into a role that he was already familiar, having previously served in 7 Parachute Regiment Royal Horse Artillery (7 Para RHA) and knew the Airborne world well. Tall and slimly built, with a deep voice and laconic style, Tony was a direct, uncompromising no-nonsense leader. He trained his battery thoroughly and relentlessly and this was to deliver dividends during the campaign. When the 'BC' spoke, in his deliberate and measured tones, everybody listened, leaving every one of us in no doubt where we stood, or what was expected of us. That said, he was fair and fully backed his team. Tony's hawkish standpoint was simply: we go where 2 Para go.

Notwithstanding the fact that we were on standby within the LPBG, Tony Rice ordered a full checklist of all stores and equipment, ordering deficiencies to be filed with the Quartermaster's departments prior to departure. He briefed us on the real possibility of our involvement as a

Battery and that we were to confirm our contact details prior to going on leave.

12 April – British impose 200-mile-wide war zone.
13 April – To Shropshire
After spending a few days in the Mess and with Jill Harrison, my girlfriend and a Lieutenant in the Women's Royal Army Corps, at her parents' house in Pirbright, we headed north to my parents' home in Shropshire, which is located on the northern outskirts of Wellington, on the edge of Telford.

15 April - The Regiment was warned for operations in the South Atlantic.
16 April – Recalled to barracks over Falkland crisis – 'Pegasus'.
'Pegasus' was the code-word sent out to all personnel for our recall to barracks. One must remember that communication back in 1982 predated the instantaneous world of the internet and mobile phones that we live in now and that it took time for the message to get through to some. The primary method was by telephone and/or telegram, but it was not uncommon to ask the local Police Force to pass on the message. The main recall went out on Saturday the 17th, with all returning by early evening the following day, many from as far afield as the North East.

Gunner Frame was a nineteen-year-old member of D Sub (Gun Detachment) and on Rear Party duties when the recall began: 'I was on guard duty in Aldershot. They sent the telegrams out with the password Pegasus and we had to get back within twenty-four hours. The buzz was unbelievable, the adrenaline and testosterone. We knew something was coming off. It was big and we were going be the first ones out there.' His first wife of just five weeks was devastated at the news, 'we were setting up a new life together and I was off to war'.

It was during the early hours of the 16th at my parents' home that I proposed to Jill. It was at 11:00 that morning that I took the very brief telephone call, calling me back, and I immediately packed to return to Aldershot. I bade my farewells and was back in barracks by mid-afternoon. Jill followed on and drove over to her parent's house, some five miles from Aldershot and waited for me there. I broke the news to Tony Rice, who arranged for me to formally see the CO as protocol dictated, as soon as he was available. Despite the developments with our forthcoming deployment, the CO found time to see me and granted me permission to marry.

After seeing the CO, I was given a few hours' grace and made my way over to Pirbright to formally see Jill's father. After a very quick celebration, I had to say my goodbyes and drove back to camp. A few days later, I was once again granted a few hours off camp, when Jill and I went into Aldershot to find a ring. Needs must in extremis and we found a ring, albeit far from spectacular, after all I was on a Second Lieutenant's wage. I made the promise to replace it one day 'with a proper one', which she held me to!

Sergeant Joe Walker, B Sub's Number 1 (the gun detachment's commander), was from the North East, where a significant number of the Battery hailed from and his story was typical of the recall: 'Once we eventually went on leave, my family and I went up North, to Seaham, Co, Durham. On receipt of the telegram, I left Denise and our two daughters and returned to camp, being on station within a few hours.

'To be honest, active service is what you train for. The chances of going are few and far between, but when it comes around it's what you want. We didn't know where the Falklands were, but we knew we had a responsibility to them. At the time a lot of patriotism kicked in'.

Whilst a significant number of the Battery hailed from the North East, some came from the opposite end of the country, one being Gunner George Kirvell, whose roots were in the South West. Gunner Kirvell was a nineteen-year-old member of Sergeant Walker's B Sub and among the Battery's younger cohort, who told of his recall to Aldershot: 'I was on leave and back home in Plymouth. At the time, I knew something going at place called the Falklands, but like most people I didn't know where it was.' The appreciation of 'what', but not 'where' was typical of the majority of the Regiment's gunners at that time.

George Kirvell continued: 'What I remember the most is, I was having a typical night out drinking with my brother and Dad. He had served during the Second World War, in North Africa and Normandy and was then also aged nineteen or twenty. We were in local pub near to where we lived and at some point during the night the local Police Officer, who my Dad knew, came in looking for me. He told me I had to return to camp and he gave a telegram with 'Pegasus' on it, which was the recall word. Anyhow, my Dad said that he and my Mum, would drive me back to Aldershot the next day and then he proceeded to get me very drunk. I can only presume that he knew what the future had in store, but I was obviously "oblivious" when my Dad said goodbye to me at camp. He offered me a piece of advice which was, if the ships get attacked I was to make my sure I was on deck and not down below; so I would at least have a chance to swim for it, if my ship was hit and started sinking!'

19 April – *Argentine sub* Santa Fe *sunk at South Georgia.*
The week was, to say the least, rather busy. Captain David Gibbins, the 'BK' and the Battery's second in command and his staff chased up, through 2 Para, all stores requisitions and issued equipment as and when it arrived. David joined the Battery after his Para training, having served predominantly in Germany, both in Air Defence and more latterly in Field Artillery with 49 Field Regiment. Now, as the Battery's senior Captain, the Unit's administration was a prime function of his position and it was an area that he excelled in. David's eye for detail and meticulous planning, ensured that our needs were met, which at times challenged his dry sense of humour.

It became very clear to us, as more and more information came to light on the Falkland Islands, that our temperate clothing was not suitable nor fit for purpose and to that end Arctic clothing was ordered. One item of equipment that did arrive in time was the new style of military bergen. The old '58 Pattern' webbing's large pack, whilst called that, was far too small to carry what was required. The new bergen was based on a new style metal frame, was considerably bigger, but still aimed at a temperate theatre. Getting all one's Arctic clothing, rations and ammunition packed would be a challenge later on and compromises had to be made. Time was spent out on the ranges zeroing our personal weapons, as well as preparing the Command Posts (CP) and guns. The biggest challenge that week was getting to grips with the new Clansman radio system and that task fell to Sergeant John Maxwell, as the Signals Sergeant, and his assistant Bombardier Malcolm Hagan. They arrived in pallets on the back of a 3-ton lorry and were unloaded outside the signals store. The delivery grew a crowd of onlookers, who were eager to see what all the fuss was about. The consensus was it looked like we had been issued with something that actually worked! These new radios were generally a fraction of the size of the old ones, with the back pack radio using the same metal frame as the new bergen. The Clansman used a dial-up frequency selector, so anybody with minimal training could work it, which is in complete contrast to the old black art of the 'frequency tuning' required with the old sets. The unexpected bonus was to be found in the, when the team removed the old bulky equipment, freeing up valuable space in the back of the CP land rover.

Behind the scenes, David Gibbins as BK worked very closely with Captain David Wood, 2 Para's Adjutant, in his capacity as the Battery UEO (movement officer), on the embarkation plan. It was identified that the guns, vehicles and stores, along with a small maintenance party, would be loaded on the MV *Europic Ferry*, at Southampton, with the main body sailing on the *Norland*. The *Europic Ferry* was a relatively small Ro-Ro ferry taken up from trade – STUFT. She had a red hull, with a white superstructure and came in at some 4,000 tons, gross weight. She was 450ft long with a 70ft beam. The BK went straight down to Southampton to meet with the ship's Captain, Chris Clarke, to discuss the loading plan. In true BK fashion, David identified the need for additional washing machines! Captain Clarke's solution was for a Portacabin to be bolted onto the deck, with a whole suite of washer/dryers hooked up.

The subject of entertainment was also brought up and left in the hands of the Captain. By the time David was to embarked, VCRs, videos and paperbacks appeared, some donated willingly from local shops. Being a STUFT ship by its very definition, meant that there was no natural link, or line of communication with the Navy and as such, STUFT ships were assigned a small Naval Party to act as the conduit. On the *Europic*, that fell to Naval Party 1720, under the command of Commander A. B. Gough RN.

20 April

Easter Leave ended at 14:00 hours, with the balance of the Regiment parading at their respective Battery Lines. Whilst our recall wasn't a secret in any way, one or two individuals were surprised to see 29 Battery in the full swing of preparations and were oblivious to our recall. It is easy to forget in today's world of instantaneous news, just how easy it was to be kept out of the loop.

22 April

Throughout this build up period, the BC was heavily involved in the planning that was taking part at 2 Para. The background administrative work was done by the BK which left the BC to concentrate on the operational planning, knowing that getting both everybody and everything embarked was well in hand. Tony Rice gave his parting instructions and leaves the Battery to fly directly to Ascension, as part of 2 Para's 'R' (reconnaissance) Group.

At 17:00 hours that afternoon, David was in Southampton and checking up on the preparations, when he received confirmation that the *Europic* was to sail at 06:00 hours the next morning. He put in a quick phone call back to Aldershot, in order to get the Battery's six 105mm Light Guns, their One Tonne vehicles and stores, along with the maintenance party, down to the docks for loading as soon as possible. David wasn't expecting this turn of events and had to rush back to Aldershot and pick up his kit, before returning. Thankfully, his journey took him past Winchester and David was able to visit his parents and say goodbye. When he returned back to the *Europic*, loading was well under way and continued right through the night, almost up until the point of sailing.

23 April

The mad rush to get everything loaded and working through the night, had taken its toll and everybody had crashed in their bunks just before they left Southampton. They were to be told later of the crowds of well-wishers waving as they sailed. Loaded on board were 29 Battery's six guns, vehicles and stores, under the command of the BK, who now acted as OC Troops, the senior military person on board, along with a small seventeen-man maintenance party. Leading the gun team was Sergeant Sprotson, assisted by Lance Bombardier Knight, along with Gunners Cowburn, Dixon, Foster, Gowland, Norris, Thompson and Wight. Lance Bombardier Saxby was there to look after the survey and command post Land Rover and equipment. Assisting David with the Battery's stores and equipment were Sergeant McGlinchey, Bombardier Elsby and Gunner Earp. The last members of this team were our REME section of Sergeant Jones, Corporal Hilderbrando and Lance Corporal Giles.

Also embarked were three Scout helicopters and a detachment from 656 Squadron Army Air Corps under Captain John Greenhalgh, along with members and equipment from a Field Hospital, which included Captain Mike von Bertele, who later caught up with 3 Para, as their doctor. It was most fortuitous in having Mike von Bertele on board, as he was able to bring everybody up to speed with First Aid Training. Stored below were 2 Para's equipment, fuel and ammunition, along with approximately 1,000 tons of artillery ammunition.

The reason for the mad rush and pressure to sail was soon explained, as the *Europic* was required to conduct a 'compass swing' calibration and sailed just around the coast to the Naval Base at Portland to complete it. It also provided an opportunity for the Naval liaison officer to sort out the fleet communications. David was informed around 17:00 hours that they would be sailing at 06:00 hours the following morning. In his capacity as OC Troops, David took the decision to grant the embarked troops a final 'run ashore', with strong words of advice of what would happen if not back by midnight.

'There were three officers on board,' recalled David Gibbins, 'me, John Greenhalgh the pilot and Mike von Bertele, 3 Para's Doc. We rang up Portland and stated that three Captains were alongside and would happily entertain three ladies for dinner that evening! Arrangements were made, especially as the Navy female officers thought we were Navy Captains. A good night was had by all, especially as Doc's brother ran a local wine bar. We missed the second tearful farewell from Blighty as we were all sleeping it off'.

24 April
Back in Aldershot we were ready to go in all respects and had said our goodbyes. We paraded in accordance with the movement instruction and awaited the arrival of the coaches. After what seemed to be an eternal wait, word finally came through that the *Norland* wasn't ready for us and that we were to be stood down for twenty-four hours. After handing our weapons back into the armoury, we dispersed back to our respective accommodation, with those married personnel going home to their families. With Jill only being five miles down the road in Pirbright, I was granted clearance to see her, but was required back by 23:59 hours.

25 April – British forces (RM) invade and recapture South Georgia.
We paraded as instructed and once again we were again stood down, following the same routine as before. The reason given was exactly the same and we again dispersed, but with the caveat that things could change and that those living off camp had to remain contactable at all times. Again, I managed to get the all clear to see Jill, who along with her parents, was most surprised to see me at the door.

Chapter 2
Sailing South

Monday, 26 April (D-25)
South Georgia capture completed. Set sail south on SS Norland *at 1300 hrs from Portsmouth. Sea very calm. Practice RAS with* Grey Rover. Intrepid *joined us off Portland Bill. Tested rear heli pad. A day for settling in and looking about. (clocks back 1 hr at midnight)*

Eventually the coaches arrived at Lille Barracks, to take us the Naval Docks in Portsmouth. The weather was fair and mild, with cloudy sunshine and spirits were high as we finally boarded the coaches. Considering that final farewells were made on the first occasion, some found the 'get on the bus ... get off the bus' scenario most frustrating, not only for members of the Battery, but for families as well. Part of the reason was that the requisitioned STUFT ship – MV *Norland*, under the command of P&O's Captain M. Ellerby, had to be converted from a North Sea ferry to a troop ship, which required the construction of two helicopter landing pads; along

On arrival at the docks on 26 April, we were issued our individual *Norland* boarding cards, detailing our cabin and assembled area. On the reverse is the deck layout particular to the cabin number. Also shown is James Watson's British Forces Identity Card, the reverse of which sets out instructions for use if captured, with the stark phrase 'Tear off duplicate portion and hand to interrogator. GIVE NO OTHER INFORMATION'.
(Courtesy of James Watson)

BRITISH FORCES IDENTITY CARD		F/IDENT/189 (Rev. 11/78)
(issued in compliance with the provisions of Article 17 of Geneva (POW) Convention 1949)		
Service No. 499787	Rank CAPT	Date of Birth 01 JAN 1956
Surname WATSON		
Forenames JAMES NICHOLAS EDWARD		

BOARDING CARD
Please have your ticket and boarding card ready.
NORTH SEA FERRIES :

ROTTERDAM – HULL
(EUROPOORT)

THIS PORTION TO BE SURRENDERED ON EMBARKATION

BERTH NUMBER 1014
ASSEMBLY STATION SNUG BAR.
'B' & 'C' DECK (Special Cabins)

with the fact that nobody seemed to understand the logistics of what was involved, in making the conversion. It was very much a case of left hand and right hand failing to communicate, hence the frustration.

Work commenced on the flight decks in Hull, but in order to prevent any unnecessary delays in completion, the work was carried out as the ship sailed from Hull to Portsmouth and was finished just prior to docking in Portsmouth. The *Norland* had a black hull, with the words 'NORTH SEA FERRY' on its sides, a white superstructure and came in at some 13,000 tons gross weight. She was 562ft long with an 83ft beam and what was being asked of her was a world away from her normal Hull - Rotterdam routine.

By the time we had reached Portsmouth most were sat in quiet contemplation. The mood was quickly broken on arrival, when we first sighted the *Norland*, with the Battery Sergeant Major (BSM) gripping the embarkation proceedings. Our BSM was Warrant Officer 2 Bernie Winch and he was the senior non-commissioned member of the Battery, who in barracks was the BC's right hand man.

The quayside was a hive of activity and no time was lost in getting on board. Despite embarking to go off to war, North Sea Ferries issued each and every one of us a standard 'Rotterdam–Hull' boarding card, detailing our berth and designated assembly area, importantly it had a deck map. We were allocated our bunks, the officers two to a cabin, with Captain James Watson and Lieutenant Bill Moore sharing, in cabin 1014 as the 'singlies', with Captain Bob Ash and I as the 'pads' in cabin 1009, which importantly for me had a porthole. The terms 'singlies' and 'pads' refers to one's marital status and as I was now engaged, I was effectively married off, with the term 'pad' the name referring to a married quarter.

Also noted on our boarding cards was our designated assembly station, which was the upper aft Snug Bar. Bob Ash was the senior Captain and Forward Observation Officer (FOO) and was the taller of the two forward observers. He was lithe and athletic, with a dry wit and a passion for tennis. Bob's stand out quality was his mellow take on life and laid-back approach, making him very easy company. James Watson was equally athletic, also enjoyed tennis and was also a keen hockey player. James's sharp, dry sense of humour worked in tandem with Bob's and the two of them were equally matched. The only difference being that James was more urbane and saw himself as the most eligible and sociable officer in the Battery.

Bill Moore was the senior Lieutenant and the Battery's Gun Position Officer (GPO), who as such, was responsible for all matters tactical and technical on the position. Bill was a graduate officer and talented sportsman, having already represented the Gunners at rugby and cricket, whilst at university. He transitioned from being one of the Command Post Officers (CPO) to GPO prior to the Northern Ireland tour some twelve months earlier, when I joined the Battery as a CPO.

The position of GPO is somewhat unique in the Army, in that on operations, the numbers under command are similar to that of an infantry company, with the level of responsibility expected of a far more senior rank, with the GPO setting the tone and temperament on the position. Bill was

Portsmouth dockside from the *Norland*'s rail, with 'Corunna's' families waving goodbye, 26 April 1982.

Para-trained and Airborne through and through, a natural leader, whose measured and deliberate leadership style, backed up with a solid tactical and technical depth of knowledge, sat well with the Gunners. Bill had high standards and rightly expected the same from everyone else and failing to not live up to them was not an option. It was clear from those early days that Bill was destined for higher command, rising to the rank of Major General and was awarded the CBE for his services, as well as holding the post of Master-General of the Ordnance, shortly before his retirement.

The Warrant Officers and Sergeants were allocated between two to four per cabin, depending on seniority. With the junior ranks being in the majority, four to a cabin was the norm. All the cabins were of a typical ferry standard, with four berths, a shower, sink and toilet and were not designed for a lengthy time at sea. After dumping kit, which for the majority due to the lack of space was in the shower cubicle, we all, to a man, went out onto the rail to watch the farewells and general proceedings.

Sergeant Joe Walker sets the scene once embarked: 'In my cabin there was Staff Sergeant John McQueenie, Sergeant Ernie Dobson, me and a Sergeant from 2 Para, who was a sniper, but I can't remember his name.'

The time came to slip the moorings and the ship shuddered as the propellers started to turn. We slipped away from the docks and passed through the forts, crammed with well-wishers, acting as sentinels at the harbour's mouth.

'I will never forget leaving from Portsmouth on board the *Norland* and actually seeing my family on the quayside.' Continued Joe Walker. 'We left them many times, sometimes for six-month Northern Ireland tours, but this felt very different.'

As the *Norland* turned to starboard and into the Solent, the ship keeled over to port and I had to go and lie down! After a short 'rest' I took my camera up onto the rear flight deck, where I captured the thin outline of southern England on the distant horizon, at the end of what seemed a very long wake. I thought at the time that this may well be my last look at 'Blighty'. As we entered the Channel, the ship rolled and I once again retired to my bunk.

Like *Europic*, the *Norland* was also assigned a Naval Party, with Lieutenant Commander C. Esplin-Jones RN commanding *Norland*'s Naval Party. The small Royal Naval detachment had the task of looking after our interests whist at sea and acted as our conduit to the Task Force. Whenever there were any messages to be passed, or news to tell during the day, it was broadcast, or 'piped' over the ship's main broadcast (tannoy). Pipes were generally both monotone and short and to the point, but attempts were made to 'lighten' them as time went on. As we sailed south, one of the naval ratings charged with making pipes, tried to put a 'Hi Di Hi campers' spin on them, which was always met with a universal grown. This individual was to be known as 'The *Norland* Nancy', reinforcing a soldier's stereotypical views of sailors. What did go down well much later, were 'Rule Britannia' and 'Ride of the Valkyries', the Para's regimental quick march.

After only a few hours sailing we met up with one of the Royal Fleet Auxiliary's (RFA's) fleet tankers, *Grey Rover* and practiced replenishment at sea (RAS) drills, which drew quite a crowd. Here, various ropes are fired over from the tanker, to both enable a fuel line to be passed, as well as a stores line. The ships gently converge until almost side by side, when they take up a parallel course for the duration of the procedure. There is a real

Last view of England coming out of the Solent, 26 April 1982.

danger of the ships colliding, as there's a critical distance between them, which if crossed, causes both ships to be sucked together. This evolution was like nothing I'd seen before. My limited maritime experiences of cross-Channel ferries had seen ships stay as far apart from each other as possible, so to have one in almost touching distance was quite a sight. The added-bonus was that it kept my mind of the fact that I was well and truly at sea.

Shortly after 'RASing', *Norland* was joined by a helicopter, which christened the rear flight deck. The officers were afforded a bird's eye view of proceedings, as the rear windows of our lounge bar overlooked this aft flight deck. We were well versed in helicopter operations and it didn't raise much interest, but I enjoyed both the spectacle, as well as the view outside. On completion, I, like everyone else, set about exploring *Norland*'s decks, passageways and stairwells in the hope of gaining some form of orientation. As the afternoon wore on, I couldn't face the thought of eating and felt somewhat queasy. That evening in the bar, we made our introductions and/or caught up with old friends, before I retired for a very poor night's sleep. I thought to myself: 'if it's this bad now, what will it be like later?'

The top rear bar and lounge, called the Snug Bar was allocated as the Officers Mess, and was run on a standard chit basis. Uniform was the order of the day; however, after 1800 planters rig (shirt and tie, no jacket) was the norm, unless on duty. It also doubled up as a classroom(s), once the myriad of lectures began. The Warrant Officers and Sergeants had a separate bar and the Junior Ranks had the Continental Lounge as their recreational space.

Tuesday, 27 April (D-24)

At 08:00 we were 150 miles off land. By midnight we hope to be out of the Bay of Biscay. Practice abandon ship drills. Sea a little bit choppy but still reasonably calm. Under a gale warning (Force 6). Felt a bit bad around 2000. Perked up and retired at 2330. A very much needed night's sleep.

To say that I wasn't a good sailor would have been a huge understatement and talk of the generally unforgiving conditions in the Bay of Biscay left me feeling completely underwhelmed. I struggled to face a cup of tea and a slice of toast for breakfast and throughout the morning, took to my bunk as often as possible. I couldn't face lunch and spent that time out on deck, trying my hardest to come to terms with my lot.

The first order of the day, as far as the RN were concerned, was that we practiced our 'Action Stations'/abandon ship drills; not only in the event of a maritime emergency, but also if we came under enemy attack. On the pipe, individuals were required to return to their accommodation, pick up their 'sea kit', before mustering to their assault stations. The sea kit was essentially your combat jacket and a warm hat, along with anything else you could fit into your pockets, in the event of taking to the lifeboats. The first drill was dire, mainly down to most being disorientated and it took some fifteen minutes to close up, whereas we were expected to complete the drill in under two minutes. Predictably, the Navy was furious. Nobody had grasped the concept of what was trying to be achieved and the Navy expected us to react as if we were sailors and were very unhappy with our performance. Clearly there was a disconnect of expectation and reality, but when it was pointed out that we were actually soldiers, and not sailors, the Naval party promised to try and understand, but was still insistent that there would have to be a huge improvement all round. Needless to say, that we would carry out numerous drills on a daily basis, often at the most inopportune moment.

By the time of the evening meal I felt empty and whilst not relishing the thought of eating, knew that I had to try and eat something. Due to the large number embarked, the messing arrangements were particularly tight. The officers had a sectioned off area of the main restaurant and took three sittings to get everybody through. Having missed lunch, I sought to get into the first sitting and after an hour found myself at the serving counter. The heat and smell of the food, not helped by the fact that I'd been stood swaying in the queue, triggered my nausea and I made a dash for fresh air and the ship's rail. After five minutes or so, I managed to compose myself and rejoined those queuing for the second sitting. Again, after about an hour, I found myself at the front and once again, the nausea returned as soon as I was faced with fare on offer. Again, I rushed topside and once more tried to regain my composure. For the third and last time, I found myself at the front of the queue and for the third time I made my topside for some fresh air. I was both hungry and nauseous in equal measures, the only certain thing was that I would have nothing to eat that night. The irony was that during all my time on board, that I was never physically sick; there was plenty of retching in those early days, but as I'd eaten so little, there was nothing to show. Looking back now, I think those early days were the lowest I felt throughout my whole time away.

It was our first full day at sea and it was evident to those trying to organise training, that there was a chronic shortage of space. Being a North Sea Ferry, *Norland* was designed for the daily run over the North Sea and catered for her passengers accordingly. What she wasn't, was a ship with spaces or voids that could readily be converted into classrooms or lecture halls. As such, with training space in very short supply, a daily training conference allocated areas accordingly and a timetable produced, detailing where and when one had to be.

Wednesday, 28 April (D-23)
At 0800 we were 130 miles off Cap Finistere. Will be travelling past Portugal all day. Sea calmer. Sun!! good weather all day. Bty training started today after Heli crash drills all AM. PM saw FAME start. Officers (RN) entertained us to drinks pre-dinner. Saw 'Life of Brian'. Last night 'The Eagle Has Landed'.

With so many now embarked and with each sub-unit with their unique specialist training requirements, space for training was at a premium. As such, a daily training conference was held, with the aim of fairly dividing up both the day into lessons and where they would take place. As the Battery Training Officer, that responsibility fell to James Watson.

Armed with the training program we divided into our two main disciplines, namely the command post and gun crews, and started on what was to become an intense training package. We all knew that the stakes were high and everyone was naturally to put in their best effort.

Bill Moore, as GPO, split the Command Post (CP) staff in two depending on their role, with the signallers splitting off and training under the direction of Sergeant Maxwell and Bombardier Hagan; whilst my CP, termed 'Hotel 1' (H1) and Warrant Officer 2 (TSM) Trevor Banton's H2 technical assistants, or TARAs came together under both Bill's and Sergeant Nigel 'Nige' Taylor's watchful eyes. FAME is a manual method of determining firing data, relying on books of firing tables and slide rules and was truly seen as a 'dark art' and is covered in detail later, but suffice it to say that on this first session, it tested our memory on its inner workings!

Sergeant Joe Walker recounted: 'Training for gun crews was varied as much as possible with the obvious limitation of not having our guns (Light Guns). It centred around PT and potted sports for fitness, general First Aid and weapon handling, including live firing. We fired our weapons off the back of the ship when the ship's crew ditched their gash.' The term 'gash' in this context is naval slang for rubbish, or waste, which was thrown over the side in black plastic bin bags. These 'gash' bags proved an invaluable aiming point, rather than the underwhelming act of shooting waves, and ditching them over the side was held back for live firing.

Thursday, 29 April (D-22)
Today at 0800 we were reported approx. 100 miles off Canary Islands (UK side). Battery training all day (FAME weapons drills and a good session of PT). The weather was good and the sea was quite calm. There were reports of porpoises and a sea turtle. Morale is still high. Tonight's film was 'All You Wanted To Know About Sex But Were Too Afraid To Ask'. Preceded by 'Electric Blue'.

These first FAME sessions showed just how rusty one can get when not in regular practice, even after our time and experiences supporting the RSA's training program. What was taking minutes to process, needed to be done in seconds. Thankfully we had time on our hands and over the coming days things soon fell into place. The rivalry between the two CPs, in particular between myself as a junior Second Lieutenant and being up against a vastly experienced Warrant Officer, helped determine bragging rights. That rivalry was all the greater as Warrant Officer 2 Trevor Banton was my Troop's Sergeant Major. The one thing in my favour which helped level the field regarding Warrant Officer 2 Banton, was that he came to the Battery having spent most of his service within the Gunner's Swingfire Anti-Tank community. It was this background that set Trevor Banton apart from my normal experiences with Warrant Officers, where the RHA's Swingfire community saw themselves as being more at home with the Cavalry; as such Trevor Banton was more 'city' than 'parade square' and life now with the Battery was worlds apart from his previous existence.

By this stage, we were, as embarked troops, settling into our surroundings and the general routine; however, we were sailing southwards and into considerably warmer weather.

See distribution

May 1982

SPORTS - SUNDAY 2 MAY 1982

1.   Other commitments permitting, it is planned to hold a Sports Competition 1400 - 1700 on Sun 2 May 82, on the upper (A and B) decks of the ship. The events, for which Coys 2IC have already selected teams, are:

   a.   Hockey   -   B Deck Rear.

   b.   Football   -   B Deck Rear.

   c.   Steeplechase   -   A Deck.

   d.   Medicine Ball Bowls - A Deck.

   e.   Tug of War   -   A Deck.

In addition, the Royal Navy and Ships Crew have also been invited to compete.

2.   All sports will be in the form of a knock - out. It is hoped to negotiate a small prize for each winning team, and a cup for the overall winners.

3.   The scoreboard will be positioned alongside the funnel on A Deck, where the draw and planned start times of events will be displayed. This will be manned by the pay staff. A rudimentary canteen will be located alongside.

4.   In addition to the sports, a shooting gallery will also be set up on the Rear Mooring Deck. The Navy and Ship's Crew are particularly invited to try their hand with our weapons.

5.   The UEO is Master of Ceremonies, and the senior PTI is responsible for Sports Co-ordination. Queries, in the first instance should be directed to them.

6.   The Aim of the afternoon is to have a relaxed but active afternoon for all, and for the Army, Navy and Crew to get to know each other in as Gala - like atmosphere as circumstances will permit. Those not participating are encouraged to watch and support.

P NEAME
Major

Distribution:

RNLO (5)

CO
Adjt
RSM
All Coys
29 Bty RA
Gdrm
Offrs Mess
Sgts Mess
Notice Boards

The instruction letter dated 1 May, for the following day's Sports event.
(Courtesy of James Watson)

'The cabins were so stifling and cramped, that we welcomed every opportunity to get out of it,' said Sergeant Joe Walker. 'Any briefings, training and recreation, anything, we even contemplated joining the boys in their lounge for a game of bingo! The sniper from 2 Para rarely spoke, he seemed very withdrawn and just worked on his clothing cam and equipment. The stuffy cabin had the occasional obnoxious smell, which we blamed on the sniper!'

Friday, 30 April (D-21)
Seemed to have been given a bum steer. Today we are 30 miles off the Canary Islands (0800). Another glorious day. Int brief today. Bty trg OK. Film 'Pretty Baby'. Wrote to Jill World news – US to help UK.

One key way to boost morale is mail and every effort was made by 'the system' to get it through. The British Forces Post Office (BFPO) was a tried and tested organisation and assigns a BFPO Number, akin to a PO Box number, to every static base, ship, unit, or operation as required, wherever they're located. The number allocated to our BFPO was '666', which felt rather apt considering the situation and the irony wasn't lost on us. They also seemed to have the uncanny knack of knowing just where you were about to arrive.

As such, mail sacks were dispatched to ports or airports en route, so helicopters could be flown on mail runs, from ship to shore, in the event of not putting into port. Once the mail is in, it's sorted and then flown and delivered around the convoy. The ubiquitous 'bluey', which was the military's version of an airmail letter, was readily available both at home and on board, and importantly free to post.

Saturday, 1 May (D-20)
Stanley airfield attacked by air and sea – Argie planes attack fleet. As at 0800 we were reported to be 110 miles off the Spanish Sahara (Cap Blanc). Weather overcast Force 3-4 little swell. Wrote home. Lectures on ship anti frogmen! Saw 'Lepke' film. Officers to entertain Naval Officers.

Despite *Norland*'s limited space, we never came across the Naval Party in our day to day turn of events. The party's officers ate with the ships officers, which also limited any interaction, so the decision was made to entertain them over a few beers in the bar tomorrow evening.

Training continued at pace and we were getting into the swing of it. What was a surprise was that we were to receive a lecture on frogmen, or at least the danger they posed and the steps to take against them. The general mutterings centred around the fact that we all thought that we had be disembarked by that time.

Sunday, 2 May (D-19)
British sub sank cruiser General Belgrano. *As at 0800 we were 110 miles off Dakar* [Senegal]. *Day off. It's a Knockout. Sun v.very hot. Sunburnt!! All over except for shorts. Ship's officers' drinks pre dinner. Tonight's film 'Magnum Force'.*

The 'It's a Knockout' competition was an inter sub-unit sports

The view from *Norland*'s top flight deck, 2 May 1982.

Sports Day deck hockey on the rear flight deck, 2 May 1982.

BATTERY TRAINING PROGRAMME - MONDAY 3 MAY 82

GROUP	0925 - 1005	1035 - 1115	1130 - 1210	1415 - 1455	1500 - 1615	1615 - 1655	1710 - 1750
Guns + Misc	RANGE PERIOD SLR/SMG/LMG LOWER MOORING DECK B DECK - BACK GROUND			AFV CONFERENCE ROOM	DETACHMENT TRAINING BTY TNG AREA	VIDEO - RESISTANCE SNUG BAR PORT SIDE	PT FUNNEL A DECK
	GUN TACT			TP COMD	NO's 1's	2 PARA	2 PARA
Sigs	HF THEORY BTY TNG AREA	MORSE SNUG BAR	MORSE	MEDICAL 2 CONTINENTAL LOUNGE	SA TNG E & F DECK	SA TNG E & F DECK	PT
	SGT BULLOCK	2 PARA		2 PARA			
OP's	HF THEORY BTY TNG AREA	MORSE SNUG BAR	MORSE	MEDICAL 2 CONTINENTAL LOUNGE	SA TNG E & F DECK	SA TNG E & F DECK	PT
	SGT BULLOCK	2 PARA		2 PARA			
T.R.	FAME BTY TNG AREA	FAME	FAME	MEDICAL 2 CONTINENTAL LOUNGE	SA TNG E & F DECK	SA TNG E & F DECK	PT
	SGT IRVING			2 PARA			

At the end of each day, Captain James Watson in his capacity as the Battery Training Officer, attended the Battalion Group training meeting, which was held to allocate the following day's very limited training space. Each day was generally split into seven forty-minute periods, with periods/lectures specifically tailored for each detachment. This is the programme for 3 May 1982. (Courtesy of James Watson)

competition based on five events: hockey, football, steeplechase, medicine ball bowls and tug of war. The event was intended to be a relaxed social affair; however, the reality was to be far from that, fostered by the intense rivalry felt between sub-units. Each event was keenly contested and no quarter was given or taken. Whilst it was very hot, it appeared to be rather overcast, with no shadow to alert you of the intensity of the sun.

By early evening I was starting to turn 'lobster' red and my skin felt very warm, despite the air-conditioning. Stood in the cabin looking at myself in the mirror, I was just like a photographic negative. I was red all over, save from my running shorts, ankle socks and trainers and my watch strap. Whilst I was sunburnt, I still felt relatively fine in myself and enjoyed the night's social.

Monday, 3 May (D-18)

Sunburn very painful. Turned bright wine red!! At 0800 we were 55 miles off nearest land on the last leg of the journey to Freetown [Sierra Leone]. Today I felt very bad, not due to sunburn, but too much sun i.e. dehydration. Very, very lethargic. A very very hot day. Met up with the Europic. Dehydration

Today's breakfast 'pipe' was to have a profound effect on all those embarked. To try and put the general mood up until this time into context, 2 Para prided itself on its aggressive fighting spirit and this ran through the Battalion Group; every success achieved against the Argentines was met with the same blowing defiance. The pipe opened with the usual internal ship's administrative announcements and then went on to read out the latest news from the BBC's World Service. The main dining area is one of the largest open areas on board and, as it was breakfast, it was packed out, with everybody intently listening to what was being said. The breaking news was that the Argentine Cruiser *General Belgrano* had been sunk, which, on hearing that news, a cheer broke out which rose to a deafening crescendo. The announcer paused, sensing the reaction, which gave everybody time to quieten down and then continued to say that the ship had been sunk with the loss of some 240 lives. In an instant the mood changed into one of total silence, as the magnitude of what had just been announced sank in. Nobody spoke, as the stark reality of what we were being sent South for hit home, and it marked the end of thoughtless celebrations. Back in England, the Sun newspaper was to run its first edition of this news, with the banner headline 'GOTCHA', with others following along similar lines; however, we were now past that, having sobered up to the realities of war and there was to be no more cheering. *Belgrano*'s sinking occurred in the afternoon of 2 May. The nuclear-powered submarine HMS *Conqueror* was shadowing the *General Belgrano* when the order was given to sink her, with the true cost being the loss of 323 lives.

The sinking of the *Belgrano* was to have a profound effect on the Argentines, in that this single action was to be the cause of them deciding to confine their Navy to its home ports. Whilst this wasn't evident at the time,

The whole morning's training programme saw the entire Battalion Group come together, for the first rehearsal of our assault stations. After lunch, the Battery mustered on the *Norland*'s forward mooring deck for the Battery photograph. Not present was the Battery Commander, Major Tony Rice, who was onboard HMS *Fearless*, and the seventeen-man maintenance party under Captain David Gibbins on *Europic*, 4 May 1982. (Courtesy of James Watson)

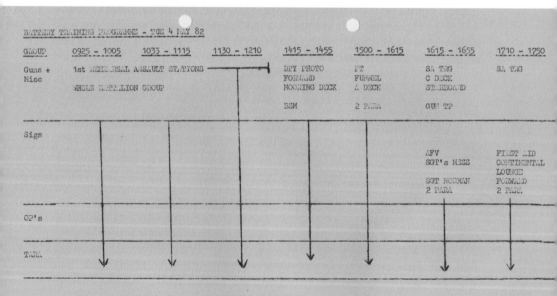

BATTERY TRAINING PROGRAMME - TUE 4 MAY 82								
GROUP	0925 - 1005	1035 - 1115	1130 - 1210	1415 - 1455	1500 - 1615	1615 - 1655	1710 - 1750
Guns + Misc	1st REHEARSAL ASSAULT STATIONS ———————			DRY PHOTO FORWARD MOORING DECK	PT FUNNEL A DECK	SA TNG C DECK STARBOARD	SA TNG
	WHOLE BATTALION GROUP			BSM	2 PARA	GUN TP	
Sigs						AFV SGT's MESS	FIRST AID CONTINENTAL LOUNGE
						SGT NORMAN 2 PARA	FORWARD 2 PARA
O2's							
TARA							

the Argentine Navy was, both during and after the landings, conspicuous by their absence.

The sunburn left me feeling very washed out and as a result of it I missed the Battery PT on the aft flight deck mid-morning. What was uncomfortable was that I was bringing to break out with thousands on micro-blisters where I was sunburnt, which painfully chaffed.

During the night, it was planned for *Norland* to be called briefly into port to take on fresh provisions and fuel.

Tuesday, 4 May (D-17)
Another air attack on Stanley and Goose Green – Argie fighter sinks HMS Sheffield *with missile. Feeling better / sea a little choppy. No sun, overcast but in the hold it is 95 deg F. At 0800 we were 20 miles off Freetown having left at 0600. Europic is with us. Training OK. Heard that HMS* Sheffield *was sunk and a Harrier lost. Very hot. Watched 'Wild Geese'. Morale still high but subdued at the news. Saw porpoises and flying fish.*

When I went below to see how the gunners were, I went past the sickbay where I saw a number of those still affected by the sun/heat. All the bays were full, with the overflow lying on stretchers in the passageway. Most had intravenous drips and were covered in huge blisters.

In the very early hours, *Norland* docked in Freetown for stores and fresh provisions. Whilst I was feeling a little better, the heat and humidity, on top of the sunburn, made it difficult to sleep and I went out onto the ship's rail to watch the activity on the dockside. I didn't stay out long, partly because of the increased humidity, but it was the nauseating stench engulfing the ship that did it.

Wednesday, 5 May (D-16)
At 0800 we were 300 miles off nearest land due south of Liberia. Weather cloudy but very hot. Sea choppy. Bty trg OK. Picked up 7 extras for the other day (heat exhaustion). Saw a pack of sharks. Watched 'Genghis Khan'. Ship started blackout, also assault stations + webbing + bergen. Crossed the Equator at 1000 & celebrated with wine and cake. Bob, me, Bill & James + photos.

As the senior Gunner on board, Bob Ash called me in for a 'chat' about getting sunburnt, which resulted in me missing PT. A number of soldiers had suffered a similar fate and were subsequently disciplined. As an Officer, I was not exempt and as such was given the extra duties. Each duty was for twenty-four hours and had to fit around the training program, requiring me to become primarily an Operations Room watch-keeper, along with the less taxing ship's 'rounds' (inspection) and checking the mess deck at meal times. I was afforded a short night's sleep!

We crossed the Equator at 1000 hours, which was marked in the traditional way. I was thankfully topside, watching a pack of sharks hold station, just off the ship's side, when the search went out for 'suitable' victims for this ritual humiliation. They were rounded up and taken out to the rear flight deck for the crossing ceremony, which was conducted with both pomp and style. What was unexpected and enjoyed by all, was the wine and cake that followed.

2303

Quartermaster Technical
4 Field Regiment RA

Ext 2398

See Distribution

6 May 82

CASUALTY ACCOUNTING

Reference:

A.   Queens Regulations Chapter 3 Section 109.1.

1.   Each sub unit is required to forward approximate heights of all personnel to facilitate the requisitioning of coffins.

2.   Numbers of personnel who would prefer to be cremated should also be forwarded, to enable the re-use of coffins.

3.   Those who require the fitting of handles to their coffin should be indicated. A charge of £2.50 will be levied for this facility. This sum will be deducted from outstanding pay.

4.   A small donation to PRI will secure the services of an honour guard.

5.   A photograph should also be forwarded for the reconstruction of your body. (This is for the benefit of relatives).

E COTTERILL
Major
Quartermaster Technical

Ac I)

Distribution:

External:

Action:

29 Bty (5)
97 Bty (5)

Internal:

Information:

RHQ   (2)
88 Bty (5)
Paymaster (2)

This is the letter concocted by Captain James Watson and Lieutenant Bill Moore, for the sole intention of winding-up the Battery Sergeant Major, Warrant Officer 2 (BSM) Bernie Winch, which was a complete success, 6 May 1982.
(Courtesy of James Watson)

Yesterday's Battery Orders had set aside part of the training program in the early afternoon, for the whole of the Battery to assemble on *Norland*'s fore deck for a group photograph. I recall that the photograph was taken by a Sergeant from the Brigade, who was embarked in his capacity to act as an official military photographer, whose sole brief was to record the events unfolding before us. Sometime later, not long after leaving Ascension, his services were requested and a call was put out for him, for it to unfold that he'd left the ship. It transpired that he'd taken it upon himself to cross to another vessel that was sailing back north to Ascension, which when we heard that news thought it a cowardly act.

We were now getting into the swing of things of life on board, only for the Naval detachment to introduce a new 'darken ship' routine, which reinforced the fact of why we were sailing South. This was coupled with having to complete the 'assault stations' drill with our webbing and bergens. Needless to say, that the passageways became very congested and the drill seemed to take an age to complete.

Thursday, 6 May (D-15)
At 0800 we were well over the Equator on our way to Ascension. The sea is normal. Again very hot, cloudy + sunshine. On Bn Orders it said 'me' 7 extras inclusive and concurrent. Film was 'Kentucky Fried Movie'. Wrote to home & to Jill, last letters to Ascension. UK & Argies looking for peaceful settlement.

Today's Battalion Orders published that I was given extra duties. Conditions were very hot, giving little to no respite, coupled with the fact that I had to remain in uniform throughout my duty, which was made all the worse by my sunburn. Having said that, I did manage to write to Jill, as we were informed of the mail closing in preparation of our arrival at Ascension, which was a welcome distraction.

One of truisms of soldiering, is that humour can be found in almost any situation, often at an individual's expense and rank isn't a factor. Earlier in the year, our BSM, Bernie Winch, had passed the selection board for promotion to Warrant Office 1, in the position of Regimental Sergeant Major (RSM) and was destined to take up his impending promotion with 50 Missile Regiment Royal Artillery over the summer. Selection for RSM is the mark of an exceptional soldier and Bernie was rightly proud of his achievement and was equally very modest about it. Inconveniently, the Argentine invasion of the Falklands happened as Bernie was wrapping up his tenure with 29 Battery and preparing for his big move. This placed Bernie in somewhat of a quandary. Bernie had spent most of his career in Corunna and to leave 'his' Battery on the eve of us going off to war, didn't sit well; in contrast, Bernie was rather keen to become an RSM. It didn't take long for him to decide, with his overriding sense of duty towards Corunna winning through. Unfortunately, this final decision wasn't down to Bernie and he had to press his case with the BC, the CO and also the postings branch. Needless to say, that he had a compelling case and was allowed to continue with the Battery. This then set the foundations for the inevitable 'fun' to be had, mainly instigated by the Battery Quarter Master Sergeant

First view of *Europic Ferry* and part of the Task Force at anchor off Ascension, 7 May 1982.

(BQMS) - Staff Sergeant John McQueenie BEM, who seemed to make it his mission in life to winding Bernie up and very successful he was too.

One of the BQMS's recurring themes always seemed to start with the phrase, 'when you become an RSM ...' In this particular example, the BQMS went on to say, 'you'll be able to save on your tailor's bill.' When questioned as to why, the BQMS replied 'because when you get your leg blown off, you'll save on trouser material'. In another, McQueenie would ask Bernie to imagine the homecoming at RAF Brize Norton or Portsmouth, with Bernie being wheeled down in a wheel chair to meet his wife Maureen. As in most cases, McQueenie used to accompany the story by acting it out and it used to send Bernie spare.

The BQMS wasn't alone here and others were to join in, with Bill and James coming up with a protracted wind up; the seeds of which were sown in the days leading up to our arrival at Ascension. The premise was that as hostilities were, at this time, looking more of a certainty, rather than just military posturing and, as such, that casualties were to be expected, the MoD through the Regiment back in Aldershot, was sending a signal directing us to establish every individual's burial preferences. To that end, the rumour was started. Naturally, Bernie rose to the bait and he wasn't backwards in telling what he thought of it.

Bill Moore remembered this incident: 'James Watson and I typed up a short note on green paper supposedly from RQMS Livingstone (4th Field

A composite panoramic view of Ascension, taken from *Norland*, with the highest point, Green Mountain, uncharacteristically not shrouded in cloud. As such, the peak is covered in thick tropical rain forest, which is in stark contrast to the island's lunar-like volcanic lower reaches, 7 May 1982.

Regiment's Warrant Officer 2 Quartermaster Sergeant) Aldershot, on behalf of the Quartermaster Technical, about coffins. We left it on Bernie Winch's bed. It asked you to fill in a form about your height and weight so that people could start planning the coffin numbers required. It also said that if you paid a bit more you could have it made of oak and for a bit more money, have brass handles. It then asked you to fill in your preferences. Bernie went mad, threatening to punch the RQMS when he returned to

Ascension and the airfield buildings just visible beyond the beach, 7 May 1982.

Two landing craft (LCUs) holding station prior to coming alongside for boat drills, 7 May 1982.

One of the LCUs awaiting 2 Para, as well as the observation parties, for a trip around the bay, which as an alien concept for those embarked, 7 May.

Aldershot. We let Bernie stew for a bit before the real story came out. Black humour at its very best/worst?'

Friday, 7 May (D-14)
Britain puts in 12 mile total exclusion zone. At 0720 we were woke by BC & told flying in 1 hr. We were at Ascension. We flew in a Sea King to airstrip on island. It's just volcanic ash. Nice beaches. Bought in 2 guns + ammo, then left. Saw Vulcan who did raid on Stanley. Wrote to Jill. MAIL IN 11 letters. Morale up and up. Saw 'Rollerball'. Beautiful day, sea calm left around 1900-2000. 2 Vulcans, 3 Harriers, 10 Victors, 2 x C130, 1 x VC10, 2 x Nimrod, many helos, Chinook, Sea King, Wessex + Scout (on airfield). Atlantic Conveyor, 2 x RFA, Intrepid, Fearless, Norland *in convoy.*

The BC flew onto the *Norland* as part of 2 Para's 'R' (Recce) Group, led by 2 Para's CO, Lieutenant Colonel 'H' Jones. After a quick brief, we mustered to fly out to the island's airstrip, Wideawake Field, with the express intent of bore-sighting (calibrating) the Guns. It was also a chance to sort out and practice the hook up drills, in preparation of the inevitable landings.

I flew out to the airfield by Sea King, landing on the edge of one of the main dispersal areas, where numerous aircraft were parked up. One of the things that immediately hit me was the intense heat, not only generated by the equatorial sun, but the vast expanse of the dispersal's black tarmac. We waited for the Guns and we were expecting all six; however, either due to the time it took those on *Europic,* or that the helicopters were re-tasked in-between flying each Gun off in turn, that the intended bore-sightings plan soon fell apart. In total, only two guns flew in and we only managed to complete one bore-sight test before the exercise was scrapped and we reversed the operation. Whilst waiting to be flown back onto *Norland*, we took shelter under the vast wing of one of the Vulcans that was involved in the bombing raids on Stanley. We stood and watched as one of the ground crew was painting the classic 'bomb' symbol on the fuselage, under the pilot's canopy. In true RAF fashion, another one of the ground crew told us that we couldn't shelter where we were and invited us to leave; however, having been stuck on a ship for some two weeks and now finding ourselves being baked in the midday sun, I suggested otherwise and he was in no doubt as to how we felt over the matter and wisely decided to leave us alone.

Once safely back on board, I went out onto the rail to watch the Paras practice their landing craft drills from one of the side cargo/loading doors. Clambering down into a landing craft is far removed from their normal modus operandi and they looked far from comfortable doing so. I then went up on *Norland*'s top flight deck, watching the activity among the fleet, when the BC came over in the company of 2 Para's CO and I was introduced. After a very brief chat, the CO and BC went off to meet up with the Battalion's senior officers.

Having spent the last two weeks at sea, we were rather out of the loop with regards to real time news. The Royal Naval detachment who were our means of communicating tried to keep us informed, as did those individuals with long wave radios trying to catch the BBC's World Service, but for most it was rumour control. Arriving at Ascension saw many having contact with individuals who were well-briefed on diplomatic developments. We also had a delivery of newspapers, which proved a welcome distraction from the rising tension. It was clear that diplomatic efforts were failing and that we would be required to do more than just sail South and wave the flag. Also waiting for us at Ascension was a bumper mail haul, which was great for morale. My tally alone was eleven letters and I wrote to Jill after reading her news.

During our time at Ascension, *Norland*'s passenger carrying capacity was pushed to breaking limits, with the addition of several hundred extra personnel. These came in a variety of different cap badges, the bulk of which were from the RAF, in the form of helicopter flight crew, RAF Harrier pilots and ground staff, whose aircraft were stored on the *Atlantic Conveyor*. The upshot was that bunking arrangements had to change and Bill and I saw us being joined by both James and Bob and not the other way around, because we had a porthole and a precious view of the outside world.

Saturday, 8 May (D-13)
We were at 0800 110 miles off Ascension to SW out in a convoy. Sea choppy Force 3-4 overcast. Duty OK, trg OK. Film 'Blue Max'.

It was the first day South from Ascension in our convoy group. We had set off from the UK alone and it was strange that we were now had company, albeit other 'non-tactical' STUFT shipping, namely *Europic* and *Atlantic Conveyor*, along with two Fleet Auxiliary support vessels, as well as the Navy's two assault ships HMS *Fearless* and HMS *Intrepid*. Our numbers were few, but it was company and equally important, was something to look at.

Leaving Ascension was a significant milestone, as it marked a noticeable mood change amongst us all, as Sergeant Walker explained: 'When we left Ascension Island, life became more tense and the mood more sombre, as we were nearing the political point of no return. The focus was on the reality that we were going to war.'

Sunday, 9 May (D-12)
At 0900 we were 420 miles on a course of 195 deg off Ascension. Still Duty Officer sea choppy swell 5'-6' Force 4-5. Day off visit to the bridge. Film 'Alien'. New ops room stag.

Whilst it was a day off, I was still required as the Duty Officer, for which we were starting to run a new and improved routine. However, I did find time to visit the bridge, which proved both interesting and a welcome distraction.

Monday, 10 May (D-11)
British warships bombard positions around Stanley – Argie tanker sunk. At 0800 we were 2000 miles approx off Brazil. Still heading south quite a way off Ascension. Bad morning of duty with silly little things. PT OK, trg OK. A little cooler in the day, strong wind. 24 hrs stag in the Ops room, between duty offr, WO + BOS – 4

hrs on 8 hrs off. Finished XPD not bad. Still hot inside ship.

I can't recall what the problems were during the morning's duty for me to make the entry, but they can't have been that significant, in the scheme of things, as they weren't specified. The new Operations Room routine was going well, as at least there was time to oneself between shifts. What did go well was our training, whilst I was over the worst of my sunburn, the PT did smart with some of the exercises. What was a blessing was the strong cooling wind, which took the edge off things, before returning back to the heat inside.

It was around this time, during one of the many small arms live firing sessions, that a most 'unfortunate' incident took place. One's stance as to how 'unfortunate' is the nature of this incident, is fundamentally rooted in one's Service and it's a flavour of what sets the Army and the Navy apart. Seemingly bored with shooting gash bags, two members of B Sub took it upon themselves to take matters into their own hands.

Joe Walker again tells this story: 'My LMG (light machine gun) team, Gunners Barney Hughes & George Kirvell, took it upon themselves to shoot at an Albatross.'

Gunner Kirvell sought to mitigate his part in proceedings: 'One of the days sailing south was spent on test firing and shooting practices of the LMG. My mate Barney Hughes had been issued with the LMG and I was his No 2, with my personal weapon being a SLR (rifle). Anyhow, on this day, we were shooting at rubbish bags dumped into the sea and we, being us, had gotten bored with this. Also in the water was a big bird, which we didn't recognise whilst it was sat floating. We both asked Joe Walker, our Sergeant, if we could shoot at the bird, which he agreed too. I and Barney Hughes both let rip at the bird with him on the LMG and me with my SLR. As the bird took off we both kept firing at it, until it started to spiral downwards into the sea. We both started claiming the shot for hitting the bird. At this point someone was shouting that the bird was an Albatross! As a result, over the next few days me and Barney had to go into hiding due the Navy wanting to string us up because of the myth of killing an Albatross as being bad luck. I certainly didn't think much of our chances after finding out that the BFPO Number for the Falklands was 666!'

Joe Walker continues: 'Shooting the Albatross caused considerable distress to the ship's officers and crew. Suffice to say firing was suspended at this point and I had the third degree.'

Tuesday, 11 May (D-10)
Weather OK, warmer – sea calm. Saw a (2) BEAR [USSR recon] flying over the convoy and at 1430 defence stations, someone sighted a periscope. Helos tasked. No danger to us. Issued arctic kit, all good stuff, on stag still – wrote to Jill, letter from Aunt Jean [Locke] and Herb &Val [Powell].

Throughout the day various pipes called us down to the lower vehicle decks and into the bowls of the ship, to be issued the bulk of our Arctic clothing and equipment. It was the first time that the majority of us has seen this equipment and we were generally very impressed. It was difficult

BATTERY PART ONE ORDERS

BY

MAJOR A J RICE RA

COMMANDING 29 (CORUNNA) BATTERY ROYAL ARTILLERY

॥॥*॥*॥*.॥*॥*॥*॥*॥*॥*.॥*॥*॥*॥*.॥*॥*॥*॥*.॥*॥*॥*॥*॥*॥*.॥*॥*

MV NORLAND   TUE 11 MAY 82   SERIAL No 013

॥॥*॥*॥*.॥*॥*॥*॥*॥*.॥*॥*॥*॥*॥*.॥*॥*॥*॥*॥*.॥*॥*॥*॥*॥*.॥*॥*

001.   ROUTINE FOR WED 12 MAY 82

        Reveille   ...   0700 hrs
        Cleaning Duties   ...   0730 hrs
        Breakfast   ...   0800 hrs
        Troop Inspections   ...   0900 hrs
        Training Programme   ...   As Attached
        Potted Sports   ...   1400 - 1800 hrs (weather permitting)

002.   DUTIES FOR WED 12 MAY 82

        Battery Orderly NCO   ...   BDR ARMSTRONG K

003.   **TRAINING PROGRAMME**

        As at Annex A. (See over).

004.   PAY PARADE

        Pay Parade for the Battery will be 1700 hrs Wed 12 May 82.

005.   FREE POST TO UK

        Free post back to UK may be used using the blue British Forces Air Mail
        letter envelopes only. This free post is limited to addressees in the UK
        and BFPO numbers only. It is stressed that all other forms of mail require
        the **full** postage rates.

006.   BLOOD DONORS

        It is intended to take blood from willing donors during the course of
        Wed 12 and Thu 13 May 82. Donors will be called forward by runner or
        Tannoy.

007.   BOOKS

        On embarkation from the UK a large quantity of books were placed in the
        bookcase at the port entrance to the continental lounge. These books have
        been taken away and not replaced. In order that everyone on board may benifit
        these books or any that have been read and no longer required should be
        placed back in this bookcase and swopped on a one for one basis.

**The Battery's daily Part One Orders, which
details specific points outside of the training
programme, 12 May 1982.**
(Courtesy of James Watson)

A J RICE
Major RA
Battery Commander

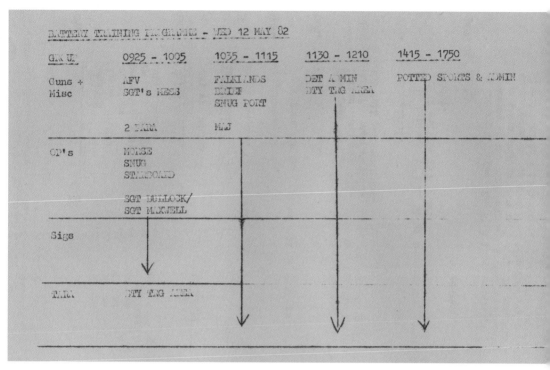

BATTERY TRAINING PROGRAMME - WED 12 MAY 82				
GROUP	0925 - 1005	1035 - 1115	1130 - 1210	1415 - 1750
Guns + Misc	AFV SGT's MESS	FALKLANDS BRIEF SNUG PORT	DET A MIN DTY TNG AREA	POTTED SPORTS & ADMIN
	2 PARA	HQ		
OP's	MOUSE SNUG STARBOARD			
	SGT BULLOCK/ SGT MAXWELL			
Sigs				
PARA	DTY TNG AREA			

This is the training Annex for 12 May, where the main focus in the afternoon was for an inter-unit potted sports competition, similar to that held on 2 May, 12 May 1982.
(Courtesy of James Watson)

Here, Lance Bombardier Ian Wyke is anchoring the Tug 'O War team on the top upper funnel deck, with Staff Sergeant (BQMS) John McQueenie coaching them on. Just visible aft is the upper helicopter flight deck, 12 May 1982.

```
                        DON'T CRY ARGENTINA

        Were off out to the Falklands,
        With the men who are the cream,
        Some of the lads don't think its WAR,
        They think it's just a dream.

        Though we are still training,
        I think were ready now,
        Cos here come the islands,
        Just off the starboard bow.

        Were always doing danger drills,
        We'll never get it right,
        Were not training to be sailors,
        Were on our way to fight.

        So look out you black daigos,
        You may be out of reach,
        Until of course those seakings,
        Start landing on the beach.

        You just won't know what hit you,
        Our guns will be red hot,
        It's just like taking candy,
        From little tiny tots.

        Our flag will soon be flying,
        As it was before,
        There aint no room for daigos,
        So just stay off the shore.


                                LBDR WYKE
                                29 (CORUNNA) FD BTY RA
```

Lance Bombardier Ian Wyke's song lyrics. 'Don't Cry Argentina'.
(Courtesy of James Watson)

to grasp some of its benefits, as the last thing we wanted to do was 'dress up' due to the heat inside. What wasn't well received were the notorious 'Ski March Boots', which looked incredibly uncomfortable. As soon as we sailed from Portsmouth the order went out from the Naval Party to wear PT shoes, as was the Navy's practice for embarked troops, which was primarily aimed at preserving the ship's decks. Notwithstanding that, everybody to a man had their regular DMS ankle boots fitting like the proverbial glove; so to be now issued with a boot that was heavy, solid and inflexible, and came with a significant boxed toecap, designed for the skis to fit onto, left everybody rather concerned. Realising the problem, a pipe soon went out, instructing everyone to wear their new boots, to break them in. Trying to

```
29 (CORUNNA) FIELD BATTERY ROYAL ARTILLERY

WEAPON STATE

SHIP                                        SHIP
MV NORLAND                                  MV EUROPIC

SLR   7.62mm   =  52                        SLR 7.62    =  5
SMG   9mm      *  39                        SMG 9mm     =  8
LMG   7.62mm   =  6
84mm A./Tk     =  3
Pitol 9mm      =  1
Pistol Signal  =  1                         MISCELLANEOUS

                                            Major AJ RICE RA   1 x SMG


GRAND TOTAL OF WEAPONS

SLR            =  57
SMG            =  48
LMG            =  6
84mm A/Tk      =  3
Pistol 9mm     =  1
Pistol Signal  =  1
```

J McQUEENIE, REM
SSGT
BQMS

This memo details the Battery's small arms holdings by type. The Battery Commander, Tony Rice, was adamant that he was not going to war armed with just his allocated 9mm pistol so a sub-machine gun was 'sourced' for him before we left Aldershot. It is listed here under 'Miscellaneous'.

break them in within the confines of a ship was nigh on impossible and it wasn't long before the complaints went in questioning their suitability. The kit issue, coupled with a mail run, kept up spirits throughout the ship, and I used my time in the Operations Room to write to Jill.

We were unsure of the Argentine intelligence capabilities, in determining both where and what we were up to. The consensus was that as we were so far north we would remain undetected; however, the fact that we were overflown by a Soviet Bear long range reconnaissance aircraft burst that bubble, as we felt that the Soviets would rush to tell Buenos Aires of our advance south. It was a memorable encounter, not for either the fact that it was a non-friendly aircraft, or for being so far out at sea, but for the fact that it flew at such a low level over us; with its 1950s four contra-rotating and very noisy turbo prop engines leaving black trail lines, as it carved its way through the fleet.

A view of a Wessex hovering over *Europic*'s helicopter landing spot. Our six Light Guns can be seen aft. (Courtesy of David Gibbins)

What did prove to be a moment of excitement was the 'sighting' of a periscope, which caused us to close up to defence stations, whilst a helicopter went over to investigate. Soon after we were stood down, with no real explanation as to whether it was a genuine sighting or not.

It was around this time and unbeknown to us on *Norland*, that one of the Battery's members had an 'incident' on *Europic*. The individual concerned was Gunner Gowland, the details of which are covered in greater detail in the aftermath, when we were back in Aldershot. In summary, Gowland, whilst on fire watch, attempted to carry out some 'grenade drills', when the detonator he was handing blew three fingers off. He was at that time

Norland **from** *Europic.* **(Courtesy of David Gibbins)**

amongst 1,000 tons of artillery ammunition and the results could have had catastrophic effects on the Task Force. He was flown off *Europic* and onto a ship that was one of the last to sail north, back to Ascension, where he repatriated back to the UK.

Wednesday, 12 May (D-9)

Argie planes attack British fleet. Weather calm – not hot, but nice. Last day of extras. Potted sports in PM. 29 Bty won overall + tug o' war, bowls + steeplechase. Nearly all kit issued. Finished peeling turned to tan. Duty OK. Gale warning later on. We are approx. 1000 miles off Argentina now, line from Cape Town to Montevideo.

The subtle change in the weather made for more bearable conditions and the Battalion Group mustered in their sub-units for the potted sports. Again, like anything that the Para's do, it was a keenly contested event, in which they took particular umbrage at losing the tug o' war, with Lance Bombardier Wyke anchoring the team to success, being urged on enthusiastically by the BQMS in his capacity as team coach.

Lance Bombardier Ian Wyke was a large yet quiet individual, who possessed considerable natural strength, whose arms were as big as my legs, but wasn't shy in expressing his delight on winning. Wyke's delight, and 2 Para's umbrage, was because they were squarely beaten in the main, in airborne vernacular, by 'crap hats'. Whilst all the Battery's forward observation parties were required to be para trained, in order to parachute in alongside their respective Parachute Battalions, the Guns were not. This was due to the fact that the Army was scaling back on its Airborne capabilities, with the Guns now solely in the air-land role and whilst desirable, it was not a requirement for members of the gun end to be para trained. The prevailing feeling within the Airborne fraternity was that anybody who didn't wear a red beret, which effectively was the rest of the Army, was held in contempt and were termed 'crap hats'. So for the Battalion to be beaten by a bunch of 'hats' was for them beyond the pale, which contrasted with the significant rise in our stock value. The reality was that the average 'Tom' (Paratrooper) never came into contact with the Guns and defaulted to type; here now, they realised that the important

A Sea King helicopter landing on the upper flight deck, typically on a mail or administrative run, shortly before the ship took on fuel, known as 'Replenishment at Sea', or RAS-ing for short, 14 May 1982.

Looking to starboard from *Norland*'s upper rail, at the fuel line now connected from the out-of-shot tanker. North Sea ferries are not fitted with an at-sea fuel system and this was modified and fitted during the frantic period that the two flight decks were fitted before we sailed from the UK, 14 May 1982. Looking to starboard from *Norland*'s upper rail, at the fuel line now connected from the out-of-shot tanker. North Sea ferries are not fitted with an at-sea fuel system and this was modified and fitted during the frantic period that the two flight decks were fitted before we sailed from the UK, 14 May 1982.

The RAS. The fuel line is clearly visible, apparently loosely hanging under the support cables. The distance between ships is critical, as there is a very real risk of a collision should the ships get too close. The slack in the fuel line allows for the ships to 'move' in station during rougher seas, 14 May 1982.

The author watching proceedings, 14 May 1982.

A closer look at *Norland*'s fuel coupling, 14 May 1982.

An indication of the swell caused by the ships being in close proximity, on a relatively calm day, 14 May 1982.

A view across to two Landing Ships, which, due to their flat bottoms, fair badly in rough seas. A warship is just visible on the horizon.

thing was the ability to deliver and we did just that.

Lance Bombardier Wyke also had a hidden talent, which came to light when he penned 'Don't Cry Argentina', a parody to the 1976 musical hit, 'Don't Cry For Me Argentina'; copies were printed off and distributed around the ship, which went to help keep spirits high.

The issue of kit came with a growing problem, in as much that the more we were issued, then the more we had to stow away in our cabins, and space was becoming a problem. Not only that, but we still were to receive our scalings of rations and ammunition. The day ended on a high note, with the end to the constant itching caused by peeling, culminating in rather a good tan. The only thing that was now taking the edge off a good day, was the pipe that we were to expect a gale sometime later.

Thursday, 13 May (D-8)
Still heading south towards Falklands, nearest land – Argentina. Still around 1400 (approx) miles. Weather cooler, sea calm & sunny day on the whole. Watched 'The Boys From Brazil'. End of extras. Op Order came out to CO + BC level. Trg not too bad. CPX not too good. Good session of PT in webbing!! Nice to be off duties!! Clocks back 1 hr.

We were almost halfway between Ascension and the Falklands, with the ironic fact that the nearest landfall now was Argentina. The weather was good and I'd thankfully finished my run of duties; as such. life seemed fair.

The unexpected 'bonus' from having the extra duties was working in the Operations Room, where I was privy to the intelligence picture, including Argentine dispositions and the possible beachheads for our landings; however, having said that, it was good to have finished my 'extras'.

One thing that did strike me, was the disproportionately larger amount of red on the maps and aerial photographs, with the density increasing the closer one went towards Stanley. Military map marking conventions show friendly forces traditionally in blue, with the enemy depicted in red symbols.

News came through that the Operational Order for the landings had

ARGENTINA – AIRFORCE NEED TO KNOW

	OFFICAL NAME	REPORT NAME	TYPE
1 BOMBER SQN	*9 CANBERRA	CANBERRA	RECC/FGA/BOMB
4 FB SQN	*60 A4 SKYHAWK	A4 SKYHAWK	FGA(CARRIER)
1 FB SQN	*18 F-86F SABRE	SABRE	FGA(CARRIER)
6 FGA SQN	*17 MIRAGE 5	MIRAGE	RECC/FGA/BOMB
	*48 MS-750A	PARIS	MULTI
	*DASSAULT ENTENDARD	ENTENDARD	MULTI(CARRIER)
1 INTERCEPT SQN	*22 MIRAGE III	MIRAGE	MULTI
2 COIN SQN	*37 IA-58 PUARA	PUCARA	MULTI
	*14 HUGHES 500m	CAYUSE	MULTI
	*8 UH-1M	IROQOIS	MULTI
5 TPT SQN	1 BOEING 707	BOEING 707	
	*7 C130 E/M	HURCULES	TRANSPORT
	*2 KC 130	HURCULES(TANKER)	
	1 SABERLINER	SABERLINER	VIP TRAN
	2 LEARJETS 35A	LEARJETS 35A	VIP TRAN
	*3 G-222	G-222	TRANSPORT
	*13 C-47	DAKOTA	PARA TRANSPORT
	10 F-27	FRIENDSHIP	LT TRANSPORT
	6 F-28	FELLOWSHIP(	LT TRANSPORT
	5 DM-6	TWIN OTTER	LT TRANSPORT
	22 IA-50	PUCARA	LT TRANSPORT
	2 MERLIN IVA	MERLIN	LT TRANSPORT
1 ANTARCTIC SQN	2 DHC-2	BEAVER	LT TRANSPORT
	3 DHC-3	OTTER	LT TRANSPORT
	1 LC-47	DAKOTA	LT TRANSPORT
	*1 S-61R	SEA KING	ASW

HELICOPTERS

	* 11 A-109	HIRUNDO	MULTI
	*7 BELL 206	JET RANGER	MULTI
	*18 UH-1M	IROQOIS	TROOPSHIP
	*4 BELL 47G	SIOUX	OBs
	*2 BELL 212	IROQOIS	MULTI
	*6 SA-315 LAMA	ALOUETTE	MULTI
	*CH-47	CHINOOK	TROOPSHIP
	*858	SEAHORSE	TROOPSHIP
	*LYNX	LYNX	MULTI
	*PUMA	PUMA	MULTI

AIRCRAFT

	5 690A		
	3 G-222		
	4 MERLIN 3A		
	5 CESSNA 207	SKY WAGON	
	15 CESSNA 182		

* DENOTES NEED TO KNOW

This document from 2 Paras' Intelligence Cell, details the Argentine air assets and those specifically designated as 'Need to Know'. The subject was covered over many lessons and was led by one of the 2 Para instructors.

been given to CO and sub-unit commander level, which proved to be the hot topic of conversation. Whilst I had no knowledge of those orders, I had just spent a week pouring over maps and helping with the intelligence picture and as such, I had more than an insight into what to expect. I was of course required throughout my time in the Operations Room, to keep what I'd learnt a secret.

Individual skills were improving daily, with the intensity of the training ramping up to match that improvement. Collectively we had come a long way since leaving Portsmouth. We had set ourselves high standards, so should any individual fail, it reflects negatively on the CP as a whole.

Gunner Steve Armour was a 19-years-old HGV driver at the time and a member of the BK and BQMS's admin and stores set up. He was to reflect on his journey so far: 'I couldn't believe why we had travelled so far to fight in such a cold, wet climate. We didn't know where is it was. We got on the *Norland*, the North Sea ferry and we thought we were going to Scotland. Two and a half weeks later, we thought where the hell are we going on this boat?'

Friday, 14 May (D-7)

Not too bad. Sea a little rough force 5. Still heading south. Op Order handed down to BC-OC to FOO type level. We RAS'ed at 1600 – very impressive. The old sea was good to watch. At night watched 'The Long Good Friday'. Put clocks back 1 hr. They say the Op Order is very unadventurous. Wrote last letter to Jill + home.

News filtered down on the orders for the retaking of the Islands, which were to be passed down by the BC/OC (Company Commander) level to their respective FOOs/Captains; whilst we were not given any detail, the little that was said was that they were 'unadventurous'.

What was impressive and drew a small crowd was watching the latest replenishment evolution, mainly due to the increased sea state, which caused the waves running between the ships to rise up to the RFA's gunwales. The most significant thing for me though was that this marked the last mail run north and I wrote two letters, one to my parents and the other to Jill.

Saturday, 15 May (D-6)

Brit Cdo's raid Pebble Island – 11 Argie aircraft destroyed. Just below Lat 45deg, nearest land South Georgia. Weather bad, Force 6-7 sea 15'-20' quite cold. Watched 'Dirty Harry'. Quite a swell – felt sea sick. as Bty is Duty Bty had a day off. During night Force 9-10 swell 20'-40'.

We were to learn that the BC attended Brigadier Thompson's (Commander 3 Commando Brigade) 'O' Group (Orders) aboard HMS *Fearless*, but not passed on to us yet.

The weather was now running true to what we had been told to expect in the Southern Ocean. It was both cold and very windy, which increased the sea state and worsened as the day went on. Thankfully we had a day off, as trying to do anything constructive was challenging in the conditions. This wasn't helped by a return of the sea-sickness that I was starting to get

LVTP 7 - APC (Marine)
AMX 10 - Armd Recce - 105mm
AMX 13 - Lt Tank - 90mm
AMXVCI - APC
M113 - APC
Moway Piranha - Lt APC/Recce
Moway Grenadier - various armaments ATK (Mor)MG
TAM 1 - Med Tk 105mm
LRC - Lt wheeled Boat, 'assault craft'

Written on the back of the Argentine Airforce's aircraft list are the Argentine land fighting vehicles we were possibly going to encounter.

to grips with. Just before last light I went out to try and get some fresh air. Whilst out on the rail, a tactic that worked for me was to watch the horizon, in the hope that it lessens the visual cues of the ship's immediate pitching and rolling. We were surrounded by other ships in the convoy, but out on the horizon were the frigates and destroyers, providing the convoy's guard screen. I have no idea of what it was like on one of those ships, but it looked very unpleasant by *Norland*'s standards. Entire ships would rise and then fall from view, hidden in the deep swell.

Whilst we had a small maintenance party on *Europic*, it was decided at an early stage during the morning and whilst the weather was still flyable, that some of the Gun Subs were to fly over and check on the 'welfare' of their guns. One of those men was Sergeant Walker: 'I recall, on one occasion, having to fly over to the *Europic Ferry* to service our guns, with some of our gun crew members and others travelling on the *Europic*. The weather turned and it was decided we should not make the flight back; all the guys were concerned about was that the bingo jackpot would be won while we were away!'

Sunday, 16 May (D-5)
Argie supply ship attacked in Falkland Sound. Air attack on Stanley airstrip. Still heading SW towards Falklands. Not far now. RV with main fleet at 1600. Very impressive sight. Weather has abated slightly, still a little rough. Watched 'Villain', 'Night Killer' and 'The Enforcer'. Clocks back 1 hr now 4 hrs behind GMT.

Meeting up with the main fleet was truly impressive, made even more so by the improvement in the weather conditions. There were ships in every

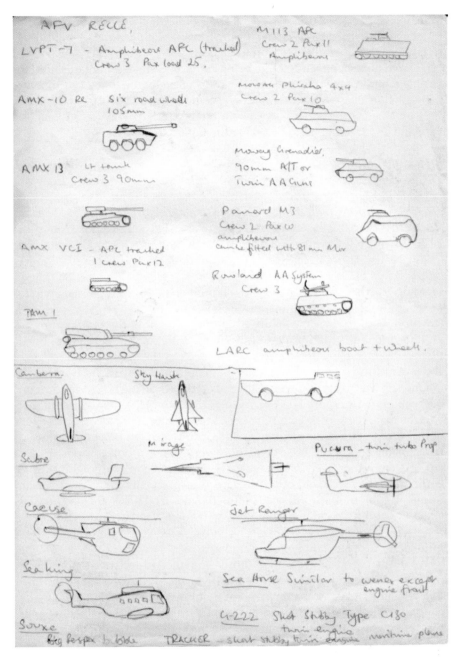

The subject of recognising enemy aircraft and fighting vehicles back in the UK, was almost exclusively based around the Cold War threat and Soviet-derived equipment. We were now faced by a more Pan-American inventory, which was far from familiar to us. As such, I made crude sketches of the various types on a sheet of A4, which I took ashore, just in case I felt the need to confirm identification.

direction out to the horizon and whilst I thought that there was quite a number of us in convoy sailing from Ascension, that number bore little resemblance to the numbers around us now.

There had been a feeling of us being rather too small an organisation to be able to undertake our given task, almost entirely due to the fact that we had sailed in relative isolation, but on seeing the growing size of the fleet, we were filled with confidence. News filtered through of operations on East Falkland and it felt good to be taking the fight to the enemy.

Monday, 17 May (D-4)

We are 680 miles from Argentina and 400 miles from the Falklands. Today we were told the plan. (West Island – Sussex Mnts) The fleet we are in totals 17 ships and we haven't RV'd with the rest. Day cold (windy) sea relatively calm. Watched 'Escape To Victory'.

Bill Moore flew over to meet up with the BC and BK, to attend Lieutenant Colonel Mike Holroyd-Smith, CO of 29 Commando Regiment's 'O' Group, on the RFA's LSL *Sir Galahad*, to be given the detailed Gunner plan. These Landing Ship Logistics (LSLs) are flat bottomed landing ships, designed to take both troops and equipment to the beachhead.

Throughout the voyage south, up until the point of the final issuing of kit and briefings, training was both intense and varied. Signallers honed their radio discipline and worked on increasing the speed of their Morse code, whilst those in the command posts continued to work on FAME.

One subject that was never really covered back in barracks was aircraft and vehicle recognition. The West was still 'fighting' the Cold War and that was the main focus of our training back home, where we repeatedly looked at the same Soviet equipment, over and over, which left most un-enthused on the subject. That mindset was now very much a polar opposite one, as we were rather keen to see what we were potentially up against. The equipment that we were about to face was predominately American in origin and unfamiliar to most. The Intelligence Cell on board produced a slide show, with a handout 'Argentina – Air Force Need to Know'; however, most were annotated as 'NEED TO KNOW'. The Argentine vehicles were more pan-European and were unfamiliar.

We all had medical training, with basic First Aid lectures taking place up until Ascension, which was made even more 'practical' by the fact that a Field Hospital was embarked at that time, which upped the ante by concentrating on gun shot and shrapnel wounds. One eye-opening part was on how to administer saline solution through a drip, without the aid of a needle – and it's not orally!

The doctors reinforced the instruction that the morphine issued to each of us, was for personal use only and we were not to be tempted to use it on others, regardless of how compelling we felt the circumstances were. They also emphasised the importance of filling out the morphine tag when administering the drug. Failure to do so could have serious repercussions or even prove fatal, should morphine be administered during the casualty evacuation or at the Field Hospital; as the medical assumption being 'no tag equals no morphine' having been administered.

One lecture that had everybody's attention, was that conducted by Major Ewen Southby-Tailyour RM. He was doing the rounds of the fleet, lecturing on survival based on the Islands themselves, along with the Falkland's flora and fauna. The Major opened the lecture by stating that he'd served down in the Islands, as part of the standing Royal Marines Naval Party, as well as having sailed around the Islands, charting and recording the entire coastline. Needless to say, that his introduction got our attention. Rather than a National Geographic style of lecture, it was aimed at the realities of surviving in the 'camp', the local term for anywhere outside of Stanley, which gave us all an insight as to what to expect on the Islands. As part of his lecture, he gave out copies of his five-page notes titled: *Notes on Survival and Living in the Camp (Falklands Islands)*.

Sergeant Walker attended the lecture: 'One of the questions asked was what if someone goes overboard and can't swim?' The answer was a stark as it was realistic, 'don't worry about that, the sea is minus twenty degrees with twenty-foot waves, you wouldn't live long enough to be rescued!'

Perhaps the most surprising speaker was 2 Para's Padre, Reverend David Cooper, who, as an international rifle shot, gave a talk on shooting at long range (sniping). One problem that unwittingly came to light, and was most confusing for the Paras, was when the 1:50,000 map of the Falklands was unboxed; showing two overlapping grid overlays, one blue and one red superimposed on the maps. The matter was resolved when Bob Ash identified that the Falklands were on a Universal Transverse Mercator (UTM) zone boundary, where it was unilaterally agreed to use the blue grid lines, as it was the blue overlay which went East to Stanley. (UTM is a type of map/chart projection, that takes mapping of a flat Earth, to allow for its real round form. The closer one gets to the poles, the greater the overlap and the islands fell between two such UTM zones.)

What was a surprise, was receiving news that we were to still to meet up with even more ships. It was about this time that individuals could visualise the size of the Task Force.

Tuesday, 18 May (D-3)

At 0640 we were woken up to defence stations. Air threat, stood down then at 0735 defence stations' Bearing Red 90 deg'. Final kit issue of saline drips, dextrose fluid, full ammo + 3 x 24 hr rats pack. Briefed on plan in detail by BC + CO 29 Cdo RA. Had a hair cut!! RV'd with main body of fleet. 'O'Gp at night from 2100-2240. Have to stay in kit all the time. Sea as calm as a mill pond.

When the second incident taking us to defence stations happened, I was on the lower vehicle deck drawing stores when the following broadcast went over the ship's tannoy: 'You hear there. This is not a drill, this is not a drill. Action stations, Action stations, Action stations. Bearing Red 90 degrees, submarine sighted off the starboard bow. Action stations, Action stations, Action stations.' To say that this focused one's mind would be an understatement and the embarked forces were in their action stations in just over ninety seconds.

A helicopter from HMS *Brilliant* was scrambled and the contact was attacked. It took some time for the results to filter through, where the RN sheepishly reported to blowing up a whale. The stark reality was that we were now considered to be vulnerable to a possible Argentine attack. As such we were required to be in uniform, as per abandon ship drills, at all time.

One area of administration that was required to be completed, but never discussed, was that of capture. To that end, individuals were ordered to hand in their military identification card and were issued with an operational 'British Forces Identity Card - F/IDENT/186'. This new card came under the auspices of the 1949 Geneva Convention, governing Prisoners of War, and it was the one thing we were allowed to take ashore. It covered the classics of: name, rank and serial number, as wells your date of birth and covered the Do's and Don'ts if captured.

The final issue of medical supplies, consisting of morphine and accompanying tag, a saline drip, a litre bag of saline fluid, three days' rations and a full issue of the expected ammunition scales, almost caused the cabin to burst at its seams. The fact that we had live ammunition of seemingly all types, in considerable quantities, lying around on our bunks was a totally surreal experience. Peacetime ammunition control is so tightly monitored and regulated for, that the fact that we had it and in such quantities brought our plight home. The biggest question that was on everyone's mind was 'where are we going to put it all!'.

Sergeant Walker: 'On the plus side, a huge sigh of relief, when we were told, at a late stage the intel reports suggested that the Argies had no NBC (nuclear or chemical warfare) capability and we could leave that kit behind!'

Considering that we had been at sea for almost four weeks, most were in need of a haircut. The 'barber' was an enterprising soldier who had scissors and clippers, but more importantly looked like he knew what he was doing and turned a tidy profit for his skills.

Chapter 3

Orders

THE ORDERS GROUP was taken by Tony Rice, who detailed the overall Brigade plan, as well as how we were to fit into that of 2 Para. It follows a strict format and is not open for discussion. Abbreviations are found in the glossary.

The following is the transcript of the 29 Commando Regiment Operations Order:

Enemy: Estimated total 11,000 (9,600 Army, 1700 Marines) - consisting of: 9 Inf Bns, 2(+) Arty Bns, 4(+) AD Units, elements of 1 Armd [Armoured] Car Sqn, 1 Cdo Coy and supporting elements.

Strengths: 2 times the numbers of 3 Bde, that they've had time to select the best ground and that they could move 200 troops in a single airlift.

Weaknesses: Logistics - limited stocks and resupply through Teal Inlet will be limited. Morale: Isolated from mainland Argentina. Cold, damp conditions. Some conscripts may be at the end of their year's service. Ratio of conscripts to marines – previous contact may worry conscripts.

Friendly Forces: The Brigade will carry out a 3 phase assault. Phase 1: By night, 40 Cdo and 2 PARA will simultaneously land by LCU, to secure SAN CARLOS SETTLEMENT and SUSSEX MOUNTAINS respectively. Phase 2: By night, 3 PARA and 45 Cdo concurrently will land by LCU and secure AJAX BAY and PORT SAN CARLOS SETTLEMENT. Phase 3: At first light, the move ashore of Artillery and Air Defence, to provide cover for the beachhead.

Mission: To support 3 Cdo Bde establish a beachhead in the PORT SAN CARLOS/ AJAX BAY AREA.

Execution
General Outline: Naval Gunfire Support will provide cover 'On Call' for Phase 1 and 2. Phase 3, first light with 29 Cdo Regt (+) flown ashore.
> *7 Bty - Direct Support 45 Cdo Gd 6092 C/A 1300 mils (6400 mils)*
> *8 Bty - Direct Support 40 Cdo Gd 5684 C/A 1600 mils (6400 mils)*
> *29 Bty - Direct Support 2 PARA Gd 5981 C/A 2700 mils (3200mils) - (6400 mils)*
> *79 Bty - Direct Support 42 Cdo Gd 5985 C/A 1 3200 mils C/A 2 4800 mils (6400 mils)*
> *RHQ, FDC, RAP - 5683*
> *LAD - 5984*
> BMA - 5984, 5585

Magnetic Variation in the FI is EAST: Gd to Mag (-) Av 80 mils
Depart with 72 hours rations, full water and puritabs by all.

The following is a summary of the 2 PARA Op Order:
Mission: *2 PARA is to land at SAN CARLOS and establish a defensive position on SUSSEX MNTS*
Execution
General Outline: 4 Phases - silent night assault.
 1. Land by LCU on Blue Beach 2 (Bonners Bay 596840)
 2. To FUP 6080
 3. Occupy Sussex Mnts
 4. Establish a defensive position on Sussex Mnts
A Coy - Initial Obj 610785
B Coy - Initial Obj 629780
D Coy - Initial Obj 609792
C (Ptl) Coy - OPS at Gds 671757, 701721, 576790, 677732, 646772, 641745,
 608756, 591766, 706693
Sp Coy - 604797
Mors - 609809 and 615802
29 Bty - All Phases - BC with TAC 1
 OP Parties to Rifle Coys
 NGFO in sp UCM
 Phase 3 - Tgt lists to follow
 Phase 4 - DF list to follow, BC to coordinate Mor, Arty and MG DFs
H Hr 0630Z 40 Cdo (land 0640Z)
 2 PARA 0315 - 0515Z
Sunrise 1130Z (approx) Sunset 2000Z (approx)

2 PARAs Artillery Target List for the San Carlos Beach Landings - OP SUTTON detailed Phases 3 and 4:
 Phase 3 - Tgt List 1 LONG RUN
 Phase 4 - Tgt List 2 TIGHT SAIL

ARTILLERY TARGET LIST - OP SUTTON

1. TARGET LIST - LONG RUN (Bn Phase 3)

Tgt No	Description	Grid	Alt [feet]
ZJ 5527	Sussex Mt West	595785	600
ZJ 5528	Sussex Mt East	608787	700
ZJ 5529	Track Junction	615783	750
ZJ 5530	High Ground	628781	900
ZJ 5531	High Ground	645772	850
ZJ 5532	Bodie Peak	669757	900
ZJ 5533	Track	628764	300
ZJ 5534	Track Junction	638734	50

2. TARGET LIST - TIGHT SAIL (BN PHASE 4)

Tgt No	Description	Grid	Alt
ZT 5310	Track	612775	600
ZJ 5533	Track	628764	300
ZJ 5534	Track Junction	638734	50
ZJ 5531	High Ground	645772	850
ZT 5311	Stream	577782	425
ZJ 5529	Track Junction	615783	750 FPF

Also given out at the orders Group was the 'Communication Electronic Instruction' (CEI), which detailed the radio infrastructure, or 'nets' and their associated frequencies, with a scaling of one per CP. A CEI is by its very nature a document that contains highly sensitive intelligence information and as such is closely guarded, with their care and security given to that of one's personal weapon – and I held H1's copy.

Having now been attached to 29 Commando Regiment as an additional gun battery, we were required to adopt their standard operating procedures formats for field administration and orders. 29 Commando Regiment's orders format was similar to those of our own in 4th Field Regiment back home, leaving whoever took down the orders needing only to fill in the blanks.

Wednesday, 19 May (D-2)
Weather still reasonably calm. Slight swell & overcast. Large number of vessels in fleet. Mail closed, wrote to Jill. Still just off the Falklands. Have Flu, on antibiotics. Political outlook bleak, looks like going in on Thursday evening and Friday morn. All kit is issued and we're waiting to go. All had or given final briefs.

The sight of the fleet was like nothing I'd ever seen before and it eclipsed what I'd previously thought as a significant number of ships. It was probably the first time that we had truly seen the scope and scale of the invasion force and it brought home the task in hand.

Being cooped up in a forced-air environment, along with the numbers on board being at maximum capacity, sniffs and snivels were becoming common place and I was to succumb to a touch of flu. Having visited the sickbay, I was put on a course of antibiotics and prayed that I would be feeling better come the time for us to go ashore.

By this stage we were essentially ready to go, bar confirmation of timings. All our training and preparations were now finished, we all had been given our orders, were packed and now ready and poised for action. The downside of this was the inevitable waiting, which was briefly put to one side when unexpectedly news came through that there was another opportunity to send mail back home.

Throughout the voyage south, homeward bound mail was regularly dispatched to whatever ship was making the return trip north back to Ascension, where it was flown back to the UK. The message we received that the mail run on the 14th was our last opportunity to send mail home proved to be a hasty one. As such, on the 14th we all wrote what we expected

SOP 24

REPORTS/RETURNS/REQUESTS - 29 CDO REGT

1. No change from previous return IS to be reported.

Ser	Report	As At	To RHQ	To Bde	Method/Remark
(a)	(b)	(c)	(d)	(e)	(f)
1.	SITREP	0600 1800 As req	0700 1900 As req	0800 2000 As req	Line/ Radio/ Hand
2.	LOCSTAT	After each change of location			Radio (in code)/Hand
3.	AIR SUPPORT REQUESTS	Preplan Immed	1400 Soonest	1500 Soonest	Radio/Hand Radio
4.	LOGREQ/OPDEM	As req		1800	Radio/Hand
5.	SHELL REP/ BOMBREP/ MORTREP	As req			Radio
6.	AMMO + BATTLE BTY STATE	0200 0800 1400 2000	0300 0900 1500 2100	0900	Radio/Hand (Shortened state only) Full Return
7.	DAILY FIGHTING STATE	2000	2359	0900	Radio/Hand
8.	DAILY GUN/VEH EQPT STATE	2000	2359	0900	Radio/Hand
9.	NBC 1	As req			Radio/Hand
10.	JAMREP	As req			
11.	DECEPTION REP	As req			

NB All formats are at Annexes to SOP 24 - 29 Cdo SOP's.

This annex shows 29 Commando Regiment's administrative Standard Operating Procedure for Reports, Returns and Requests. It details what return is sent, to whom and by what means. It's in A5 format and it made up part of my officer's A5 Nirex pocket folder.

to be our last letters home. What we didn't know was that another ship was now detaching itself from the convoy and making that round trip back to Ascension. Consequently, a pipe was made to the effect that we were allowed another 'last' mail run and to that end, I wrote my last letter to Jill.

As part of the detailed planning for the re-invasion, the obvious question for the Battery was how were we to get ashore and this fell to Bill Moore. By this stage in proceedings, the OP Parties had joined up with their respective

Companies and we had effectively parted company. There were two ships' 'fly in' programs to consider, with the bulk of the personnel on *Norland* and all our equipment on *Europic*. The plan was to commence the fly-in from *Norland*, with the protection/clearing party loading first, followed by Bill Moore and Sergeant Taylor, as the Reconnaissance Party, in a Gazelle helicopter. Once all were airborne, we had be flown towards the drop-off point, where the Gazelle would fly over and mark the position by dropping a smoke grenade. This would be followed by myself in the lead Sea King of two (fifteen persons each), with orders to be prepared to fight for and secure the position in preparation of the main gun group flying in. Three further Sea Kings sorties (fifteen, fifteen and fourteen persons) would then follow on some twenty-five to thirty minutes later.

The detail of Bill's plan was as follows:

We were all to be flown from the rear flight deck, with all 'sticks', namely the group of individuals pre-flight, being required to be nearby at least five minutes beforehand, ready to board as a 'chalk', or flight detail once on board and allocated a 'serial' or flight number/callsign, as designated on the timeline. For this to happen, my stick was to muster in the Continental Lounge by L-30 (11:00), even if in defence stations, to then move to our assault station by L-15 (11:15), which required the standard five minutes' built-in safety factor. As the stick commander, I had a white card on white were listed, our assault station, the times of mustering and leaving, and our order of priority. The military assign letters to phases in an operation: H Hour would be the time to begin an assault by crossing the start line. Similarly P Hour would be the time set for a parachute assault drop and L Hour the time of a heli-borne assault landing. L Hour was set for first light which was 11:30 Zulu, where Zulu time is the military's term for GMT.

Serial	Loading	Leaving	Land	C/S Helo
1171B	L-10	L-8	L+4	V1 (Sea King)
1171C	L-8	L-6	L+4	V2 (Sea King)
1171A	L-5	L-3	L+4	C3 (Gazelle)
1172C	L+24	L+26	L+31	V2, V3 V4 (3x Sea King)
1172J	?			
1172U	?			

From then on the serials came from *Europic*, with A Sub leading the way, followed by two pallets of ammunition. The CP Land Rover Trailer was to follow, containing all the CPs tentage and equipment, with the PADS/FFR Radio Land Rover next. The PADS Land Rover housed a vehicle-mounted survey box of tricks used to determine one's position to the meter, it was radio fitted and was the only vehicle we were allowed the luxury of for the CPs. The next load was for one solitary Gun's 1-Tonne Land Rover. The Gun Subs B to F then followed in turn, mirroring A Sub's fly-in. After F Sub, two serials of gun store followed by the Battery's latest acquisition of two 250cc dispatch riders' motorbikes, to be used for reconnaissance. Fifteen loads of two pallets per net, followed by a last single pallet net saw

OP DEM / LOG REQ
OP Dem / Log Req N° on at DTG (Z)

ALPHA - C/S

BRAVO - 1. Vocab Sect
2. Part N°
3. Description
4. Eqpt Type
5. Qty
6. Addl Remarks

CHARLIE - 1. Delivery Grid
2. DTG Delivery Required
3. Unit Collection.

only diff from Flyin to Bty Scale is 1368 He

LOG REQ - 24hrs before (80 rds/gun)
OP DEM - Immed priority (50 rds/gun)
IMMEDIATE - 50% of non He Nature RPG

				RPG
A	HÉ	720		120
B	HE PLUGED			
C	SMK	96		16
D	ILLUM	24		4
E	HESH	48		8
G	MARKER - RED	12		2
H	-"- ORANGE	12		2
I	CARTG NORM	912		32
J	-"- SUPER	228		38
L	L33	144		23
M	L27	480		80
N	L32	200		
—	SPOTTERS	228		48

This handwritten 'OPDEM/LOGREQ' annex shows the same format for each request/demand depending on ammunition stocks held on the position. The format is broken down into 'headings and sub-headings' for brevity during radio communications. It shows the numbers of types of artillery round required to be held at Battery level and it's broken down to each gun's holding. Importantly, it specifies when stock levels require the routine request be upgraded to an operational demand. A late pencil entry details that the 'only difference from fly in to Battery scales is 1368 rounds of HE'. This also was part of my A5 pocket folder.

This shows the first part of my handwritten Orders form, which, like the others, is broken down for brevity. There's no time to write down the headings during Orders and its preset format means nothing is missed. In Serial 7, the '19, 29, 39 ... 69' relate to the Battery Centre's locations; similarly, Serial 23 detailing '1 to 6' gives the grid references of the individual battery positions. 29 Battery was designated 'Callsign 6' and its derivatives. Orders are only passed from officer to officer and as such, it was the first section in my pocket folder.

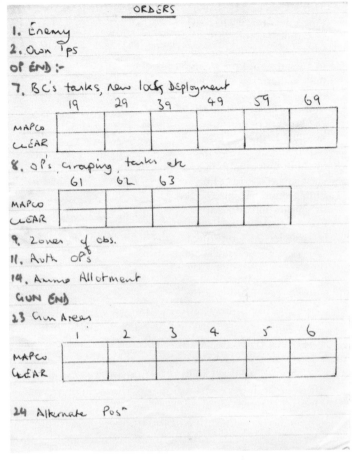

us nearly set up. The last load was the Battery's store, with the last serial being those eleven men left on *Europic* who did the hooking up.

The tactic behind sending just one gun ahead is to establish the position as 'Battery Ready'. The practice is that as soon as the CPs set up and the first gun is in 'Action', then the position is in Gunner terms 'ready', albeit that it's only one gun. This is more of a throw-back to traditional gun position occupations, where the Guns drove onto the position in turn, so the delay from guns 2 to 6 is acceptable. The Gunner kudos is all in the battery which calls their 'Battery Ready' first, as is for each Gun Sub to call 'Ready' during a Fire Mission. During firing, the CP that can process the firing solution first and pass it out to the Guns and the Gun Sub that calls 'Ready' first, allows the CP to call 'Battery Ready' first and take the lead in any multi-Battery or Regimental Fire Mission.

With paper expected to be in short supply, the orders detailing the flying program were written down on the reverse side of the kit list, with the admin and reporting timings on the front.

By mid-evening the mood was very subdued for a number of reasons. The two main ones being that any political solution appeared to have run its

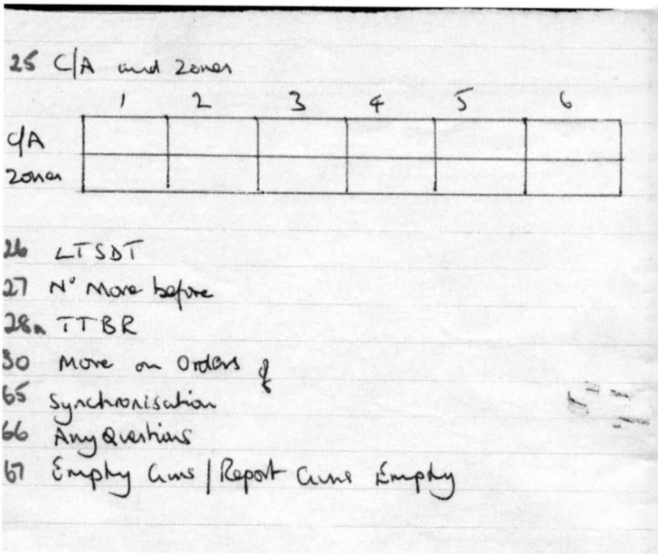

This shows part two of the Orders form. This part contains the more technical aspects of gunnery, in order to meet the support we must deliver. Serial 25 specifies the main direction of orientation of the position, with Serial 26 giving the minimum possible target distance required, known as a line-to-shoot-down-to. Being too close to a crest/ridge line, or high ground, might void the firing solution and a non-firing worked example must be completed to confirm any specification. Serial 28a details the time to be ready by.

25 C/A and Zones

C/A	1	2	3	4	5	6
Zones						

26 LTSDT
27 N° More before
28a TTBR
30 Move on Orders of
65 Synchronisation
66 Any Questions
67 Empty Guns / Report Guns Empty

course, with military action seemingly inevitable. The second reason being much closer to us here and at the news, which filtered through the ship, of a tragic flying accident involving the Special Air Service (SAS). A Sea King was cross-decking members of the SAS, when it was reported to have crashed into the sea with a significant loss of life. Thankfully there were survivors, but the exact number of those on board was not given. Rumours varied, but the consistent numbers talked about, were that the crew of three had survived as had five of the troopers, but tragically eighteen to twenty SAS died. The later brought home the stark reality of what we were doing, coupled with the fact that is was so close to where we were. This news, on top of the loss of HMS *Sheffield* on 4 May, meant that mood was black.
Thursday, 20 May (D-1)

Also filled away in my pocket folder was my handwritten note for the emergency HF frequencies, should the need arise.

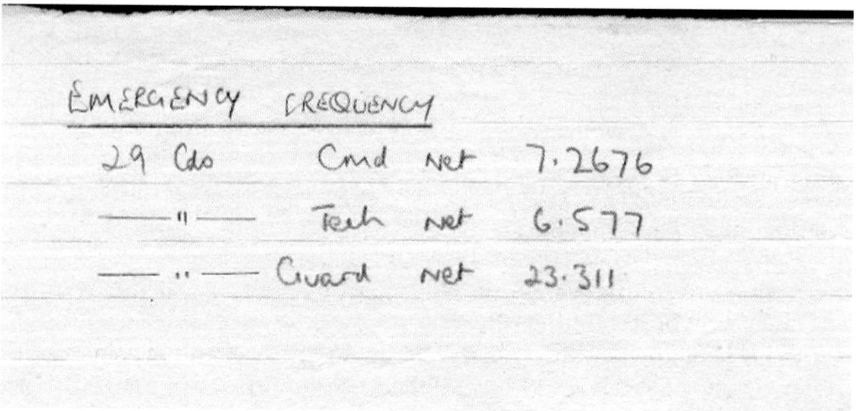

EMERGENCY FREQUENCY

29 Cdo	Cmd Net	7.2676
—— " ——	Tech Net	6.577
—— " ——	Guard Net	23.311

ARTILLERY TARGET LIST - OP SUTTON

1. TARGET LIST - LONG RUN (In Phase 3)

Tgt No	Description	Grid	Alt
ZJ 5527	Sussex Mt West	595785	600'
ZJ 5528	Sussex Mt East	608787	700'
ZJ 5529	Track Junction	615783	750'
ZJ 5530	High Ground	628781	900'
ZJ 5531	High Ground	645772	850'
ZJ 5532	Bodie Peak	669757	900'
ZJ 5533	Track	628764	300'
ZJ 5534	Track Junction	638734	50'

2. TARGET LIST - TIGHT SAIL (In Phase 4)

Tgt No	Description	Grid	Alt	
ZT 5310	Track	612775	600'	
ZJ 5533	Track	628764	300'	
ZJ5534	Track Junction	638734	50'	
ZJ 5531	High Ground	645772	850'	
ZT 5311	Stream	577782	425'	
ZJ 5529	Track Junction	615783	750'	FPF

As part of the initial landings on the 21st May, codename 'OP Sutton', an Artillery Target List was drawn up by the Battery Commander to support 2 Paras' phased move ashore. This was handed out when our main orders were given to go ashore. Once ashore, I was my role as a CPO to plot the targets in readiness for a call for fire.

Again awoken to defence stations. Now routine. Weather cloudy and with rain, swell was 8'-10'. At 1500 local (1900Z) we were given the order to move. We are heading due west all day. All timings at 1800 (local) to 2200Z. We hand in all personal admin at 1700 local. Final brief. Leave at 1130Z on Friday 21st.

Due to an error in Naval communications, it wasn't until the 20th that the final decision to land at San Carlos was received; however, preparations were well under way and in true military fashion, we had go where ever we were sent. What was clear was that we were in the final stages of deployment, as we sailed towards the Falklands. We were acutely aware of our vulnerability and we spent much of the day at Defence Stations, which revolved around lying on your bunk, with your helmet on and wearing a life jacket.

By this time, having spent so long at sea, if you had asked anyone to invade, regardless of what they were potentially about to face, the answer would have been a resounding 'yes'. The fact was that we just wanted to get ashore.

Sergeant Walker felt as we all did: 'The worst parts of the voyage down was the length of time on board, toward the end, being confined to the cabins in full kit, being on the ship/North Sea Ferry, with the threat of an air strike.'

The air threat was probably one of the embarked troops' greatest worries,

My morphine tag. It was emphasised that morphine was strictly an individual issue and that it wasn't to be used on others, despite their need. My recollection was that the morphine was taped to one's 'dog tags' and the form would be filled out by the person administering it. Failing to record administering morphine could lead to the casualty being given an overdose by the medical teams, as by default, no tag equals no morphine, hence the danger.

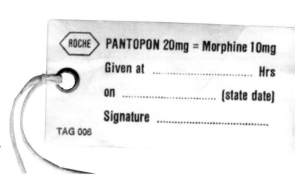

This is the first of five pages of the Communication Electronic Instruction (CEI), which details the artillery radio communications networks and the frequencies assigned to each. This document was highly sensitive and afforded the same level of care as your weapon. The two CPOs were given one of the two copies issued to the position. Mine lived in my pocket folder.

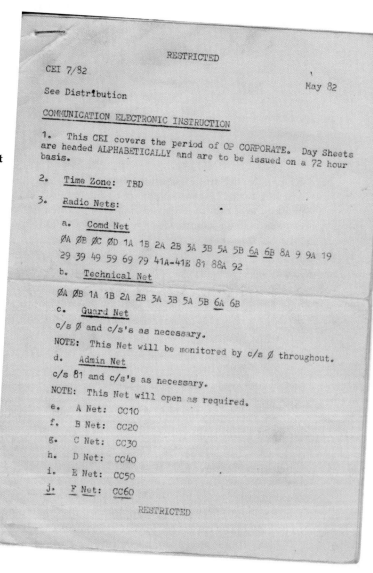

RESTRICTED

CEI 7/82

See Distribution

May 82

COMMUNICATION ELECTRONIC INSTRUCTION

1. This CEI covers the period of OP CORPORATE. Day Sheets are headed ALPHABETICALLY and are to be issued on a 72 hour basis.

2. Time Zone: TBD

3. Radio Nets:

a. Comd Net

ØA ØB ØC ØD 1A 1B 2A 2B 3A 3B 5A 5B 6A 6B 8A 9 9A 19 29 39 49 59 69 79 41A-41E 81 88A 92

b. Technical Net

ØA ØB 1A 1B 2A 2B 3A 3B 5A 5B 6A 6B

c. Guard Net

c/s Ø and c/s's as necessary.

NOTE: This Net will be monitored by c/s Ø throughout.

d. Admin Net

c/s 81 and c/s's as necessary.

NOTE: This Net will open as required.

e. A Net: CC10

f. B Net: CC20

g. C Net: CC30

h. D Net: CC40

i. E Net: CC50

j. F Net: CC60

RESTRICTED

with Gunner Kirvell repeating his Father's advice to always try to get on deck during air warnings. 'He only ever gave me three bits of advice in my time in the Army and that was one of them.'

Outside, the air defence crews were manning the rails, but thankfully the weather was poor and the risk of air attacks minimal.

At the end of the afternoon, the entire Battalion Group was assembled in 'The Continental Lounge', which was by far the largest space on board, for Lieutenant Colonel 'H' Jones final address. This was followed by a brief church service conducted by the Padre. The atmosphere was most sombre. 'H' Jones's address steeled everyone to the task ahead, while David Cooper prepared everyone, not only to the reality of what we were about to do, but allowed individuals to contemplate and make peace with their maker. At the end, there was no overt show of bravado, as everyone was focused on what they had to do and we all filed out in relative silence.

After we had dispersed, the last thing to do was the personal administration referred to, which was the stay behind, non-military things destined for the ubiquitous standard army suitcase, such as, sports kit, books, personal radios and those items replaced by the issue of the Arctic clothing. We were all rather dubious of the promise that we had see them again, as Sergeant Walker remembered: 'We were told to leave all personal effects behind in our suit cases, which should have included cameras. Judging by the amount of photo's appearing at reunions and on social media now, that did not happen!'

The final timings, as I noted them down:

Kitbags – 17:15

Tea – 17:30-19:00 Officers 18:00-19:00

18:00 to Zulu Time

23:00Z - All below D Deck to Forward Lounge

11:00Z - Breakfast

Fly Ashore

The change at 18:00 hours to Zulu Time, was to change from the ship's local time, to operational time. This was to ensure communications between the UK and the Falkland Islands didn't result in any misunderstandings because of being in different time zones. The requirement to move everyone up below D Deck was to get them above the waterline.

Friday, 21 May (D-Day)
At this point my notes transfer from my Desk Diary to my War Dairy.

Note: The current 1:50,000 maps of the Falklands show an eastings grid displacement of 200m from those issued in 1982, therefore the true grid on the current map is 200m west (left) of the plotted one. For example: A grid reference given in this book as Grid 123847, would need to be adjusted to grid 121847 on a modern map. The grid locations given throughout this book relate to the maps as issued in 1982.

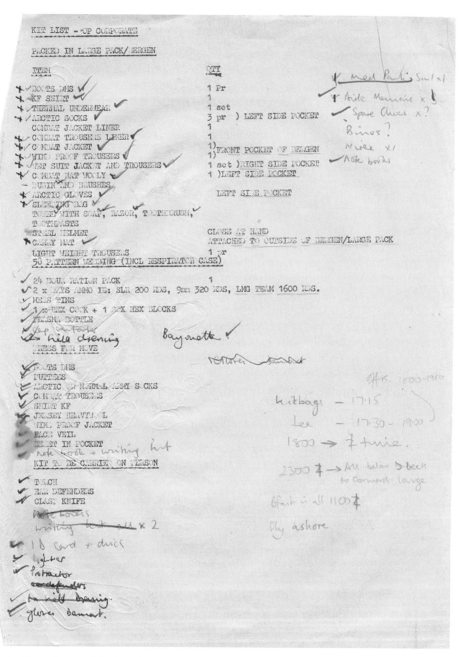

At first glance, this just looks like it's our standard kit list for going ashore, which it predominantly is. Items were checked and double-checked, as seen by the number of marks against each item, but it also covers my specific CPO kit, aid memoir and pocket folder, along with officer-assigned equipment such as binoculars. The handwritten pencil entry on the right-hand side details the final timings as part of Bill Moore's plan to helicopter us off the ships and onto our first gun position. Paper was at a premium by this stage, so when we were given these final details, all I had to hand was my kit list, 20 May 1982.

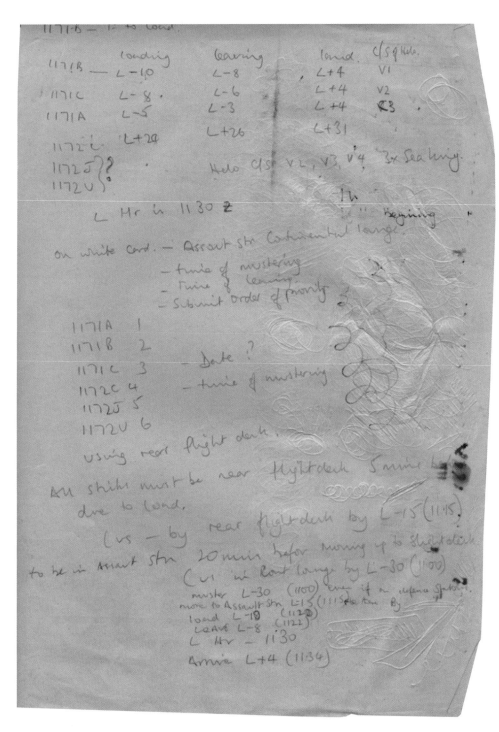

Bill's Moore's orders, detailing the flying programme, copied down on the then blank reverse side of my kit list, as given to the detachment commanders. The full transcript of the plan is covered in the text, 19 May 1982.

SHIP NORLAND 29 BTY

SERIAL ASSIGN NUMBER	Serial No		PAX	U/SLING	WEIGHT (kgs)	REMARKS.
1171 A	1	GPO +1	2		600	FORCE / GAZELLE
B	2	PAX	15		4500	PROT / GEARING
C	3	PAX	15		4500	— • —
1172 C	6	PAX	15		4500	
J	12	PAX	15		4500	
U	23	PAX	14		4200	

This is a copy of Bill Moore's plan, detailing the main personnel move off *Norland*. I was on Serial 1171B, along with Serial 1171C, in a pair of Sea Kings, leading a thirty-man protection/clearing patrol for the initial wave leading the Battery ashore. We were prepared to fight for our foothold on the island, 19 May 1982.

SHIP EUROPIC 29 BTY

SERIAL OF	Serial No		PAX	U/SLING	WEIGHT (kgs)	REMARKS.
1172 A	4	GUN		GUN	4200	A SUB
B	5	AMMO		NET	4500	2 × PALLETS
D	7	¾ Tn TLR		TLR	3000	CP
E	8	¾ Tn UR		UR	5200	PADS / FFR
F	9	1 TONNE		UR	4300	
G	10	GUN		GUN	4200	B SUB
H	11	AMMO (2)		NET	4500	2 × PALLETS
K	13	GUN		GUN	4200	C SUB
L	14	AMMO (3)		NET	4500	2 × PALLETS
M	15	GUN		GUN	4200	D SUB
N	16	AMMO (4)		NET	4500	2 × PALLETS
O	17	GUN		GUN	4200	E SUB
P	18	AMMO (5)		NET	4500	2 × PALLETS
Q	19	GUN		GUN	4200	F SUB
R	20	AMMO (6)		NET	4500	2 × PALLETS
S	21	GUN STORES		NET	2000	
T	22	GUN STORES		NET	2000	
V	24	MOTORBIKES		NET		2 × CANAMS
1173 A	25	AMMO (7)		NET	4500	2 × PALLETS
B	26	"	8			
C	27	"	9			
D	28	"	10			
E	29	"	11			
F	30	"	12			
G	31	"	18			
H	32	"	14			
J	33	"	15			
K	34	"	16			
L	35	"	13			
M	36	"	18			
N	37	"	19			
O	38	"	20			
P	39	"	21			
Q	40	"	22		2200	1 × PALLET
R	41	STORES		NET	2000	
S	42	PAX	11		3300	

This was the technical part of Bill Moore's plan, namely getting the guns and ammunition off *Europic*, importantly in an order designed for us to get straight into action in support of the main invasion, should the need arise, 19 May 1982.

Chapter 4

War Diary

MY KIT FOR landing was considerable. It included full Arctic windproof clothing, Arctic underwear, waterproofs (including waterproof gloves), spare clothing and boots as per the kit list. Helmet, my new trial helmet was not officially cleared for operational use, but considerably better than the standard steel 'battle bowler' issue, so I took it. Belt fighting order, with bayonet and bergen. Sleeping bag and roll mat, 'kip' sheet with bungees/para-cord. Medical kit, with 1litre of saline solution, two x 1litre water bottles, three days' rations (including Hexamine (hexi) at a rate of one box per day). Personal weapon – 9mm SMG sub-machine gun, four x 30 rounds magazines, plus sixty spare rounds of 9mm ammunition, two (four) x L2 grenades, two (four) x 84mm Carl Gustav Anti-Tank rounds, 1-inch Very flare pistol with thirty-six (seventy-two) rounds of mixed coloured flares. RAF style 'Nav Bag' [Navigators canvas briefcase] with the Command Post's technical documentation, consisting of: Firing Tables, three gun-slide rules, Nirex folders, which are folders containing clear plastic sleeves (orders/reports & returns/technical forms) and stationary.

The initial twenty-four-hour Arctic rations scales were for three days. After the first twenty-four hours, a stores request, knowns as a LOGREP would be sent for a further three days, with the rations request dispatched the following day, and the cycle repeated.

Whilst this was my scaling of personal kit, weapon and ammunitions, it was not dissimilar to that of others, save for the technical Nav Bag. Most carried 84mm rounds and the gun crews carried extra 7.62mm for our six Light Machine Guns - LMGs.

The numbers in brackets relating to ammunition were the initial scalings, but halved due to lack of space/weight. There just wasn't enough room in my personal equipment to pack everything away; and initially when I did try to stow the smaller items, as well as externally attach the four Carl Gustav rounds, from the original ammunition issue, I couldn't physically pick up my bergen. I couldn't understand as to why we, or more importantly that I, had been issued with the Very pistol and so many flare rounds in the first place. I had never seen one before and to be issued with it at the last moment seemed to be more of an afterthought than tactical.

It was, just like the flares, albeit now halved, heavy and it took up valuable space in my bergen and seemed totally pointless. Whilst the pistol came with a large heavy leather shoulder holster, there was no such provision for the flares, which was irritating to say the least. I found a small number of plastic bags to split them into for packing, which at least kept them in one place.

The issue of the cold weather clothing was very well received, as mentioned earlier, with the exception of the Ski March Boots, which we universally failed to break in after leaving Ascension and were left on board. They were causing a number of foot complaints and it was decided a few days earlier to go in wearing our DMS boots. Unfortunately, our DMS ankle boots were neither never intended, nor capable of withstanding prolonged use in such boggy conditions, possessing no waterproofing capability and provided little to no comfort to the wearer. The issue of Arctic socks helped to offset the problem of the boots; the acrylic temperate issue socks would have been useless in these conditions. The clothing was by-and-large well suited to the conditions that we now found ourselves in, with the windproof jacket and trousers greatly reducing the effects of the bitterly cold wind. The Arctic underwear proved to be a good base layer. The only problem we found was with the fully reversible (white/green) waterproofs, constructed from of a non-breathable material, which caused you to sweat under moderate activity.

The Arctic Rations were a new experience and were also generally well received, whilst there were similarities in their content to the temperate (North West Europe) issue of the day, they did require one to actually cook the meals. Both ration types boxes were the same size and both came in eight menu variations, with the temperate style's meals contained in tins, which could be eaten cold, whilst the Arctic meals were dehydrated and/ or freeze dried, hence the cooking requirement. Both contained sundries of biscuits, spreads, chocolate and nuts, complemented with a beverage pack of tea, coffee, powdered milk and sugar, as well as packets of soup and squash. The main difference was that the Arctic pack had effectively double the sundry snacks, as they were designed to compromise the need to cook and be eaten 'on the go'. The bonus in the Arctic ration was the inclusion on a pint's worth of hot chocolate powder, which when some of it was added to the sachet of porridge, it made chocolate porridge. This little and seemingly minor delight helped raise spirits at breakfast.

Both types of ration used the solid fuel Hexamine, which came in a box of eight tablets, which fitted into a fold-out pre-formed lightweight metal cooker. Hexamine tablets can best be described as looking like a fire lighter, were very difficult to light in the wind and almost impossible to light when wet. They also gave of toxic fumes, requiring cooking to be done in a ventilated area. The problem that we faced, was that the temperate ration pack came with a single box of Hexamine, whereas the Arctic pack requires a second box – due to its dehydrated contents and increased beverages pack – and we were only given one pack per day. This was either an oversight, or the supply chain having insufficient quantities in the first instance. The reality of our situation was that on a day-to-day basis, we had to sacrifice the cooking times to stretch out our meagre resources. On occasions, it was a choice of having either a hot drink or to eat.

One other problem was that the menus only varied in their main meal content and whilst there are technically eight varieties, they can become repetitive over a period of time. The issue we faced was that menu rotation took absolutely no time at all. I spent my entire time, except for approximately five days' respite of chicken supreme, eating the mutton granules menu. The one trick often used to 'combat' the monotony of the menu, was to carrying a small container of curry powder. Mine was kept in a small plastic spice pot, secured by the ubiquitous 'harry black maskers', a military grade black sticky tape. Despite the addition of a pinch of curry powder to the pot, it took some ten years after getting back to rediscover the delights of both lamb and mutton.

As an additional gun battery with 29 Commando Regiment, 29 Battery went ashore without the use of the Land Rover based FACE, which was available to 29 Regiment's 7, 8 & 79 Batteries, each of which they took ashore. FACE is a large vehicle mounted artillery computer, the sole purpose of which is to produce firing data for the Guns and it was the universally preferred option for this. As a consequence of not taking our Command Post FACE-equipped Land Rovers, we were required to use the manual back-up known as FAME for the processing of firing solutions. Under 'normal' circumstances, i.e. pre-deployment, there was an almost total reliance placed on FACE. The back-up to FACE was FACE, i.e. the other CP. FAME was rarely used, took time to recollect the complexities/processes required and considered archaic.

What proved to be invaluable training, was the period when the 4th Regiment supported the Royal School of Artillery, Larkhill; whilst the School's supporting regiment changed over, in the period shortly before the Argentine invasion of the Falkland Islands. During this transitional period, 29 Battery spent a considerable time supporting the field training for the SMIG Course on Salisbury Plain. SMIGs, or Sergeant Major Instructors of Gunnery to give them their full title, are Warrant Officers 2 of considerable gunnery experience, who have a mastery of all matters technical, making them the Artillery's arbiter of fact on a Gun Position. Every live firing training camp has a SMIG allocated and all bad practices, or poor drill are unceremoniously quickly stamped out. Here, the SMIGs Course takes experienced senior Non-Commissioned Officers, normally with the rank of Staff Sergeant, through an exacting and technical course, to become such technical authorities, rewarding them with promotion to Warrant Officer 2 on competing the course. Through supporting such a course, the general professionalism of the Battery was raised, as a direct result of being under the watchful eye of potential instructors, who were themselves under the microscope. Emphasis was placed on the finer points and less practiced aspects of gunnery and that's where we gained, in tandem with the student instructors. What seemed to be a considerable part of the SMIG's Command Post's field training, was that FACE continually went 'down' and therefore unavailable, requiring us to resort to FAME. This seemed to be the methodology whereby the black art of FAME was passed on from one generation of SMIG to another. Consequently, the Battery's Command Posts became extremely proficient in the use of FAME, having demystified it on Salisbury Plain and saw it for what it was, which was refreshed and refined during the long sea voyage south.

During a fire mission, when an initial target grid is sent to the Command Post, the first action is to plot it onto a plotting board. The plotting board is a very low tech solution, which provides the basics for the firing solution. Essentially, it's a large 6400 mil (or 360 degree) protractor, which is placed over either a 1:50,000 map, or even just simple 2 cm square gridded graph paper, either of which is under clear Perspex. If it's placed over plain gridded paper, the actual Eastings and Northings of the area can be written on the Perspex cover. The key to this is to accurately place the centre of the protractor over the grid of the Battery Centre and firmly secure the protractor down. The Battery Centre is vitally important, as it is the grid datum point when calculating the Battery's weight of fire. A ranging arm, similar to a ruler, is attached to the centre of the protractor and can rotate around as required, immediately determining both the target's range and bearing.

The plotted target grid, as well as providing a bearing and distance to the target, also doubles as a gross error safety check. In the case of FACE, after the initial gross error check on the plotting board, the target's grid would be entered into FACE, which in turn would provide the computer's firing solution. Here the Command Post Officer's (CPO) technical assistant would enter the data into the computer's keyboard and the CPO would have to check this input data, before pressing the umbilical 'enter' key. With regards to FAME, the initial plot was the firing solution, with the distance being converted to a generic elevation by use of a range/charge slide-rule, thereby time was saved by not having to enter data into FACE. The required charge for the rounds can also be determined during the initial plot, by extrapolating and superimposing the charge's range bracket on the ranging arm. So where the plotted grid falls along the range arm, the corresponding charge can be read off, allowing the CPO to get the ammunition preparation order to the Guns without delay.

At this time, a number of factors must be taken into consideration, in order to complete the firing solution. Firstly, that the Battery's weight of fire is calculated from 'Battery Centre' and the disposition of how the Guns are dispersed needs to be factored, in order to concentrate that weight of fire. Not doing so would mean that each gun's fall of shot would reflect the mirror image of how they are positioned. Secondly, there are minor differences in gun muzzle velocities, again failing to correct for them builds in errors at the target. Whilst the differences in bearing and/or elevation may only be a few mils, it can make a difference on the footprint of how the rounds land. Other variables, such as differences in shell weight and charge temperature, can be worked out in advance using Firing Tables, a series of weighty tomes containing a tabular version of almost every firing variable, allowing adjustments to CPO's calculations. The variable that was impossible to determine was the 'met', or more specifically the wind and how it affects the trajectory. There was a simple fix to all of these factors and that was to simply shoot them out. Depending on the proximity of own troops, the Forward Observation Officer can, providing it's 'safe' to do so, make the initial target grid – one that allows for a degree of latitude in the opening grid, which absorbs these variables, hence 'shooting them out'.

In essence, FACE required one to enter the data twice, once for the plotter's gross error check and secondly into FACE itself. In reality, the differences can be measured in seconds; however, as a direct result of just working with FAME, when any multi-battery call for fire came, 29 Battery invariably called 'ready' first, in the race for the adjustment.

Chapter 5
Going Ashore

Friday, 21 May (D-Day)
Landed at 'Head of the Bay' almost 1km out and had to tab in. Initial deployment went wrong, choppers to the wrong place. You can see the ships in the bay; and their sirens sound as air attack is imminent. En forces tgt'ed airstrike. Mirage flew over our position. No casualties. 3 Mirages attacked OC's loc but missed. 2 planes shot down (Pucara). No real en threat in the area. But there were a few cases of activity around to the North. Staging 4 on 8 off & digging takes priority. All is well after day 1. Weather not too bad, windy & cold, frost in AM. When we re-invaded not too bad. Rain.

Having dispersed from the CO's final briefing yesterday afternoon, we were required to wait in our bunks/cabins until called forward to assault stations. The morning pipe that signalled the start of proceedings was 'Ride of the Valkyries', which focused one and all. I was detailed to go in at first light (1130 Zulu), in the lead Sea King of two, to lead a clearing/fighting party of thirty, fifteen in each, made up from the command post crews and gun numbers, in order to secure the position close to the farmstead – Head of the Bay House – prior to the Battery flying in. On completion, I was then to assist in setting up the position, under the direction of the GPO. At the appointed time, we made our way to our nominated muster station, where we were guided to the flight deck. The mood was dark and nobody spoke as we made our way out, each filled with the feeling of 'right, this is it'.

As we made our way to the waiting helicopter, I could make out our new surroundings and thought, much as others, of its striking similarity to Scotland's Hebrides. Being the first in the chalk, I took up position by the cabin door, helping each in turn to climb aboard, and then assist the aircrewman to load the stack of bergens left as each climbed in. Having been helped aboard myself, I took my position by the door, to be first off and to reverse the procedure.

We took off from *Norland*, but instead of flying straight to our intended drop off point as expected, the pilot landed on the rear of the assault ship HMS *Intrepid*, which we believed to be as a result of a possible air attack. I don't recall any Argentine air attacks coming in at first light, as to achieve that, they would have attempted to fly under the radar at very low level at night over the sea and then negotiate the island's terrain, before pressing home their attack. The more probable explanation was that we landed on the back of *Intrepid*, whilst the second Sea King loaded, thereby we could land as a pair at the drop off point.

After skimming over the water for only a few minutes, we arrived at our 'drop off point' and disembarked at great speed into a hasty defensive position, with the helicopters wasting no time to get away from the uncertainty of the shore line. The silence that followed the noise of the

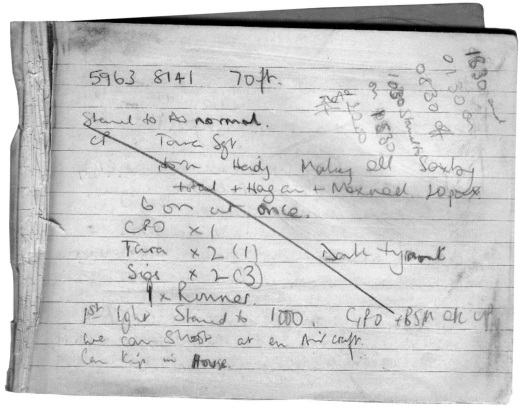

This is the first page of my operational notebook, which importantly gives the grid reference of our first gun position at Head of the Bay House. As part of the immediate setting up drills, my job as a CPO was to do an independent check of the centre of the position, known as Battery Centre (BC), to determine the grid reference, against that worked out by Bill Moore, the Gun Position Officer (GPO). Each and every firing solution is based on BC and as such it's vital that it's accurately worked out. I'd previously cut out the earlier pages, as they related to previous notes from back home in the UK. Care must be taken when plotting the grid references given in this book on a contemporary 1:50,000 map, as the grid lines on the maps of 1982 show an offset of some 200m to the west, 21 May 1982.

helicopter's departure was intense, as each scoured the immediate area for signs of danger.

It was a welcome feeling finally setting foot on dry land, every sense was heightened as we scanned our immediate vicinity in total silence. Apprehension fuelled by not knowing what's happening can be a debilitating feeling. We knew nothing of what to expect in the immediate area surrounding us; whilst the pre-landing intelligence led us to expect little to no opposition, it wasn't a cast-iron assurance. It's not fear as such, adrenaline overcomes that feeling, it's that the need to perform that drives the fight and the requirement not to show weakness. After waiting for a few minutes, I assessed the situation and called the party to hand. The initial adrenalin surge had subsided, but with my heart was still pounding I took a deep breath in and stood up. It felt like a defining point in my life, my officer training, in particular at Sandhurst, was all about leadership and this was now the real thing. I gave a quick order to move and we began our walk in.

The initial landing did not go quite as smoothly as planned. Unfortunately, due to a combination of going in at first light and the very short distance, in aviation terms from ship to shore, identification and orientation between the numerous inlets/headlands was difficult, considering the air raid threat (note my diary reference to the Mirage above) and the desire to get all ashore as soon as possible, the old adage of 'close enough is good enough' springs to mind. We were dropped off some distance from the position to the west and were forced to make our way in. By the time that we reached the position, the position was well on its way to being set up. That early feeling of apprehension we felt when first dropped off, eased as we closed in and saw familiar faces, coupled with a collective feeling of strength in numbers.

Gunner Frame was one of those in my party: 'We got picked up by a chopper, landed in the wrong position and had a long walk to where our guns were.'

Bill Moore commandeered a Sea King and landed with his own party at Head of the Bay House: 'it was not the planned gun position, but because of the air raid, the Navy just dropped us there. Without any vehicles it proved to be the only place to set up.' Similarly, the initial intention was to site the main Command Post away from the main house; however, the decision was quickly made due to the conditions to occupy the property and run the main Command Post from within. The gun position's Command Post is the nerve centre of the position and its siting is a key factor for GPOs to consider. The early morning weather was fair, but cold and relatively calm, with a touch of frost on the ground; however, the wind was soon to pick up and bring in driving rain. One bonus from being indoors was that the Command Post's room had a pot belly stove, with a mountain of peat outside for fuel.

The move ashore was for the majority 'unopposed' and as such, had the feel of being just another training evolution in those very early stages, as Gunner Kirvell tells of his arrival onto the Falklands: 'My first day landing on the Island, after being pushed into the helicopter due to the amount of kit we were carrying, seemed all very surreal. In my head it was just like being on Exercise, even when the first enemy aeroplane flew over us and started shooting at the ships in San Carlos Bay.'

Not every flight was an uneventful lift ashore, as Sergeant Walker recounts of his move. He references the collective feeling of vulnerability from being 'cooped up' on a North Sea Ferry, at the moment that an air attack came in: 'Because we were the first ones down there, apart from the Marines who had taken South Georgia, it was a relief to get off the boat. We had been on three weeks and on the last day when we were sailing into Falkland Sound we were very vulnerable. Because it was a North Sea ferry, it didn't have an awful lot of protection.

This was a SITREP taken by myself, once the Regiment was ashore and everyone was in place. Importantly, it confirmed the forward locations of 2 Paras' Patrols Company. What was evident when we plotted everything out and onto the map in the Command Post, was that we were the only guns in range to their front, 21 May 1982.

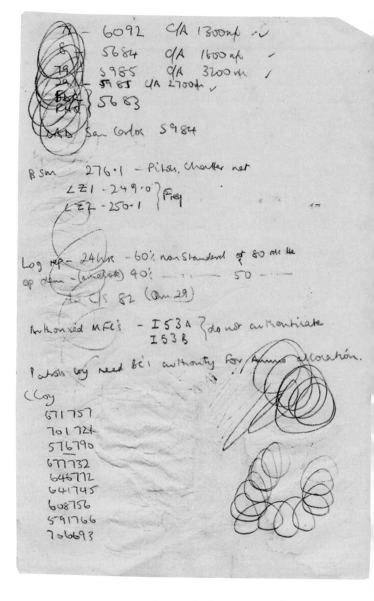

'The later came to fruition as we were about to board the helicopter when an air strike came in! Bits of fuselage hitting the ship's deck, as our air defence boys shot down a Pucara', leaving them in no doubt that "this is for real"'.

The Battery Centre was effectively just outside of the house and the Guns were sited on the edges of the farmstead. The position [Grid 5963 8141 Alt 70ft] now centred around the abandoned farmstead and from a technical perspective was ideal. We estimated that the house had been abandoned some seven months before our arrival, based on discarded newspapers, used presumably for packing. The farmstead sat in a 'clear' grassed area,

Head of the Bay House's rear aspect, looking south to north up San Carlos Water, with Fanning Head in the far distance, behind the far warship. The highly visible colour scheme proved to be an ideal line-up marker for the attacking Argentine aircraft. One of the guns under its camouflage net is set up at the rear of the position (north-west), on the northern perimeter, 21 May 1982.

The same view now, or lack of it. The house has a new roof and the chimney stacks have gone. The large green oil fired heating tank has taken over from burning peat, 7 January 2017.

smaller than a football pitch, with the house set off to one side. It had a small front garden, with a vegetable patch/garden, with a few small scrubby bushes at the rear, surrounded by an unpainted American-style post and rail fence. The house itself was a modest, but sturdy property, with the main living space downstairs, with the addition of two bedrooms built into the sloping roof. Outside, there were a number of small sheds and out buildings and a small domed roofed garage. One building that was almost as well received as the house, was the outside privy.

All the buildings conformed to the non-tactical highly-visible paint scheme of white walls and red roofs! The house also provided shelter for

Resultant recoil forces requiring C Sub to be dug out - see page 178.
(Courtesy of Steve Sprotson)

the other members of the position to conduct their personal admin within. Small paddocks, fenced off with barbed-wire surrounded the edge of the 'grassy' area, and beyond that lay the 'Camp'. The 'Camp' is known by the islanders as being any area outside of Stanley; however, to us it meant the barren, heavily tussock-grassed and often boggy land.

The initial gun position was selected with the first and specific intention of not being actually located at the deserted farmstead, but close by. The brightly coloured buildings would have been an easy target identifier for any Argentine aircraft. As it was, events overtook the initial planned deployment, mainly due to the terrain, in as much that due to the tussock grass, that the Guns remained in the position that they were helicoptered in. The absolute requirement to site the Guns first time, brought on extra pressure during the fly-in, in particular for the GPO.

As BK, David Gibbins was the senior officer on the position and was responsible for, not only for his 'normal' administrative role of rationing, water and general stores, but also for that of local defence. David worked closely with Bill as GPO, who had total responsibility for all gunnery and technical matters and was responsible for the layout of the position. It's a

This composite photo is looking south-east and south from the front of the gun position at Head of the Bay House, showing the two most forward guns; with the second command post (H1) in the foreground of the right-hand gun by the corral, its 5m mast aerials visible. The valley behind the left-hand gun go the south-east shows the main Argentine jets route in, with Mount Usborne visible behind. Sussex Mountains are rising to the right in the south-west, with 2 Paras' locations occupying the ridge line on the high ground, as seen in the distance, between the two guns. The outbuilding to the right houses the farm's generator, 21 May to 5 June 1982.

The same view today, 7 January 2017.

Looking out from the front garden of Head of the Bay House, northwards up San Carlos Water. What is noticeable is the apparent lack of ships at anchor. The rear left gun is seen behind the kennels, 21 May to 5 June 1982.

The same view today, with part of the dog kennels still remaining; note the extremely low angle of the satellite dish. The entrance to San Carlos Water is on the left of the sound, with the high ground of Fanning Head just behind, 7 January 2017.

slightly odd situation, as Bill was the next in line and the position's second in command, but as the GPO, it was his responsibility to site (position) the Guns, considering their technical firing aspect, but also bearing in mind their defence. Once the GPO is satisfied with the layout, along with its general defence, the responsibility for that defence is devolved to the BK; however, once established, Bill whilst moving around between guns, assisted David in this task.

Supporting them both was the BSM, Warrant Officer 2 Bernie Winch. In barracks, Bernie worked very closely with the BC; however, with the BC positioned well forward with 2 Para, his role was that of primarily supporting the BK. It is far too simplistic to think of his position of being just about the finer points of polished boots and pressed uniform, as being BSM, Bernie Winch was a Regimental Sergeant Major in waiting, he was the one who sets the tone and temperament of the Gunners. He had, by the very nature of his appointment, 'been it, seen it, done it' and had a wealth of experience. Whilst the GPO effectively was working alone and certainly from a technical aspect, the BK and BSM worked very closely together.

My five-man team in H1 was fronted by Bombardier Phil Marsh, who was a very competent and able technical assistant. Phil Marsh was my 'go to' man, who I could place my trust in helping me make the right call. He had an eye for detail, which considering the fine margins we worked in, was priceless. Bombardier Marsh was assisted by Gunner Jim Finlay, who despite being relatively new to his role, was both enthusiastic and cheerful in equal measures. Jim Finlay was Canadian by birth and could revert to type, but to all intents and purposes was an honorary Geordie. The one thing that Finlay possessed in abundance was an optimistic view on his lot and always seemed to have a smile on his face. The signals side of the Command Post was the domain of Lance Bombardiers Trevor Woodgate and Gregory 'Cozy' Powell, who shared the workload, by alternating from the intensity of the operational net to the more routine administrative one. Both experienced signallers, they thrived off the competition between themselves; however, Cozy Powell's handwriting did take some deciphering at times! They were assisted by Gunner Mick Botterill, who like Finlay was new to his role and was of an equal disposition. I also was also allocated Gunner Hadjicostas from the GPO's party, who acted as a 'runner' or messenger.

The 'opposition' six-man team of H2, led by Warrant Officer 2 (TSM) Trevor Banton as the CPO, was fronted by Bombardier Armstrong 'K' (Keith), who was very similar to Bombardier Marsh; who also took on the 'official' role of Battery photographer, with the aim of recording events now we were ashore. Bombardier Armstrong was assisted by Gunner Truswell, who like Gunner Findlay was relatively inexperienced. Lance Bombardier Dave Handley led the signals side, with the much lesser experienced Gunners Simpson and Kemp assisting, who like Gunner Botterill, were both equally new to the signals world. This shortfall in signals experience was made up with the addition of Gunner Tony Horn from the GPO's party. Tony Horn was an experienced signaller, who worked well above

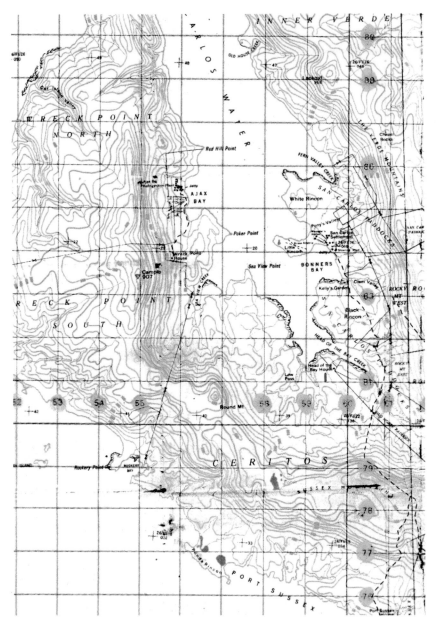

San Carlos Water and the first position (1) at Head of the Bay House. This map is a copy of James Watson's original 1.50,000 forward observers map.
(Courtesy of James Watson)

what was expected of him as a Gunner and could hold his own against the Lance Bombardiers and provided that second string in H2's signals make up. Similarly, the signallers in H1, Lance Bombardier Handley and Gunner Horn, shared their workload.

Acting as over-watch for the technical gunnery side to both Command

Taken from the corral is the forward left-hand gun, 21 May to 5 June 1982.

Posts was Sergeant Nigel 'Nige' Taylor. Technical Assistants Royal Artillery (TARAs) assisted the CPO within the Command Post in helping to produce the firing solution for the Guns. General tasks were given to those less experienced TARAs, with the Bombardiers concentrating on the fine detail of the firing table books and graphical slide rules. As a relatively young TARA Sergeant, Nige Taylor was quietly spoken and highly proficient in the Command Post and was ready to stand in as CPO, should the need have arisen. Sergeant Taylor was my Troop Sergeant when I first joined the Battery, during the later stages of the Battery's deployment to Northern Ireland, some twelve months earlier and we worked well together. Now, as Bill Moore's technical assistant, he both set and expected the highest of standards from those involved both around and in the Command Post. He was an experienced operator who kept a keen eye on the younger technical assistants' performances, offering his help and advice when needed.

In a similar role to Sergeant Taylor, the signals aspect fell to Sergeant John Maxwell, who was equally at the top of his game. Unlike Sergeant Taylor, who effectively worked alone, Sergeant Maxwell, a short barrel-chested and jovial individual, was assisted by Bombardier Malcolm Hagan, who was also equally adept. Bombardier Hagan carried a few extra pounds and whilst he found it hard to keep up when out on Battery PT, possessed a will and resolve which saw him through. He was sharp-and quick witted and an excellent operator. With communications being fundamental to what we do, these two aligned themselves, one to each Command Post; with Sergeant Maxwell going to Warrant Officer 2 Banton's H2 and Bombardier Hagan with me in H1.

Whilst individual Batteries may consider themselves to be the best, they

Head of the Bay House main building, with the small vegetable patch at its rear and the outside toilet just off the garden, overlooking San Carlos Water to the north. An LSL's stern is just visible over the 'long drop', with the rear left gun at the rear. The generator outhouse is seen to the right. The Air Defence sentry was posted on the water tank after the first air attack, 21 May to 5 June 1982.

The same rear view of the house today. The 'long drop' has long since gone, which in its day was a most valuable asset, 7 January 2017.

are completely ineffectual if they can't communicate either between each other, or forward to the Observation Parties. As such the Gunners prided themselves in their signals skills and communicating throughout the battlefield. Whilst the radio infrastructure of the infantry they support may falter, the Gunner's didn't. A truism amongst commanders at whatever level, was if they wanted to know what was going on, they would ask a Gunner!

The Survey team was responsible for the PADS; however, outside the requirement for establishing our position on initially occupying a gun position, there was little to be done. The team of Lance Bombardier Nigel Saxby, an experienced technical assistant who specialised in the PADs survey equipment, assisted by Gunners Dave Mackey and Ell both junior technical assistants of varying levels of experience and their services, was put to use by augmenting the Command Post's technical team.

Due to our only method of deployment being by air, the role of Battery Guide, as filled by Staff Sergeant Dave 'Muttley' Mutter, was somewhat redundant. Dave Mutter was one of the most experienced Gunners on the position. He was a short, stocky individual with a cheerful disposition; who was known as 'Muttley', due to possessing a laugh not too dissimilar to Dick Dastardly's dog Muttley in the cartoon Wacky Races. Traditionally, the Battery Guide would work with the GPO during the reconnaissance phase of setting up a Battery move and would then wait and guide the vehicles into their allotted position, when they followed on. As there were no vehicles, Staff Sergeant Mutter's wealth of experience was put to use by assisting Bill as the GPO, by helping to coordinate the Gun Line Commanders (GLCs), as well as helping the BK with local defence, along with welfare and morale.

The structure and make up of a six-gun Battery, means that it has the ability to be split in half, into two 3-gun sections, with each section taking one of the Command Posts, as well as the gun line coming under the supervision of a GLC. GLCs were, by definition, all highly experienced Sergeants, whose prime role is to supervise their 3-gun section. They would also manage the ammunition stocks and help to coordinate the movements when a gun would come out of action, under the direction of the GPO, to complete its daily maintenance, with the aim of having only one gun out at any time. GLCs were also experienced Detachment Commanders, or Number 1s, in their own right, having moved up from Number 1 to GLC. This gave the Battery resilience in the event of casualties. The positions of GLC were filled by Sergeant Tony Irvine and Sergeant Ernie Dobson.

Sergeant Tony Irvine was ex-7 Para RHA and another one who was Airborne to the core. He was a highly capable and forthright GLC, with an acerbic wit. Sergeant Irvine re-joined us from the RSA's Gunnery Staff Course (SMIG) just before the conflict and provided a wealth of technical knowledge across the position. If ever there was to be mischief to be had, Tony Irvine would be front and centre, but that didn't stop him from rising to become a Regimental Sergeant Major.

Sergeant Ernie Dobson was an imposing individual with a quiet

Snow. The alternate command post (H1) dug in under a camouflage net. My very own sleeping area! 21 May to 5 June 1982.

disposition. Ernie Dobson naturally transitioned, with a wealth of experience from being a Number 1, to that of GLC. Towards the end of his Army career, Ernie Dobson was awarded the MBE, a true reflection of the individual.

What was evident was that the role of a GLC was 24/7 and that he needed help in order to function over a protracted period of time. To that end, two unlikely candidates had 'on the job' training, in becoming auxiliary GLCs, particularly during darkness; with our senior cook, Sergeant Scott of the Army Catering Corps (ACC), and our senior maintainer, Sergeant Jones of the Royal Electrical and Mechanical Engineers (REME), stepping up to their new role, as well as featuring in the local defence party and plan. Whilst they lacked the pure technical skills found on a Gun Detachment, they could monitor shell stocks and ensure that the ammunition was evenly distributed.

The Guns, known as a 'Sub' and lettered from A-F were each primarily served by a detachment, averaging a seven-man crew and were commanded by a mixture of 'youth' and experience, with the absolute emphasis on ability, rather than on rank. The Detachment Commanders, or Number 1s as they were referred to were:

A Sub: Sergeant Kenny Morgan, ex-7 Para RHA and Airborne in every fibre of his body. He was precise, no nonsense and straight down the line as a Number 1.

B Sub: Sergeant Joe Walker, a gritty terrier-like Northerner, who strove to set the standards as the senior Number 1 and was calm under pressure. Bill Moore sums it up by saying, 'he was the person I would always turn to for advice; he had also been my Troop Sergeant in Northern Ireland'. Like Bill, when I eventually took over as GPO, when we returned to the UK, I was also to rely on him for his counsel.

A wider view of the house and the immediate surrounding area. The rear left-hand gun's camouflage net and members of the sub are just visible to the far right of the house, as is the southern part of the anchorage. Ajax Bay lies directly behind the house and is some 5km along the left shoreline. The thin strip of land on the right, with the adjacent warship close by, is San Carlos's airstrip jutting out into the sound, with the settlement some 3km on the right, 21 May to 5 June 1982.

The same view today. The airstrip on the thin strip of land running out into the sound more clearly shown here is no longer in use. Walking to the tip gives the illusion of being in the middle of the water, but still being on dry land and shows just how narrow the anchorage was in real terms, 7 January 2017.

The front aspect of the house, along with the main outbuildings. The start of the main ammunition drop off area is seen in the foreground. The round roofed building to the left was used by the BQMS for our stores. The dark mound to the left of the house is the peat stack. The Air Defence sentry can be seen on the water tank, 21 May to 5 June 1982.

The same view now. The rounded building has gone, however some of the original buildings remain. The front porch has gone, which shows where the command post was located. Solar panels, a wind turbine and satellite dishes show the trappings of modern living, 7 January 2017.

C Sub: Sergeant Steve 'Sprossie' Sprotson, a fit, bright and highly capable Number 1, who had not long before rejoined the Battery from being an adventure training instructor. Shortly after returning to Aldershot, Sprossie Sprotson went back to his previous position, as he didn't see a future in the Army and left the following year.

D Sub: Bombardier George 'Pig' Armstrong, another ex-7 Para RHA, and Airborne through and through. He was thickset, solid and dependable, the sort of individual who if asked to move a mountain would simply ask how far? He was known by one and all as 'The Pig' and walked round with the gun's knock-off wheel hammer in his hand for effect, not that he needed it.

E Sub: Lance Bombardier Willie 'Willie B' Butler was the junior and least experienced Number 1, but behind that lay a bright and determined individual, who competed with every Number 1 and what Willie B lacked in experience, he more than made up for it with youthful enthusiasm.

F Sub: Bombardier Paul 'Schoie' Schofield was another gritty terrier-like Northerner with a dry wit, short and stocky, who sported a huge moustache; who later in his career, rose through the ranks to become a Regimental Sergeant Major and eventually went on to be commissioned.

The Number 1s were the more senior members on the gun line; however, being a Number 1 required ability in role as a defining quality, not just rank. As such, Lance Bombardier Butler was very much treated as an equal along with the vastly more experienced Sergeants. As Number 1s, they had not only to deal with the technical gunnery aspect of their role, as well as looking after their individual Light Guns, but also the welfare, hygiene, medical and morale of their gun crews. Ensuring that individuals kept on top of their personal administration, when permitted, and keeping their weapon clean, kept everyone focused and spirits up. One thing that was going to be particularly challenging for every one of them as a detachment, was coping with sleep deprivation.

The position's admin team tasked with helping the BK was led by the Battery Quarter Master Sergeant (BQMS) Staff Sergeant John McQueenie BEM. John McQueenie was rapidly coming to the end of his service and had spent his career within the Airborne Forces and was somewhat of a legend within its fold. He had fingers in more pies and was involved in more scams than anybody I'd ever come across, then or since, and was exactly the person we needed in such circumstances. How the BQMS came up with some of his 'goodies' was best left unquestioned, but we were all very grateful of his efforts.

Assisting the BQMS were Gunners Jardine and Brown, who spent their time controlling / stockpiling our rations, water and meagre stores.

Of our REME section, Sergeant Jones became a GLC, Corporal Hilderbrando and Craftsman Bracegirdle went to the Guns, with Corporal Giles working miracles throughout in keeping the Guns in a serviceable state and in action. Our catering section followed similar lines, with Sergeant Scott also becoming a GLC and both Lance Corporal Bailey and Private Lee augmenting the Guns. Sergeant Walker noted that having untrained members of the Battery on their guns did not alleviate the work required of the detachment but that the additional numbers were a good help in other ways.

The remainder of the Battery was intended to form the local defence force, with the more senior of the non-commissioned officers acting as section commanders.

Joe Walker described the initial deployment: 'Eventually we lifted off and landed, followed by the Guns. Immediately the gunnery training and skills kicked in, in action, recorded and line ran out to the Command Post, the Battery was ready very quickly. Apart from the usual 29 Battery competitive spirt between guns, we wanted to report ready before 29 Commando Regiment and be first to fire.' Walker describes the slick core drills, from getting the gun into action, being 'recorded' or surveyed in, to connecting the communications line to the Command Post, which were honed from years of practice. Gunner kudos is that every Gun Sub wanted to be first into action, which in turn put the Battery in the race to call 'Battery Ready' first, as it confers bragging rights and is hotly contested.

We were set up by mid-afternoon, however the fly-in of all our stores and ammunition was hampered by the arrival of the Argentine jets.

During these first few hours ashore there was little or no advanced warning of any incoming hostile aircraft. The only notice we had was when they were almost upon us, as they screamed down and past us, from the valley to our front hugging the terrain. The combination of the prevailing wind and their ultra-low-level flying helped mask their path of attack and this first wave caught everyone by surprise. Most of us were heavily involved in getting on with our individual and detachment tasks, to take in what was going on around us and we were effectively spectators for the Argentine first wave. Most had either a pick or shovel in their hands than a weapon, when we first had any inkling of these incoming aircraft, which for some that by the time that were swapped out the moment was gone. I'd never seen such flying and as they flew so low and close to us that you could see the pilots and their aircraft's every detail and the roar of the engines reached a deafening crescendo as they flew by. That initial pause taken to process and comprehend what was happening was in reality only a few seconds, but it gave the Argentine aircraft time to pass through; however, it gave a fair number the chance to open up with their rifles and light machine-guns and take the fight to the enemy.

This was our first direct contact with the enemy and it lasted a mere few seconds. We continued to stand and watch the jets press home their attack, to the sounds of explosions and anti-aircraft fire; they continued to fly so low that we could see them having to pull up to drop their bombs, not only to avoid slamming into the sides of the ships, but also as they weaved their way around the anchorage, before they disappeared from sight further up the sound. As a result of being almost caught out by the incoming enemy aircraft, Bill placed an 'Air Sentry' on top of the house's water tank, being the highest point around, in the hope that it would buy us vital seconds in any future attack. As trenches were being dug and individuals took more interest in the ground around them, should there be a need to dive for cover, being stuck on top of the water tank made for a very lonely and vulnerable post.

As a position, we had marked the time when we took our first offensive action and morale was high. In fact, as the Mirage mentioned in my diary flew over, Gunner Hughes was to ask Bill if we were allowed to shoot at it!

Gunner Kirvell's earlier expression of how he felt going ashore, was brought sharply into focus, as the Argentine jets flew over the position and attacked the anchorage: 'When the first enemy aeroplane flew over us and started shooting at the ships in San Carlos Bay that changed and was soon replaced with shoot at them, after Lieutenant Moore shouted that we could shoot at them if we wanted. I did not need telling twice.'

Gunner Frame summed up the general feeling felt throughout the position, as we came to terms with our surroundings: 'It was a culture shock and within ten minutes the first Argie jet came over. There were hundreds of lads looking up at this jet. We could see the Argentine markings and you could tell everybody wanted to open up. And then the first round went off and the whole sky went red with tracers. You could hear the rounds pinging off it.'

The position at Head of the Bay House was to see scales of ammunition that we had never seen before. Peacetime firing camps would see the allocation of ammunition given out to the Guns almost in single figures, with training eking out the frugal amount, often with 'dry firing' being the primary method of training. Here, ammunition was flown in at a rate and scale never encountered. Peacetime Gun Sub manning for a Light Gun was for a six-man crew, which was thought to be sufficient, based on training practices; however, the sheer scale of the ammunition before us made David and Bill rethink numbers. The fact of the matter was that the position was now holding hundreds of rounds per gun, which because we had no vehicles, was left where it was dropped off by helicopter and everything had to be moved by hand. 105mm ammunition comes in two parts, the shell itself and its brass shell case containing the charge, each of which are packaged separately and come two per metal ammunition box. The standard High Explosive (HE) shell weighs 35lbs (16kg) and with its pair, each packed in a hard, black plastic tube/container, the ammunition box weighs in at 94lbs (42.6kg). Whilst not as heavy, the box containing the charges weighs 48lbs (22kg), with the empty brass shell cases alone weighing in at 7lbs each. Each box also contained the ubiquitous plastic inserts and cardboard packaging, which added to the volume of waste.

The plan was that each Battery went ashore with 912 rounds, or 152 rounds per gun. The logistical 'OPDEM/LOG REQ' form shows how it was broken down into the various 'natures' or types, with the following rounds shown per gun. The bulk of the ammunition was HE – 120 rounds, followed by 'SMK'(Smoke) – sixteen rounds, 'ILLUM' (an illumination parachute flare) – four rounds, 'HESH' (High Explosive Anti-Tank) – eight rounds, and 'MARKER' of which there were two red and two orange shells, which stained the area on impact and provide a highly visible reference point. As explained above, for each shell there's a corresponding standard cartridge case, designated 'CARTS NORM'; however, to fire out to maximum range, we needed to use 'CARTS SUPER' (Charge Super), for which there was an extra allocation of 228 rounds per Battery, or thirty-eight per gun. Normal range firing back in the UK meant that most firing practices were done at relatively low charges. Whilst the report, or bang, from firing is still loud, it was nowhere near that matched when firing Charge Super. Here, the report was absolutely deafening, causing tinnitus and the shock wave that hits you goes through to one's core. Standing adjacent to a gun, or in front of it when firing such a high charge is a very uncomfortable experience. The fuses came in different types - L32 HE point detonating, with the airburst options of the L33 Mechanical Time and L27 Proximity radar fuse giving various combinations, depending on the request for fire. The HESH round does not have a separate nose-fitted fuse and was not used. These anti-tank rounds are fired directly at the intended target and were taken as a precaution against any suspected Argentine armoured threat. The form also details 'SPOILERS', which we had a small stock of, where a ring is fitted over the nose of the shell as it's loaded, which is used to disrupt, or spoil the shell's aerodynamics, causing it fall short, particularly with close range and high angle missions, again which we never used.

The operational and Artillery planners soon realised that this was insufficient and we were up-scaled to fly in with 1,368 rounds, increasing from 152 to 228 rounds per gun.

Little did we realise that the amount of ammunition we had on the position was only a taste of what was to come in the weeks ahead. Towards the end, we were resupplied with 2,000 rounds, or some 64.5 tonnes for the final push towards Stanley.

The physical effort required to move such an amount was new territory for the crews, as rounds tended to be flown into a central drop-off point, or at least by section. Flying in ammunition and stockpiling it pro-rata behind each gun poses three problems. Firstly, having so much ammunition out in the open and next to a gun increases exponentially the Gun Sub's vulnerability to hostile fire. Secondly, flying in these underslung loads so close to each gun, was that the helicopter's downwash was destroying the camouflage nets, which were already suffering in the wind. Lastly, during the bigger resupplies, we were not in control of what was in each underslung load by type and there certainly was no time to check.

David and Bill were faced not only with the problem of getting rounds to the Guns, but also with the dilemma of how to conceal the stockpile of ammunition. Every effort was made to site the ammunition out of direct line of sight, by using the natural folds in the ground, but this was not always an option. Not only were there now hundreds of rounds on the position, but the reality of scale was the sheer amount of salvage or waste that is generated. The day to day management of the problem with regards to both ammunition and salvage was delegated to the GLC.

The conundrum of manning the Guns, as a result of the impending increased scaling of ammunition that we were about to be faced with, was alleviated by redeploying those administrative non-specified members of the Battery, such as the cooks, REME and other admin staff, to augment the Gun Subs. The simple reality was that the cooks had no cooking to do, as we were on individual twenty-four-hour ration packs and we had no vehicles (apart from the PADS Land Rover) for the REME to maintain; some however, were held back to form the local defence section.

Once established, Orders were held in the house and were given by David, with Bill setting out the details pertaining to the technical running of the position, with those non-essential Command Post personnel having to leave, in order to make space. In summary: We were to 'Stand To' as normal. 'Stand To' is a tried and tested practice conducted throughout the Army and it is a time, usually lasting thirty minutes, when a position is brought to 100 per cent readiness. Typically, this happens around first and

FALKLAND ISLANDS TIMES

Distribution: All Units

Press Trench
HQ 3 Cdo Bde RM

Sun 23 May 82

29 85

1. <u>General.</u> A quiet day on the Military Front. Several A4 aircraft were identified over the Falkland Islands however only 1/2 x A4 Sky Hawks came near San Carlos water. It dropped a bomb way out in the sound and returned from whence it came. A submarine sighting was reported by 2 PARA South of our area. Pinger helicopters went out to search but found nothing. There was no Naval Gunfire Support activities. Harriers attacked Goose Green but with limited success. No servicable aircraft were seen but a possible fuel dump was hit and secondary explosion reported. On the civil radio we heard a Arg pilot with broken arm and badly injured leg was picked up by locals at Hill Cove (West Falkland).

2. <u>At Sea.</u> CANBERRA left San Carlos yesterday and is unlikely to return in the near future. Some equipment will be cross decked to another ship. STROMNESS and NORDLAND visit us today.

3. <u>Ashore.</u> The Arg weapons and ammo captured on Fanning Head were destroyed yesterday. They included 2 x 105mm Rds and other ammunition. An Arg soldier surrendered to 3 PARA yesterday. He was one of those who got away on the Fanning Head operation.

4. <u>World News 211800Z.</u>

    a. UN resolution passed called for an immediate ceasefire and withdrawal of both sides.

    b. The producer of the controversial Panorama programme about the FI crisis has resigned.

    c. FA cup final. Spurs V Queens Park Rangers, drew 1 all. Replay on Thursday. Requests for tickets to CANBERRA.

    d. Mr NOTT, Sec of State (Defence) said we had achieved tactical suprise with the landing, we have 5,000 troops ashore, 3 Royal Marines Commando units and 2 Para Battalions.

    e. <u>Arg Claims:</u>

        (1) British vulnerable to counter attack.

        (2) Arg troops attacking us.

        (3) Our supply line to sea severed.

    f. Arg spokesman said Arg Navy unlikely to leave 12 mile limit because of British submarines.

    g. Costa Mendez, Arg foreign sec at the UN today.

    h. Pope calls for immediate ceasefire and peaceful solution.

Thats all till tomorrow, keep your peckers up on those windy hill sides.

This is a copy of one of the 'Press Trench's' newsletters, which were distributed throughout the brigade. It supplemented the BBC's World Service and was well received, unfortunately only four were produced.

last light, which are the periods thought to be most vulnerable, or likely to be attacked, and defensive positions are manned in readiness.

Early notice in preparation for our first light 'Stand To' tomorrow morning was set for 10:00 hours, with the GPO and BSM and others to be up and about. The time for our first light 'Stand To' was set for 10:30 hours. 'Stand To' is a period of some thirty minutes around first and last light, when everybody on the position, save for the on-duty Command Post crew, comes to readiness in their defensive positions. Historically, first and last light have been the favoured times for mounting an attack and as such, standing-to is a time-honoured practice to prepare for such an attack. The current Command Post crew were to end the current watch at 18:30 hours, with shift changes to take place at 01:30 hours, 08:30 hours, 15:30 hours and 22:00hours through the night and into tomorrow.

The following were to augment the already established Command Post crews of H1 and H2: Sergeant Taylor, Lance Bombardier Saxby, Gunners Horn, Hadjicostas, Makey and Ell; giving a total of twenty all ranks, including Sergeant Maxwell and Bombardier Hagan. Of the total available, there were to be a minimum of six on at any one time, made up of the CPO, two technical assistants, two signallers, and a runner. With the extra personnel, Sergeants Taylor and Maxwell were able to allow some relief to the duty crew, that however, did not run to the CPOs themselves.

We were also given clearance to shoot at low flying enemy aircraft. It was here that the decision was announced that sleeping in the house was permitted. We were now faced with our first night ashore, with no hard intelligence to say that it was free from an Argentine presence. To that end, tight discipline was paramount and finding one's way around in the dark was a challenge. As such, only those requiring to move around the position were permitted to do so. It was common practice to call over the tannoys 'Number 1's' which was the order from the Command Post to muster there at best speed. Just as it was in every Number 1's mindset to be the first to be ready, so it was their aim to be the first at the Command Post. Their competitive spirit set the tone and nobody wanted to be last, as Sergeant Walker remembered: 'The problem for us Number 1's was finding our way to and from the Command Post at night, for briefings and 'O' Groups (formal Orders). The simple solution was we used the Don 10 line'. Don 10 is akin to a telephone wire and each gun connected their gun's tannoy, via a spool of Don 10 to a junction box in the Command Post, providing a simple and effective means of communications over the dispersed position. Even connecting these wires to the Command Post was a competitive event.

At the end of the day I took a short situation report, known as a SITREP over the radio, which both briefly updated the situation and confirmed the other three Battery dispositions. Brevity on the radio is key and the use of acronyms is heavily used to reduce transmission times. Equally, these acronyms sum up in one word the expected message content. I didn't need to record the situational update, as the narrative was simply along the lines that all went with the landings and continues to go well. Also, the locations of 2 Para's 'Patrols' or forward reconnaissance sub-units, as well as the observation parties from C Company were given and plotted on the battle map for deconfliction. It also clarified the aviation UHF frequencies used by the helicopters, which is a separate and specific radio from those used by the ground forces which we held; along with confirming which Mortar Fire Controllers were authorised to call for fire. Mortar Fire Controllers controlled their Battalion's mortars, much the same as the Forward Observation Officers controlled the artillery's fire.

Within the Battalion, the Mortar Fire Controllers could direct their own 'internal' fire, but were required to be authorised when requesting external fire support. This was a blunt way of both controlling fire support stock control, whereby only those authorised to request fire support did so. Perhaps more importantly for the Command Posts was the requirement to monitor ammunition stocks, which directly called on the services of the GLCs and Bill as GPO. We were required to submit a standard logistical request – LOG REP – every twenty-our hours, should ammunition stocks fall below sixty per cent of non-standard shell types, such as smoke or illuminating rounds, or eighty rounds per gun; however, we were to upgrade this to the more urgent operational demand report – OPDEM should stocks fall to forty per cent or forty rounds per gun.

Saturday, 22 May (D+1)
Day 2. Windy and cold. Priority is digging protection for pax. The day was dogged by Air Threat Red, but no en aircraft went over the position. Took a clearing patrol out but no joy. Spent the afternoon adjusting targets (Regn Pts) for future use.

losses:	*2 x Harriers } ? Probable*
	2 x Gazelle }
	1 ship abandoned
	3 ships damaged
en losses:	*7 x Skyhawk*
	11 x Mirage
	3 x Pucara
	1 x Chinook
	2 x Puma

Morale is still quite high and no one is suffering.

The 'digging in' was far from easy, as the farmstead was located on a well-drained part of the shoreline, with bedrock not too far from the surface, and only personal entrenching tools at hand. The priority was for personal trenches; however, the decision was made shortly after landing to dig in the second Command Post. The main Command Post, now in the house, was to have a large trench just outside of the property, with the second Command Post, initially identified for H1 as the main, being sited some distance away. The requirement for a 9ft x 9ft hole and chest deep is no mean undertaking, with what feels like a teaspoon to dig with. If you weren't on duty in the Command Post you were digging.

The work was split between the Command Post crews, with H1 excavating the second Command Post and H2 digging the trench outside the house. After going down about four feet we hit bedrock and called it there. It didn't take long for the weather to play its part and the decision to allow those off watch to sleep in the house, was well received; however, that luxury was denied to the Gun Subs, who had to remain at their guns, due to their required state of readiness. There was a concern of having all one's eggs in one basket and I was required to sleep in the second Command Post, as it was technically H1. I do recall having a feeling of isolation inside the now semi-dug in Command Post tent, as there were no volunteers to keep me company.

The first Clearing Patrol fell to me as the junior officer. Bill, as GPO, couldn't leave at such an early stage in setting out the position, as he was responsible for all matters technical and tactical. The BK, David, whilst the Battery's Second in Command, had responsibilities for the administration of the position, along with the coordination of the position's self defence. As a Second Lieutenant and one of two CPOs, it was an easy choice to send me out. I briefed the small party of six of what we were going to do and left the position to sweep some 4-500m out from the farmstead.

Stepping out from the relative safety of the position raised the pulse somewhat, but we soon settled into the task any initial angst quickly faded. No body spoke and the Gunners knew exactly what to do.

It wasn't before long that the inevitable call for fire came in and it was a good to get these first technical fire missions under our belts, not only from my point in the Command Post, but also for the Guns; as it brought into focus their role and snapped them back into the world of gunnery, having effectively spent the last month at sea.

Whist it felt full-on when the call first came in, these missions were run in comparatively slow time, compared to what was to come. This was the first time that the Royal Artillery had fired in its conventional role in action since Malaya, in 1960, although Gunners did fire in a limited capacity during the crisis in Aden, which ended in 1967. The reality was that 29 Battery was the first to fire its guns and it was me that was in the hot seat. There was a real feeling in the Command Post that we were being 'watched' by 29 Commando Regiment en mass and that our performance was being assessed.

Sergeant Walker: 'The story told at reunions is that Sergeant Ken Morgan and A Sub fired the first round. I know my own gun fired a lot of adjustments; I had a very slick crew, which had recently won the Best Gun Competition in Larkhill, at Westdown Camp.'

My diaries do not note whether it was Sergeant Morgan's A Sub that fired the adjustment of the Registration mission, only that 29 Battery and my crew of H1 were the first to respond to the call for fire, albeit on a purely technical mission. Regardless of that fact, we were the first to fire and unlike the other gun batteries and with only FAME to work with, which was testament to the amount of effort put into the Command Post's training during the voyage south.

One thing that was very well received, was a briefing sheet of A4 paper which was distributed to all units, in the form of an operational news sheet, from 3 Commando Brigade's Headquarters, styled from 'The Press Trench, HQ 3 Cdo Bde RM'. The first edition was only dated 'May 82'; however, the news relayed within would suggest that it came 'off the press' on the 22nd May.

The following is the transcript of the first news sheet:

Press Trench
HQ 3 Cdo Bde RM
Distribution: All Units   May 82

NEWS SHEET

1. **General.** We hope to produce this News Sheet on a regular basis to keep all informed of major developments. Due to our initial facilities we cannot produce large numbers so please use it to brief others at O Groups so that information is disseminated to the lowest level.

2. **Britain's SAN CARLOS Landings.** The Brigade went into action yesterday with Red and Green berets working side by side to re-establish a British presence on the Falkland Islands. A big thank you to the Royal Navy for delivering us safely to the Falklands after our 8,000-mile voyage together. Yesterday's landings went smoothly, as planned, with supporting arms (Rapier and Guns) being flown ashore about midday. The action ashore including Naval Gunfire Support/SBS operation (Pre-landing) on FANNING HEAD in which 9 prisoners were taken, of which 3 were wounded, in addition weapons and equipment were captured. 40 enemy approximately fled from Port San Carlos Community Hall leaving most of their kit and equipment. Two gazelle helicopters following them up were shot down by these enemy. Sgt A EVANS RM, Lt H FRANCIS RM and LCpl B GRIFFIN lost their lives and Sgt E CANDLIS was injured. The SAS destroyed a Pucara with small arms North of Darwin during a diversionary operation. In the air the Navy did a magnificent job defending us from the Arg air strikes. Numerous wave attacks of A4 Sky Hawks, Mirage jets and Pucara aircraft attacked our ships. Five ships were damaged defending us, ANTRIM, ARDENT, ARGONAUT, BROADSWORD and BRILLIANT. ARGONAUT was immobilised but can defend herself, ARDENT was sunk after the crew was taken off. Enemy aircraft destroyed by our ships, harriers and ground forces were: 7 Mirage, 5 A4 jets, 3 Pucara, 1 Chinook and 1 Puma which brings the total of enemy aircraft destroyed so far to 46. Good stuff lads keep it up.

3. **Secretary of State's Statement Yesterday.** (unclass)
    a. Following statement made by C of S for defence at 211920Z seven weeks after the Argentine aggression, British forces are tonight firmly established back on the Falkland Islands.
    b. Following the raids which we announced earlier today, British forces have now established a firm bridgehead on the Falkland Islands. Royal Marines Commandoes and the Parachute Regiment are now ashore in substantial numbers, with artillery, air defence

weapons and other heavy equipment already disembarked from our ships. These landings were unopposed. A secure land base is being consolidated.

c. During the night several landings and raids were made by our forces in different parts of the Falkland Islands, some of the forces remained ashore. Argentine forces have suffered casualties and some prisoners have been taken these operations continue.

d. As we expected our ships have come under heavy air attack, five have been damaged, two seriously. There will have been British casualties but we have no details. Our Harriers and missiles have destroyed 7 Mirage, 5 Sky Hawks and 2 Pucaras, 2 Argentine Helicopters, a Chinook and Puma have been destroyed on the ground. We have lost two of our small helicopters.

e. I will make a further statement tomorrow and take questions at that time."

Apart from such sheets, we were, to say the least, in a news information vacuum. There was no TV, daily newspapers or such like, and the only real up to date news we had came from the BBC's World Service. Finding the station wasn't easy and required careful tuning, but its instantly recognisable signature opening tune of the 'Lilliburlero March' before the news confirmed it. Whilst this was invaluable, there is only so much that can be either said or crammed into a short news segment. Equally, it transpired through letters from home that events, certainly the early deployment south and the initial landing stages, were being drip-fed to the public back home at a glacial pace. In letters to Jill, events I was writing about gave her first-hand knowledge before the official Ministry of Defence (MoD) announcements.

The MoD chose to keep a stranglehold on news from the South Atlantic; and when it was deemed appropriate, often many days after the fact, it was delivered by their erudite spokesman – Ian McDonald, a civil servant, whose steady, but dry and doleful briefings, provided most of the available news of a conflict 8,000 miles away. We clearly had no access to this, but how news broke and the style, were told in my letters from home. In a conflict whose media coverage was tightly controlled, Ian McDonald's press conferences at the MoD headquarters in London had not only the nation, but the rest of the English-speaking world, on the edge of its seat for news of the campaign. What we weren't aware of, was the breakdown in trust between the MoD and the press and media. Not only was there distrust back in London, but also towards the embedded reports sailing south. Here, reporters had the embittered experience of hearing 'their' news being broken for them on the World Service. Reports were censored, delayed, occasionally lost, and at best sent back by surface mail. When relations between the press and the Navy on board HMS *Hermes* were at their worst, Michael Nicholson of ITN and Peter Archer of the Press Association, prefaced their bulletins with the rider that they were being censored, the irony being was that this fact was itself censored! The price of such censorship against the desire for timely news and the consequence of such actions was to be paid later in the forthcoming battle at Goose Green.

Chapter 6
'Air Raid Warning – Red'

Sunday, 23 May (D+2)
Day 3. Weather overcast and windy. Rained during the night. Many enemy air waves on the fleet. Many enemy cas and planes shot down. A Mirage flew over the position, Rapier and Blowpipe engaged but missed. Rapier claimed 2 kills, ships 2 x kills, 1 x dog fight with a Harrier. Engaged the 1st Fire Mission Battery at around 1600Z and fired the first rounds in anger; at light armoured Recce vehs – target was neutralised. Rained during the night. Various explosions in the bay. Could be a ship blowing up. Battery re-engaged the previous targets (ZS6150) with C/S 63. C/S 63 then consolidated there.

By this stage, the Rapier Air Defence missile system was set up around the anchorage, on slightly elevated bluffs, affording them the best line of sight and angles of fire. We watched on as the Argentine jets flew in and were engaged by our air defenders and were somewhat disappointed at their lack of success in hitting their targets, in these very early stages. During my initial young officer training at Larkhill, the Rapier's sales pitch was 'one shot – one kill' and to see the system not live up to expectation left us with a feeling of vulnerability.

The first offensive mission came curtesy of Bob Ash, whose Observation Party was high on the ridge of Sussex Mountains, with 2 Para's B Company and was monitoring activity to his south. The atmosphere beforehand had been light and jovial; however, when the radio came to life and the words: 'Fire Mission Battery' came through, you could have cut the immediate tension with the proverbial knife. I felt a huge rush of adrenalin as I took my position at the table, waiting for Bob's instruction, knowing that all eyes were on me. It was down to me to co-ordinate the collective efforts on the Gun Position and deliver the first Gunner rounds in anger. The format of fire orders is prescriptive, quick and the actions both in the Command Post and on the Guns are very well rehearsed. At either end of the table sat the signallers, with the Regimental (operational/firing) net to my left. Bombardier Marsh stood to my right and waited to plot the grid, as soon as it came in. On first hearing the call, I immediately picked up the gun tannoy handset and called the Guns to readiness, by repeating the order 'Fire Mission Battery'.

Out on the position, the gun sentries acknowledge the order, the gun crews immediately stop whatever they are doing and close up for action. As the Guns check in, I eagerly watch the signaller take down the detail and repeat it back. This is done in a form of shorthand and is effectively done at a fast conversational pace. As soon as the grid comes in, Bombardier Marsh plots it and I double check his work. I instantly knew that we were the only Battery in range and that the entire Gunner radio network would be listening intently to our collective efforts.

After the grid comes the target's description and the method, i.e. does the Forward Observer require the target to be adjusted, or to be hit by all guns at once? or any further control orders. Concurrently, as soon as I hear the method, I determine the ammunition instruction for the Guns of shell type and weight, along with the fuse type to match the request. In this case, it was by default set to 'Quick', the standard point detonating 'HE' and I pass that out to the Guns: 'HE 2 Square, L32', thereby eliminating any unnecessary delay.

The shells were weighed and batched at source, here '2 Square' required the gun's ammunition numbers to source shells matching that order. There may be on the position shells of '2 and a half, or 3 Squares' stockpiled, whose minor weight differences must be allowed for in the firing solution's calculations. Mixing shell weights and not accounting for it would cause target errors, which may have disastrous consequences, hence the need to specify. At the same, Bombardier Marsh swings the plotter's rotating arm and I watch to confirm both the range and bearing. From the range, I determine the charge, which in this mission was 'Charge Super' and I immediately pass it out as part of the ammunition preparation order. Depending on the level of control imposed and/or adjustment anticipated by the Forward Observer, the order to load is given to the Guns, who in turn acknowledge the order.

Out on the Guns, having been given the ammunition and charge orders, the Detachment Commander, or Number 1, orders the Numbers 5 (ammunition number) and 6 ('Cover' or detachment second in command) to prepare the shells and cartridge's charges. The Numbers 5 and 6 have the responsibility for the care and preparation of the ammunition throughout. The Numbers 5 and 6 each then presents the shell and brass cartridge case in turn for inspection by the Number 1. The Number 1, depending on whether the order to load has been given, orders the Numbers 5 and 6 to either hold the shell and brass shell case, or pass them over in turn to the Number 4, who is standing inside the trail to the left of the breech. The trails are the gun's fixed outward-bowing towing arms. The Number 4 then first places the shell in the breech for the Number 2, also standing inside the trail, but to the right, to ram home the shell with his ramrod; the Number 4 then places the brass case in the breech and the Number 2 then close the breech mechanism, with both standing clear after loading.

Having worked out the individual bearings and elevation, I pass them out to the Guns, whose Number 1s in turn acknowledge the order by repeating it back, as specific to them. On receiving the bearing and elevation, the Number 1 orders the Number 3 to 'lay the gun'. The Number 3 sits on a small fixed seat on the left of the trail, which is where the sighting and laying mechanisms are located. The Number 3 sets the sights with the bearing and elevation on to the sub-scales and uses the azimuth and elevation winding handles, turning them until a small bubble, similar to that of a spirit level, is centralised within its marks. The numbers on the gun sight are checked by the Number 1, who also checks through the sight, to confirm both the accuracy of the lay, as well as the sight glass bubbles being central within their marks. Immediately that the Number 1 is satisfied that his gun is ready, he reports back, with the Number 3's hand waiting on the firing handle in readiness.

Depending on the control in place the signaller reports back to the Forward Observer, with the round's time of flight, or I order the gun(s) to fire and the time of flight is then passed. In this mission, Bob wanted the first round adjusted by one gun and then all guns to initially fire one round each simultaneously, when ordered to do so; the adjustment of which was to be done without delay. This meant that there was no 'At My Command' order in force placed by Bob. I was waiting for the first gun to check in as being ready, which took very little time, which I in turn acknowledged. The competition between the Gun Subs to be the first to report 'Ready' was as keen as ever and in this first offensive Fire Mission, that prize went to Sergeant Walker and B Sub.

The Command Post is silent waiting for me, save any radio calls coming in from Bob's Observation Party. As there was no 'At My Command', the first gun to report as ready should have been my cue to order it to fire; however, I paused momentarily. The reality was that I was conditioned to peacetime range firing, where everything is subjected to a double check, of which the last check is an independent 'Safety Check'. Once 'Safety' has given the all clear, rounds can be fired off. Failing to comply with this fundamental element of range discipline, or indeed fire though a control order, is career limiting, or at worst, career ending. Identifying that I'd briefly paused and suspecting the reason for it, Bombardier Marsh leant over and quietly said 'Sir, there's no Safety, you can fire the Guns' and I gave the order: 'Number 2 FIRE'. An idiosyncrasy of gun line communications is that when referring to guns individually, they are referred to as A to F Sub; however, during a fire mission, they are referred to as Number 1 to 6 respectively.

As soon as the report of the gun is heard, then the signaller reports to the Forward Observation Party as such, including the time of flight – 'Shot XX', for which he had been primed to transmit. Giving the time of flight in seconds (for example where XX is twenty-eight seconds) helps the Forward Observer to determine his rounds, as in the event of a number of fire missions happening in the same area, that the ones impacting from the time given are more easily identified. In the example just given, we would transmit 'Shot 28' at the time of firing, with the Observers Party noting the time and giving a five-second warning of impact at the twenty-three second mark. As the round lands, Bob made his adjustments and his signaller passes it on. Adjustments are done first for line and then for range and a typical order is such as 'Left 100, Add 200 Repeat'. As these adjustments come in, both myself and Bombardier Marsh reprocess the solution and I reorder the bearings and elevations out to the Guns. Here, not wanting to lose the element of surprise too much, Bob quickly went for the full weight of the Battery and ordered '1 Round Fire For Effect'. With all guns being ready, I in turn order 'Fire' and the position fires in unison. Bob makes another adjustment and orders 'Repeat', which is the executive order for me to recalculate, pass both the ammunition order and the new data out to the Guns, which when applied, I order the Guns to fire again with 1 Round Fire For Effect.

It felt that as soon as the mission came in, that it was over, as Bob orders 'End of Mission'; which I in turn pass on to the Guns. Typically, at the point at the end of the mission, the Forward Observation Officer gives any result from what's just occurred; however, in this case Bob broke with tradition and simply called an end to proceedings. The target's initial description and the mission's result are important for two reasons. Firstly, it gives all those on the radio net, in particular those in higher command, a picture of the battlefield and any subsequent battle damage inflicted; and secondly, it gives the gun crews an insight into what they were firing at. In this instance, it was believed to be light armoured reconnaissance vehicles, LVPT-7s, from an Argentine Marine patrol. To give a description and no result was far from the norm and I pressed for a result. To say that Bob was being evasive was an understatement and after repeated requests to clarify the situation, he came clean and reported that a horse and foal were seen to be galloping away!

In his defence, the target was at least 10km from his observation point and 16km away from us and what he thought he saw was a vehicle and trailer. It was an honest call to make, but importantly, it got us on the front foot with the other Batteries.

A valuable lesson had been learnt in the process; in that the hard work put into the Command Post crews training was now paying dividends and that the procedures worked. Everybody in the Command Post felt at ease with FAME and that first fire mission proved that we responded without any delay whatsoever. As a Command Post we had survived our baptism of fire, one never knows how one will react in such circumstances and we all thankfully proved up to the task. What I was acutely aware of was that being the CPO, at the gun end, the buck stopped with me.

I recall being in the Command Post when we called Headquarters on the 'admin net', which is used for all routine non-operational radio traffic, asking for an update on the ration resupply, to which there was no satisfactory reply. We were now two thirds of our way through our rations and we were becoming increasingly concerned at the lack of a positive response.

It was surreal watching the attacks on the anchorage, from our position at the farmstead, at the southern tip of San Carlos Water. Whilst we received 'Air Raid Warning – Red' over the radio, as precursor to the imminent air attacks, the jets seemed to just appear over the position; with the prevailing strong winds helping to mask the sound of their arrival. Because the farmstead was on a slightly raised part of the shoreline, the jets continued their decent past us over the water, on their northerly run in. Being that we were by this time on a similar level, but some way behind, the surreal part was that we could clearly see them open-up with their cannons at the closest vessels. The line of cannon shells could be seen ripping up the water, tearing towards the target at anchor; with the splashes turning to bright orange sparks, as the cannon shells found their mark on the ship's superstructure. As we had witnessed on numerous occasions by now, the jets would then be forced to take avoiding action, for fear of slamming into the ship's side.

Later that night, I was standing outside the house along with Bill when we witnessed the night time explosion of HMS *Antelope*. The first thing that we knew was seeing an extremely large bright flash, centred on *Antelope*, which lit up the whole of the Sound for a few seconds, and was followed almost immediately by an almighty explosion. We stood in stunned silence trying to comprehend what we had just seen and tried to explain what had happened to those coming out of the house to investigate.

The following is the transcript of the second news sheet:

FALKLAND ISLAND TIMES

Distribution: All Units

Press Trench
HQ 3 Cdo Bde RM
Sun 23 May 82

General. A quiet day on the Military Front. Several A4 aircraft were identified over the Falkland Islands however only 1/2 x A4 Sky Hawks came near San Carlos Water. It dropped a bomb way out in the sound and returned from whence it came. A submarine sighting was reported by 2 PARA South of our area. Pinger helicopters went out to search but found nothing. There was no Naval Gunfire Support activities. Harriers attacked Goose Green but with limited success. No serviceable aircraft were seen but a possible fuel dump was hit and secondary explosions reported. On the civil radio we heard a Arg pilot with broken arm and badly injured leg was picked up by locals at Hill Cove (West Falkland).

At Sea. CANBERRA left San Carlos yesterday and is unlikely to return in the near future. Some equipment will be cross decked to another ship. STORMINESS and NORLAND visit us today.

Ashore. The Arg weapons and ammo captured on Fanning Head were destroyed yesterday. They included 2 x 105 mm Rds and other ammunition. An Arg soldier surrendered to 3 PARA yesterday. He was one of those who got away on the Fanning Head operation.

World News 211800Z
a. UN resolution passed called for an immediate ceasefire and withdrawal of both sides.
b. The producer of the controversial Panorama program about the FI crisis has resigned.
c. FA cup final. Spurs v Queens Park Rangers, drew 1 all. Replay on

Thursday. Requests for tickets to CANBERRA.

d. Mr Nott, Sec of State (Defence) said we had achieved tactical surprise with the landing, we have 5,000 troops ashore, 3 Royal Marine Commando units and 2 Para Battalions.

e. Arg Claims.

(1) British vulnerable to counter attack.

(2) Arg troops attacking us.

(3) Our supply line to sea severed.

f. Arg spokesman said Arg Navy unlikely to leave 12 mile limit because of British submarines.

g. Costa Mendez, Arg foreign sec at the UN today.

h. Pope called for immediate ceasefire and peaceful solution.

That's all till tomorrow, keep your peckers up on those windy hill sides.

Monday, 24 May (D+3)

Day 4. A glorious day. Hardly a cloud in sight, the sun is up and really quite warm. We have run out of scales for food (72 hrs) and are awaiting a replen, also water. Morale is very high. This morning after our 7 hr evening stag, were greeted by a wave of en Miragés. Small arms fire was returned. One aircraft left the position with smoke trailing; they attacked the fleet. During the morning HMS Antelope *sank in the Bay. 2 more waves of Skyhawks and Miragés took place. One was shot with smoke trailing, from a Rapier. We heard that 90% of all aircraft that attack the Fleet are shot down. Saw Sir* Galahad *being bombed, let off more rounds at a low flying Skyhawk (Mirage). Heard that my Fire Mission destroyed 2 x LVPT7s and shells landed 10m from the vehs. At around 0900 we engaged FM Bty, 16000m Ch S, 1 rd FFE Prox, followed by 4 rds Fire for Effect. C/S 69 very happy that all rounds landed on target and the quick response. Re-engaged later 3 rds FFE. Target Rds.*

I should point out at this stage that whilst I recorded that the weather was glorious and really quite warm, it was more of a relative statement of the prevailing conditions. The reality was that it was not that warm at all, it just felt that way when the biting wind slackened.

I noted in my diary that I thought that they were Miragés; however, Bill Moore clarifies this: 'I don't think we saw any Miragés after Day 1. The Mirage had delta wings and I think that was an air-to-air fighter. The A4 Skyhawks were fighter ground-attack aircraft and it was these that attacked the shipping in Falkland Sound.'

As left the house after coming off watch, I stopped to look back down the sound to see what had happened to *Antelope*, from the massive explosion seen ripping her apart a few hours earlier. It was a truly sorry sight to see thick black smoke still coming from her and she looked to be low in the water, in the certain knowledge that there must have been casualties and it was a melancholy experience.

A minute later I was out by the reserve Command Post and was thinking about doing some personal administration, when the warning came for the first wave of Argentine jets; which was met with a hurried response by the position to grab their weapons, in readiness to engage the enemy.

The change in mindset was immediate, as I picked up my 9mm sub-machine gun, pulled back the cocking lever and moved the safety catch from Safe to Fire. From an early teenager, I would class myself as an accomplished shot, from being in the school shooting team, to passing my weapons tests in the Army at marksman level. I was also very experienced with a shotgun and having missed out on the previous chance to fire at the Argentine jets, I resolved not to miss this opportunity. The lead aircraft of the first wave came down and off the position's edge and I gauged it to be just out of the effective range, as well as having a very high crossing rate. The second aircraft flew a little closer and, at approximately 100m distance, I knew this was my chance. I instantly determined that to stand any chance of hitting the aircraft, that I'd have to give it some lead, as if I were firing my shotgun. I brought my weapon up to aim, followed the line through the aircraft to a point just ahead of it and squeezed the trigger. I held the trigger and fired a continuous burst, which required me to continually adjust my point of aim, to overcome the weapon's recoil, which naturally wanted to draw each subsequent round off target. This was a world away from the sterile range work that we were used to, not only from firing single shots at a static target, but also from a lack of range safety supervision. The moderate rate of fire offered meant that it didn't take long, although everything seemed to be in slow motion, for me to expend my thirty-round magazine and by the time I'd reloaded, the aircraft had passed through the position. After the engagement, I picked up one of the empty shell cases that lay just off to one side and put it in my pocket.

Channeled aggression through the act of firing at the incoming aircraft was a massive release, it's a cold emotion and I didn't take a moment's second thought to pull the trigger. It took the general situation of the anchorage being attacked and bringing it down to a personal level, where one's actively taking the fight directly to the enemy. Individually it may have been a futile act, but collectively it was huge, as it made a statement of intent at to what we stood for and it certainly raised morale.

Buoyed by the response, the position was in a heightened of readiness, in anticipation of any subsequent raids. It wasn't long before another wave came by and I manage to fire off another fifteen-round continuous burst, before I assessed it as being out of range, watching it continuing on to attack *Galahad*.

I don't recall which aircraft it was in which wave, but one left the position with smoke trailing from it and Bombardier Schofield and his crew claimed it; however, I suggest that it was more of the collective response and the sheer weight of fire we put up that did it. We couldn't claim the hit as such, as the aircraft continued to press home its attack and we were unable to see if it was subsequently destroyed.

One aircraft had a 'lucky' escape, as it was engaged by one of the nearby Rapier sites, whose missile exploded close by it, but it didn't bring it down and the jet flew on clearly damaged with smoke trailing. Notwithstanding that, it was reported that we were doing very well against incoming air raids, with a success rate of some ninety per cent.

Bill Moore continues: 'After several days of air raids, it became clear that the Argentines were using the house as a reference point, on their way to attack the ships. That's when Gunner Crompton asked why we had to set up next to such a prominent and obvious object!'

It was believed that there was an Argentine Forward Air Control (FAC) Party situated on Mount Usborne which, at just over 2,000ft, gave an ideal vantage point for them to direct the attacking jets onto the ships at anchor. San Carlos Water was almost completely protected by the surrounding mountains. There was, however, one weak point in the natural defence, which was a valley that led into it from the south to southeast, where at the end of the valley and at the bottom of San Carlos Water, were the only red and white buildings for miles around and those of Head of the Bay House, situated right in the middle of our gun position. The FAC would direct the very low level incoming enemy aircraft from the relative safety of the east, down the valley and over this unique and prominent IP (Initial Point), which would act as a run-in marker, before their final attack heading into the anchorage.

An unforeseen danger of having the Argentines use the house as an IP, was that the overflying jets would start firing their cannons as they over flew the position, strafing the ships in their final bomb run. The danger was not from the rounds themselves, but the discarded empty shell cases that rained down from on high. A Skyhawk's 20mm, or Mirage's 30mm shell case exiting the aircraft at speeds anywhere between 300-420knots, is as bad as being shot at. The Guns situated at the rear of the position were most vulnerable and the gun crews soon learnt to take cover during an air attack.

Another unforeseen problem came to light after a few days, and related to the hours on stag or watch. When on exercise it's relatively easy to work through the cycle of being on/off duty, mainly down to the fact that there's always an end of exercise – 'ENDEX' – in sight. Here, that was a completely unknown factor and trying to work under 'exercise' conditions just didn't work. We initially adopted a four-on-four-off pattern in the Command Post, typically as on exercise; however, when you factor in the very real requirement for one and all to be in their defensive position at 'Stand To,' around dawn and dusk, the same Command Post crew (mine!) found itself losing out on a significant amount of sleep. The off time available has to be managed to complete all of one's personal administration, i.e. feeding, washing, weapon cleaning and sleeping. So, to have the latter significantly reduced by 'standing to' was beginning to have a negative impact on everyone's performance. This was compounded during the early set up phase, due to the defence's digging in requirement and having 'set' duty times, as per the first Orders Group. To that end, we considered adopting a five-hour turnabout, but in the end elected where possible to stretch it to seven. The key to the issue was the fact that it was an odd number, meaning that both Command Post crews cycled through the twenty-four-hour day as the days progressed, with each liable to be off when called to 'Stand To'. Consequently, individual performances improved almost straight away.

Unlike the first fire mission, this one was a devastating success, not only in terms of accuracy in working with FAME, but in the position's response. Any feelings of angst or worry in coordinating the gun end response were a distant memory, as our collective confidences grew with every mission. Our position at the bottom of San Carlos Water put us closest of all the four Batteries, to any significant numbers of Argentines, which in turn kept the spotlight on us.

It is worth taking a few moments to explain the differences between the three different types of fuse used on the standard HE shell, as their effects are somewhat different. Having said that, all three utilise the same simple arming method, which is initially based on the 'set back' (g) force of firing the shell. As well as using 'set back', they also used centrifugal force, caused by the rifling in the barrel spinning the shell in the second arming process.

The act of firing off the shell arms it, with the fuse type determining how it explodes. The default setting 'Quick' was standard on the general purpose point detonating L32 Fuse, which, as it's description suggests, explodes on impact. The drawback with this method, is that it's reliant on the surface it lands on, and the harder the better. This is because if the initial contact of the nose isn't sufficient to initiate the shell's detonation, depending on how soft the ground is, it allows the shell to continue down and bury itself, up to the point that the fuse does what it's designed to do. Here the ensuing explosion is absorbed by the earth, with a high percentage of the intended shrapnel rendered ineffective. The soft peaty ground was the saving of many, both friends and enemies alike. In direct contrast, the hard, rocky surface was devastatingly unforgiving. There is an alternate setting, 'Delay', which intentionally allows the shell to penetrate the surface before detonating, but this must be specifically ordered in the mission orders, as it required the Gun Subs ammunition numbers to individually change the fuse's setting. Typically, 'Delay' is utilised when the blast energy of the exploding shell is intended to be contained and travel through the earth, destroying trenches and bunkers.

The next two fuses are designed for the shells to explode in the air, or 'air bursts' for short. The fail-safe action of point detonation for both air burst fuses, is ensured during the initial stages, and guarantees that the round isn't wasted, even if it fails to air burst, particularly with Mechanical Time Fuse (MT).

The older technology uses an L33 MT Fuse, or mechanical time fuse and is effectively a clock timer, which is hand-set depending on the CPO's calculations. The aim here is to calculate the shell's time of flight and subtract the short period it takes to get from forty feet above the target, to the target. The numbers are in tenths of a second and have to be calculated for each gun individually, due to variations in muzzle velocity. This method requires an accurate assessment of the weather, in particular the prevailing wind, as any tail-wind will require the base calculation of the time of flight to be shortened and vice versa for a head wind. Not knowing the exact time of flight, not even to the nearest second or two, when one's talking about the detail of aiming for tenth or hundredth of a second, makes it almost impossible for the Forward Observers to get it spot on with the first round. The penalty for not getting it right is losing the element of surprise. The L33 also had the advantage in that it could be set for point detonating; however, this would only be considered should stocks of the standard L32 become exhausted.

The third method uses the L27 Proximity, or 'Prox' fuse. Here, the element of determining that point in space over the target, is done by having a very small radar unit built into the fuse. The fuse's radar is designed to initiate ten meters above the target and eliminates the vagrancies of wind and weather, as its calculation is the same as that of the standard HE. Here, the point of detonation is almost guaranteed every time, the only problem was that we didn't have enough of them.

We were to be subjected to enemy shelling from a 155mm field gun firing MT at a later date, which thankfully was ineffectual, as their fall of shot was not witnessed by the Argentine Forward Observers, consequentially they were not in a position to correct their initial guess work. In direct contrast, we were to use the L27 Proximity fuse to great effect.

Again, we contacted Brigade Headquarters regarding our precarious ration situation, stating to no avail, that we were four days into an initial three-day issue, which was made even more frustrating by the fact that we could effectively 'see' them further up the sound. Our frustration was completed by the response: 'My priority is to move this Headquarters', which was met with utter disbelief and when pressed again, the response was the same: 'My priority is to move this Headquarters', as if it were a stuck record. I recall some of us who would have liked to have made his acquaintance!

Bill Moore recalls events: 'We did run out of rations because 29 Commando Regiment forgot to resupply us. I remember their 2IC (second-in-command) visiting us and explaining that he only had a sausage for breakfast – there was silence in the Command Post when he said it.'

The 2IC sensed the mood following his crass comment and soon made his 'escape'! As such, contingency planning was in place.

During the day that we watched *Antelope* sink further into the icy waters of San Carlos Waters, until she finally sank shortly before last light. Those that saw her go down just stood and watched in silence.

Chapter 7
Sheep Stew in a Dustbin

Tuesday, 25 May (D+4)
*Day 5. Started day off at 0730 by being on duty till 1430. C/S 0 reported 4 man
en patrol to our South. I [India] C/S's tasked. It was enemy, 300 m away from
our posn. I C/S were tasked. We fired again on ZS6151, Prox this morning at
a Command Area. An early afternoon attack by 4 en planes – 3 x Skyhawks 1
x Mirage. Saw them bomb & strafe an LSL. A plane was shot down & the pilot
ejected. Later another wave came and 2 more were shot down. The 1st wave took us
completely by surprise. At 1600 we were given our 1st resupply of food. None since
yesterday morning. Digging as usual, did a little bit more on the trench!! Mail
run – 2 letters, 1 from Jill & 1 from ADAT!! Very morale boosting. Just the tonic.
Yesterday, someone killed a sheep and tonight we had a dustbin full of mutton stew.
A quiet day where nothing exciting happened.*

Bill Moore and I were standing outside the house, close by a fire trench,
when the raid caught us by surprise. Bernie Winch was standing in the
open nearby, but still some distance away, when he showed a fair turn of
speed and barged us out of the way to get into the trench first. As Bill Moore
reflected later, 'it was totally understandable in the circumstances!', Bernie
was after all, still as determined as ever to become an RSM.

I have two very clear memories of aircraft being shot down by Rapier
today, having watched them from the moment they flew in, until their
eventual destruction. The pilot who I saw eject did so at the last safe
possible moment, presumably with a continuous radar warning tone going
off in his helmet prioritising his thought processes.

He'd flown over our position at low level and was lining up for his
bombing run in the anchorage. As he levelled out for his final run in,
two simultaneous flashes could be seen coming from the recently set up
Rapier firing points on the southern flanks of San Carlos Water, with them
tracking in at Mach 2, approximately forty-five degrees behind. Just before
they both hit and the plane exploding, the pilot ejected, with the fireball
continued forward and down into the water. His parachute deployed, but it
was questionable as to what extent, and *Fearless* sent a boat to his aid. It was
reported back that the pilot had survived, with 'badly smashed legs' and
was taken to the Task Force's Field Hospital, located in an old refrigeration
plant complex at Ajax Bay for medical treatment; which was all that he
could have hoped for, with his life expectancy measured in milliseconds
prior to his ejection.

The second aircraft, again having flown over our position, managed to
weave a course through the anchorage at very low level and having made
its attack, sought to egress over the mountains to the west. As he dodged
and weaved some of the ships tried to engage, presumably with Sea Dart
missiles, but were thwarted by his low-level flying skills. Just before he

reached the crest of the mountain ridge, a solitary flash was seen from the opposite side of the Sound; the Rapier missile caught the underside of the jet as it attempted to roll over the crest line, with less than a second from safety. The news hacks tagged San Carlos Water as 'Bomb Alley'; I have no idea what the Argentine pilots called it, but I can only assume it was some form of hell on earth. What wasn't questioned was their incredible bravery, which was clear from the way we saw them press home their attack.

Considering where we were in the overall scheme of things, there wasn't a lot of enemy activity out to our 'front'. Most of the Fire Missions were in support of 2 Paras Patrol Company, which had the task of locating any Argentine patrol bases. Due to the nature of the operation, most missions were at the very limit of our range and required us to use Charge Super. This was starting to take its toll on the Guns, due to the stresses of firing such a powerful charge and 29 Commando Regiment's CO stepped in and banned its use unless expressly authorised by him. It's estimated that we fired approximately seventy-five rounds per gun during this phase.

The rationing situation was by this stage dire and a sheep was shot by the BK and butchered by Sergeant Scott (ACC), who reverted to being an Army Chef for the making of the 'all in' stew. A dustbin was cleaned by Private Lee (ACC), using wire wool from the gun-line, until 'gleaming', Army slang for spotless. Lee joined the Battery straight from Basic Training, had never been on exercise outside barracks in Aldershot, had never seen the inside of a 24 Hour Arctic Ration Pack prior to the landings and his first night in the field was the initial invasion!

Although the settlement at Head of the Bay House had been vacant for an estimated seven month, it still had the remains of a vegetable patch, which contained potatoes and carrots, which were collected and added. The BK, GPO and BSM also went round every individual asking for 'donations' i.e. unused rations such as soup sachets, stock cubes, dried pea sachets etc., to supplement the stew. Anything and everything was thrown into a black bin liner and by the end they'd quite a haul. Every man had at least one full mess tin of hearty stew, with the exception of the BSM, who cited that 'you'll go down with the shits if you have that'. The only person to suffer was the BSM!

Bill Moore provides an interesting post note: 'As a 2 Star I went round the Army Catering Corps College at Omar Barracks in Aldershot and they are still practicing such cooking, in a separate area just outside of the College, as a result of the Falklands' experience'.

There was a report of a four-man Argentine FAC party in the area between our position and Sussex Mountains, that was considered to be directing the enemy jets on the ships in the anchorage. As such, a fighting patrol from 2 Para was sent to sweep the area. The fire-fight that took place just off the position between the patrol from 2 Para and the 'enemy patrol,' was abruptly ended when the Para's patrol commander shouted, in a parade ground manner, 'STOP' to his men, in order to assess the situation. When both parties stopped on command the penny dropped. The 'enemy' was in fact a forward operating base for one of the AAC's Scout helicopters, with the patrol coming across the landing site's ground crew. It was common practice to disperse these helicopter landing sites into individual operating bases, using every gully or fold in the ground to conceal their position. In this instance, considering the high volume of helicopter traffic going on around the anchorage, nobody had realised that one had set up so close; equally, nobody at Brigade had considered letting the troops on the ground know either! Luckily there were no casualties and a valuable lesson was learnt.

Wednesday, 26 May (D+5)

Day 6. 252130 to 260430 stag. Very tired during the zombie stag. Off till 1330. Afternoon stag we fired a FM Bty on a group of vehs (tgt rds). Stag OK 1 FM Bty was bad all round, later on in the afternoon we had an altitude (height unknown [Mirage]) bombing. Presumably for us but it landed about 1000m South, nearer C/S 150's [Mortars] area and people soon dived for cover!!! No air attacks from fighters and generally a quiet day. 2 PARA moved out to attack Darwin & Goose Green. It will be a hard Op, let's hope it goes alright for them, as our C/Ss are with the Coys. At night it was very quiet on stag. Moral is still high, but we are getting a little tired.

The Fire Mission in question was due to an unseen number of factors. Firstly, 'H' Jones and our BC, Tony Rice, came up with a plan to have an FPF (Final Protective Fire) mission as a form of 'flak', using mechanical time fuses (MT). These FPF missions have a special part to play within artillery circles. Rather than the Guns laying idle, they are 'laid' on the FPF target, there's only one at a time and preventing any confusion, as means of last resort. In extremis, all a Forward Observer has to do is call 'FPF Fire', which will exact an immediate response from the Gun Position. The mission was centred on a grid reference in the middle of the valley that the Argentine fighter planes were using as a low-level route into San Carlos Water, as directed by the Argentine FAC Party hidden on Mount Usborne. The concept was that when enemy aircraft were sighted, the FPF would be called, when allowing for the time of flight, that aircraft and rounds would come together. Unfortunately, the FPF mission was adjusted on a day where the time of flight of the rounds was markedly reduced, because of a significant tail wind from gun to target. All guns were laid and loaded with this 'reduced' time of flight for this FPF mission. When the call for fire came to the south over Sussex Mountains, the Guns were switched to the new target; however, I did not fire because of the shell 'nature' being set for the FPF and not as now requested, and I had to consider the options. When asked for the reason for the delay, as there was no 'At My Command' in place, the Forward Observation Party was informed that we were loaded with MT. When ordered to fire off the MT as per the fire mission, a 'safe grid' was requested, so as not to alert the enemy to our intentions. We were instructed that the target grid was a 'safe grid' and cleared to fire, with the line of fire directly over 2 Para's position on Sussex Mountains. The Guns were now firing into a significant head wind and it was calculated that all would safely clear the troops based on the mountains. The unfortunate oversight was the head wind component, which coupled with the 'reduced' time of flight set on the fuses, meant that rounds that were expected to go off well past Sussex Mountains –and actually exploded directly overhead 2 Para's B Company position. The shrapnel blasts lacerated their defensive position, but thankfully there were no casualties. The only positive outcome was that of demonstrating to the troops of the need to dig in!

Bill Moore was to meet the Platoon Commander some years later: 'It was from B Company and the Platoon Commander was Geoff Weighill (a journalist who had a TA Commission and was doing his regular service with 2 Para). Some three years later whilst on JDSC (the Army's Captain's Staff Course) he said to me at the bar, that 'some bastard had shelled his Platoon position shredding all the ponchos'. I put my arm around him, bought him a drink and explained all.'

The bombing had quite an effect on the position, as it was the first time we had seen, relatively close up, any Argentine return fire. The explosions were very loud and threw up great clods of peat and rock into the air and caused one and all to dive for cover. If you needed convincing as to why you dig for protection, you only had to look just over to what had just occurred. Thankfully, the bombs landed between our location and the mortars and there were no injuries, but had one of them found their mark it would have been catastrophic. At the time, there was some conjecture as to what was responsible for the high-altitude bombing. Perhaps the high loss rate endured by the persistent low-level attacks in San Carlos Water, caused the Argentines to change tactics. It was suggested that *Canberra's* were used at night around this time. We were later to have it confirmed in the Press Trench's edition of the 27th May: 'Harrier CAP patrols drove off two Argentine Mirages which dumped their bombs near 2 PARA and fled.'

With preparations underway for 2 Para's forthcoming operation, Bill was summoned by the BC to Sussex Mountains for orders. Whilst a simple instruction, the practicalities of getting up there were far from easy, made even more difficult by the distance and terrain. For Bill to go by foot over the Camp would have taken him away from the position for far longer than was desirable. Having flown in with only the PADS Land Rover, transport was, to say the least, limited; however it wasn't the only means of getting around. Just prior to our embarkation, cuts in the Defence Budget saw the Battery's holding of 3/4 Ton Land Rovers cut by two, with two Can Am Bombardier 250cc Dispatch Rider Motorcycles issued in lieu. These were now the obvious solution. Previously unused, they were flown ashore as part of our scalings and were now ready to be put to use. It would be fair to say that Bill wasn't a 'biker' and the thought of riding a bike, not only locally around the position, but cross-country filled him with trepidation. What was clear, was that Bill was not going to make the journey alone, requiring an escort on the second bike. Bombardier Hagan claimed to have some motorcycle experience and volunteered his services and, being effectively out of the Command Post's manning, he was available to accompany him. Bombardier Hagan literally gave Bill a crash-course, within the confines of the position, much to the amusement of the gun crews, especially at the state of him on his return!

Bill Moore recalled the experience: 'I was given a Can Am 250 just before we left Aldershot, I had never ridden before which is why I took Bombardier Hagan with me. I went on several long rides over the peat bog – not the easiest thing with a heavy bike and road tires. I did go to Sussex Mountain to see Tony, we parked at the foot and tabbed up the hill, in order to receive orders. I also went to 3 Commando Brigade's Headquarters which was a much longer ride and came off a few times during it.'

At the 'O' Group that night, a quick round up of events set off proceedings: Two Exocet missiles were launched at the carrier *Invincible*, which were defeated by deploying the anti-missile countermeasure called CHAFF, which deployed a cloud of tiny strips/particles designed to 'confuse' the missile's radar seeking head. HMS *Coventry* was reported as being sunk on 25 May, killing twenty of her crew. On our side, Harriers in the ground-attack role destroyed an Argentine infantry company position, as well as a gun battery location.

We also had Naval Gunfire Support (NGS), with the ship's 4.5-inch gun firing in the Fox Bay area. We were also given notice that 2 Para was going to attack the settlements of Darwin and Goose Green; however, it was made clear that 8 Battery would be supporting them and not us. The reason given was that it was 29 Command Regiment's Batteries that were trained for night moves and we weren't. The upshot was that 8 Battery would send twenty-four men, consisting of a Command Post, local defence and three guns; with the operation scheduled for the attack to go in tomorrow midnight.

There was concern at Brigade about our stocks of Charge Super ammunition, and instructions were given that where possible, Mortars were to be used for small targets. Also, that our low-level code system was to change over to the random 'nick number' system.

Over the next few days, the BSM, GPO and BK were going to collaborate on logistical planning, including the possibility of a night move, also on light equipment scales. We were told of the plan for more NGS at Port Howard and that 8 Battery were relocating to Camilla Creek House. Lastly that the SAS were moving into the area for future operations.

Domestically, the Royal Engineers had fixed the water supply; however, it was't for drinking. As far as our rationing situation was, we had two days remaining and we were to expect a resupply on Friday. Sergeant Scott was detailed off to monitor the 'shit house' outside toilet, to prevent it becoming the proverbial minefield! Equally he was to get the message out that individuals were to take a shaded light at night. One or two individuals had failed to appreciate that light was escaping from within and that our security was being compromised. With regards to mail, all outgoing mail was to go to the BQMS and that there may well be a bar on mail going out.

Generally communications were going well, but we were to switch to hand-held sets, akin to the old style telephone, from now on and were not to use the trusty gun tannoys. We in the Command Post were reminded to use the Regimental Command radio net for such events as coming under attack. Individuals were reminded of the lack of a supply line, to which we had already fallen foul of, and to discourage waste. Also, individuals were to keep on top of their personal administration, in as much as keeping their weapons clean, kit packed and to generally just look after it.

The following is the transcript of the third news sheet:

FALKLAND ISLAND TIMES

PRESS TRENCH
Headquarters
3rd Commando Brigade
26 May 82

Argentina's ruling junta announced yesterday that they would agree to a three-day cease-fire in the Falklands as proposed by Ireland in the United Nations. The Irish proposals call for further talks between the British and Argentine Governments followed by a withdrawal of forces from both sides.

In London, Prime Minister, Mrs Thatcher stressed to the House of Commons that no negotiations with Argentina could be considered until the Argentinians withdrew their troops. She rejected Labour's calls for a cease-fire.

The Argentine air force again ran the gauntlet of the San Carlos Bridgehead. The price yesterday was one Skyhawk downed by HMS *Coventry*, a Skyhawk shot down by a Sea Harrier and three Skyhawks destroyed by Rapier missiles plus one probable. One A4 pilot ejected and was picked up by a boat from HMS *Fearless*. He had a badly smashed leg and was taken to Ajax Bay for medical treatment.

But it was a sad day again for the Royal Navy. HMS *Coventry* was attacked by waves of Skyhawks and had to be abandoned. HMS *Broadsword* is reported damaged and the gallant supply ship *Atlantic Conveyor* was badly hit out in the 'Exclusion Zone". Fortunately her invaluable Harrier strike aircraft were off-loaded onto the carriers along with some of her cargo of helicopters.

The Argies announced they had damaged *Canberra* in San Carlos Water but this was only in their imagination.

Yesterday was of course the 25th May, a day of Argie independence celebrations, and according to the junta the forces on the Falklands were joyfully singing their national anthem. But the junta did announce this year's celebrations were in a more sober look than usual because Argentina found herself in a war she did not want against a colonial aggressor.

Meanwhile on the Falklands there are several Argie pilots who missed the celebrations because they are still wandering about after parachuting from their aircraft. Those we know of are in the Pebble Island, North Arm and Kepple areas as well as the one who landed alongside HMS *Fearless* yesterday.

Speculation is growing about the British Sea King wreckage

found on Chilean territory on Tierra Del Fuego. Sources in Chile say the British helicopter crew were spirited away to safety with the help of Chilean Officers who a commando group moved to attack Argentinian air bases. Tension is said to be growing between Chile and Argentina; and Chile has concentrated her fleet in the south and moved Mirage squadrons to the area. A BBC correspondent said every Chilean he met was hoping for a British victory in the Falklands.

Britain announced yesterday that an Argentine officer captured on SOUTH GEORGIA, a Captain ASTIZ, would be taken from ASCENSION ISLAND to the UK. Captain ASTIZ is wanted for questioning by French and Swedish authorities about the disappearances of French nuns and a Swedish girl in ARGENTINA. There is some doubt, however, about whether the UK will be able to hand over Captain ASTIZ under the terms of the Geneva Convention.

Captain ASTIZ is one unhappy Argie at the moment. Before too long there will be 10,000 very unhappy Argies around here.'

Thursday, 27 May (D+6)

Day 7. The early hours are very quiet, with 2 PARA still on their way to Darwin. (Yesterday I heard that the Atlantic Conveyor *was hit by 2 x Exocet and HMS* Coventry *was sunk.) The BQMS had just told me that we have had 35 airstrikes in the area i.e. us and the fleet in the bay. Quiet all day no fire missions as at 2000, but at around 1830 2 x Skyhawks and 2 x Mirage attacked. Bombs dropped near C/S 2's location – 1 x casualty due to small arms fire! C/S 'Alpha' at Red Beach [Ajax Bay] reported 4 x dead and 20 injured. The Paras are still around Darwin (5 miles). 3 PARA are on their way to Teal Inlet, 45 Cdo are going to attack Douglas. (3 PARA's tab is 40 km, same as 45 Cdo's.) Just before last light Air Raid Warning Red. The waves that attacked the Bay: 2 x Mirage shot down, saw 1 being ditched (shot down by Rapier). Told in a brief that we are moving forward. Generally a corridor is being made East towards Teal Inlet and from then the advance to Stanley. Wrote to Jill.*

As a result of this casualty at call-sign '2's' location, somewhere mid-point up San Carlos Water, all small arms anti-aircraft fire was stopped, to prevent 'blue on blue' across the bay when aircraft fly between engaging units. As units opened fire at the approaching Argentine aircraft, there comes a point when these units are actually firing towards each other, as the enemy jets fly between them. It was the fall of shot from the rounds that each unit was inadvertently firing at each that caused the 'blue on blue'.

There is always scope, even in war, to find humour in one's lot and this was not lost on the gun crews. Each and every one of them looked up to Bernie Winch and knew of his waiting promotion, but it didn't stop the banter when the Argentine jets came by, as Sergeant Walker again recalled: 'During Air Raid Warning Reds, some of the LMG teams were finding the BSM in their trench from out of nowhere!'

At the 'O' Group, details were given as to the Brigade plan for the expected move out from our initial landing areas. It was a phased plan, with the first element covering 2 Para's return to Sussex Mountains, after their operation at Darwin and Goose Green. Next, 45 Commando were now to move by Landing Craft Utility (LCU) to Port Douglas; along with 3 Para, who were now to 'tab' (forced march) to Teal Inlet. LCUs are flat bottomed landing craft, with a drop-down ramp, and are perfect for beach or shallow water landings. Next there came the broad statement: 'Advance on Stanley'.

To cover the positions of the units moving out, 40 Commando was to stay behind and reoccupy them, with one Company in each of the three main locations. Lastly, 42 Commando was also to provide one Company to the defensive positions on Sussex Mountains, with the remainder of the Commando to be held as the Brigade reserve. With regards to 2 Para, they were to be given twenty-four hours rest and recuperation back in San Carlos, when they had completed their operation in Darwin; after which they were to fly to the area of Mount Kent, some 40kms away. 7 Battery was placed at 'Priority Call' (first response) to 45 Commando, whilst the Commando stayed in range, likewise with 79 Battery and 3 Para; after which they were to fly forward into the area to support their attack, which may be tomorrow night. 29 Battery was to prepare to fly to the area of Mount Kent, to support 2 Para; however, 29 Battery may be required to move before 2 Para, which was yet to be confirmed. There was also news that 7 Battery may go by LCU.

With regards to the administration and support, the Brigade Headquarters was going to relocate to Teal Inlet. Artillery ammunition was going to be at a premium, with the Fleet Auxiliary's LSL at Teal Inlet only having limited stocks, but there was to be at least 100 rounds per gun per day. 29 Battery was to be placed at 'Priority Call' to 2 Para, even when 2 Para returned to San Carlos and it was emphasised that we were to be prepared to move out at short notice. 79 Battery was detailed to relocate to grid square 9189 and to be prepared to fire in all directions. Emphasis was placed on the fact that when we go, we ensure that we go with the correct scales of equipment from the start and were to go with not less than 100 rounds per gun. Again, it was emphasised, that when we go, we're not coming back here, so we were to stockpile petrol for the Command Post's generators in anticipation, as there would be no resupply when we're up there.

Regarding water, we were told that there was no resupply and that we were to use local sources, suggesting that individuals used their issue of purification tablets, as supplied in the ration pack. It was briefed that helicopters were only to be used at night, but that we were to be prepared to go at any time.

For us to be able to concentrate on our personal administration, we were encouraged, where possible, to try and get a 'day off'. This was more of an aspiration than a literal expectation. Our ration holding was detailed at three days and a LOGREP was to be sent, to ensure that we had sufficient stocks for our impending move. With the ever-present hostile air, individuals were reminded not to be 'wandering about' unnecessarily. With regards to communications, long messages are not to be used, with the emphasis placed on brevity, but not at the expense of clarity.

We were to be all packed up in forty-eight hours and be ready to move by last light on Saturday. As such, our personal kit was to be kept in a ready state. All outgoing mail was to be in by last light tomorrow.

There was to be a minimum of five on duty in the Command Post at 'Stand To', with the remainder to take their positions at the trench outside the house. The CPOs were reminded to tell the GPO of any change of our 'Priority Call'.

A summary of the flying serials was detailed, with the first chalk being expected to go by Chinook. It was to take: The PADS Land Rover, the Command Post trailer, the GPO and Sergeant Taylor, myself, H1 and staff, the six Gun Covers (Detachment second in command), the BSM, the remainder of the Reconnaissance Party and Lance Bombardier Saxby. The remainder of the Battery would follow on by Sea King, using the same chalks as per the initial fly in, with the exception of Sergeant Maxwell, who was to fly in Chalk 5.

On completion of the 'O' Group and following on from the announcement regarding mail, I wrote to Jill, suspecting that it may be some time before we get another chance to.

Later that night, we were to listen in horror and disbelief as the BBC's World Service was to announce, that British Forces were on the outskirts of Darwin and Goose Green and making final preparations to attack. This was a crass lack of security, not only by the MoD for briefing reporters, but equally by the BBC for not comprehending the danger that they had just put our troops into. Unsurprisingly the Argentines also heard this breaking news and sent reinforcements to their garrison, in an attempt to bolster their numbers and thwart 2 Para's assault.

I was on duty during the night when the call came in over the radio: 'SITREP – fetch Officer', I was handed the radio and responded that I was ready to receive it. The following is the transcript of that Situation Report, that I took during the battle, written on the back of one of the Press Trench newsletters. Burntside House is situated on the approach to Darwin and Goose Green and its location was just passed 2 Para's start line for the coming attack:

> *Darwin OK - 1st battle Burntside House till midday I[India]3*
> *I[India]2 had to be reinforced by I[India]4 and got through.*
> *They wheeled left to Goose Green where they are being held up*
> *by mor[tar] fire & heavy wpns [weapons] + A/A weapons*
> *They want Cymbaline C/S3*
> *They will try and move C/S3 Cymbaline tonight.*
> *The CO said they have Goose Green, casualties are slight*
> *over 100 prisoners 40+ killed but they are still*
> *under mor fire. Also A/A fire in the direct role &*
> *the PARAs are just waiting.*

The mood was somber after I had relayed it out to the position. The following is the transcript of the fourth and final news sheet:

FALKLAND ISLAND TIMES

PRESS TRENCH
HQ 3 CDO BDE RM
N[B]FPO 666

27 MAY 82

BRITAIN and ARGENTINA are both ready to agree to an amended Irish resolution in the United Nations aimed at settling the Falklands dispute, it was announced yesterday. The UN General Secretary will hold talks with both sides and report back to the UN within 7 days. The Irish call for a cease-fire was dropped from the resolution because BRITAIN intended to veto it. The UN General Secretary confirmed his mission to find mutual ground between the two countries would be very difficult. ARGENTINA said the Irish resolution was barely acceptable but it could be tolerated.

In a major speech, Mrs Thatcher declared BRITAIN's resolve and confidence in her cause is just. Ours is the cause of freedom, and rule of law and support for the weak against the aggression of the strong, the Prime Minister said.

Defence Secretary Mr John Nott speaking in the House of Commons confirmed the loss of HMS COVENTRY and the ATLANTIC CONVEYOR. He said 20 men were killed and 20 injured on HMS COVENTRY and 4 killed in the ATLANTIC CONVEYOR. Four hundred and fifty men were rescued from both ships.

Mr Nott also said three successive British air raids had been made on targets in the Port Stanley area. British forces, he said, were poised for further operations and the military objectives of the task force were being pursued as planned. Mr Nott said the loss of more ships was tragic but losses have been expected and mercifully casualties were lower than might have been expected. Ten more warships, he said, had joined the force in the last two days.

Ex Labour front bench spokesman Mr Andrew Faulds – he was sacked by Michael Foot this week – was banned from the Commons for 5 days for accusing the Speaker of not letting enough pro-cease-fire MPs speak during Falklands debates. Most MPs still support the Governments policy and there have been renewed calls for bombing of Argentine air force bases on the mainland.

Britain's Foreign Secretary, Mr Francis Pym, said BRITAIN had no quarrel with the Argentine people, just with the ruling military junta. BRITAIN still hoped a cease-fire and a withdrawal of Argentine forces could be achieved. Mr Pym said BRITAIN would close no door on diplomatic negotiations, although experience had shown ARGENTINA had not been willing to alter her position.

AMERICA is supplying BRITAIN with missiles for use in the Falklands fighting according to press reports in the USA but this has not been officially confirmed.

On the Falklands yesterday, Harriers attacked a HQ Complex, tents and vehicles at Port Howard and claimed the target destroyed. Harrier CAP patrols drove off two Argentine Mirages which dumped their bombs near 2 Para and fled. The night before last HMS PLYMOUTH fired 174 salvos at Fox Bay. HMS GLAMORGAN fired 140 salvos onto Stanley's airfield at a Super Entendard on the air strip. This was probably the aircraft that fired exocet missiles which hit ATLANTIC CONVEYOR. Last night HMS ARROW fired on Port Howard while HMS YARMOUTH fired at enemy forces north of Port Howard.

Friday, 28 May (D+7)

Friday Day 8. After a lying-in! And getting up at 0900, found out that 2 PARA have killed many en and taken prisoners, no mention of own cas. 12 men from this location to 2 'Bravo's' location loc for prisoner handling, via 2 x BV Snow Cats. Sitrep – Attack on Darwin successful. Battle at Boca House (1 ¼ km) west of Darwin with C Coy till mid-day. 'India'2 had to be reinforced by D Coy and they got through. They wheeled left to Goose Green where they were held up by mortar fire and heavy wpns, also A/A fire in the direct role. Bravo C/S wants a Cymbaline from C/S 3. The CO 29 Cdo said they have taken Goose Green. Casualties are slight, over 100 prisoners and 40 plus killed. They are still under mor fire and are just waiting. One air strike against the Bay but nowhere near us. Managed to get as much sleep as possible. Very quiet night's stag.

Offensive action is all about winning, with planners understandably focusing their efforts to ensure that aim. One of the lesser considerations is dealing with the aftermath, with a sense of 'seeing what's left' to be dealt with, being somewhat of an afterthought. 2 Para's victory had taken its toll, not only because of their own dead and wounded, but also for their exhausted men. As such, we were tasked to supply a twelve-man working party to assist 2 Para in the immediate aftermath, principally dealing with the Argentine PoWs and were allocated two BV 'Snow Cats' to take them there. These BVs were unarmored tracked vehicles used by the Royal Marines to transport a typical eight-man section. They were designed to have a very low ground pressure weight distribution and were ideally suited for the Marines to operate in the Arctic snow, but were equally at home on the Falkland 'Camp'. Gunners Frame, Armour and Kirvell were part of the party selected: 'We travelled down on a 'Snow Cat', loaded up with mortar arms, small arms and rations and we got opened up by a Pucara and it turned over and I thought I broke my back,' recalled Frame. 'I was winded, my gun was stuck in the ground. I had a weapon which I couldn't fire. I just hoped other people could cover us. We were lucky. When we got there they were still well into it. It was a hell of a shock. We are not normally that far up front, usually ten miles or so away. As we got down to the gorse line, there was a chopper taking off with 'H' (CO 2 Para) on. It was a total eye-opener, seeing the Argie prisoners. They were in a right state. Massive head wounds, field dressings dripping with blood. The

Paras were so exhausted they couldn't give them the care they needed. But they were the enemy. I didn't feel that much for them and they were still alive'.

Steve Armour also recorded these events: 'We saw the results of what we were doing. When we first started capturing the Argentinians they were just like what we were. We were all scared in a way, but knew we had a job so we just went and did it.'

Bill Frame continued: 'They were telling us what our rounds were doing and that was a great buzz. It's good to be told. It's the adrenalin keeps you alive, you live by every day. The objective was Stanley and we were thumping on.'

Individual's perceptions change in adversity and Gunner Kirvell's recollection of going forward to help with the aftermath was no exception: 'I just never gave it much thought about what was happening at the dangerous times which were numerous, like the time we went through a minefield after volunteering to go forward to help 2 Para during the Battle of Goose Green.'

Bill Moore makes the worthwhile point, 'that we (the gun group) did not accompany 2 Para, as we had apparently "no experience of night flying". It's ironic when the section of three guns [8 Battery], under Mark Wearing, that did fly forward, broke one of their gun's LBMs [breech levers] when lifting the gun (up by helicopter). It was a poor decision to separate the gun line from the battalion with whom they had worked. It was unnecessary and introduced risk where it was not needed'. The fact of the matter was that the Battery was current and practiced in moving by helicopter, by both day and night. The collective feeling on the position was that the Commandos did not want the attack at Darwin and Goose Green to be an entirely Airborne affair and ensured a Commando presence, by substituting a section of guns from 29 Commando Regiment. We felt aggrieved at the lack of trust in our ability to complete the task, but felt vindicated, albeit a somewhat hollow feeling, of the news that the 'experts' had lost one third of their guns' firepower in the night move.

The request for Cymbeline was not realistic in the circumstances. Cymbeline was a trailer-mounted radar used by the Gunners for locating mortars, although most of us doubted its effectiveness. The high angled trajectory of a mortar round is traced back to its point of origin and as such, provides the location of the firing point. However, to call forward such a cumbersome piece of equipment, would require it to be underslung, which in turn would have jeopardised the helicopter and its crew.

Saturday, 29 May (D+8)

Day 9. A very quiet early morning's stag all the way till stand to. Heard that C/S 2 are moving to C/S 2B's location at 1st light. One Air Warning Red this afternoon. Heard that 1 Skyhawk was shot down. Managed to get both fires going in the house & cooked some jacket potatoes. Heard that 250 Airmen + 1000 Army & Navy Argies taken prisoner. Also that the CO, Adjt + A Coy 2IC (Col H, Capt Wood, Capt Dent) + 20 Toms killed also more seriously injured. Bad news. Good news in that the Union Jack was raised in Darwin at 1430 GMT. Came on stag again at 2330 to hear that Teal Inlet was taken and that there were no Argies there. Sounds like 2 PARA had quite a rough time down at Darwin.

The fires in the house allowed individuals to rotate through and was a huge boost for moral. The jacket potatoes came from the few potatoes left in the fallow vegetable patch at the rear of the property, that were left when we had the rubbish bin of mutton stew. They were cooked on the peat-fired pot-belly stove in the room occupied by the Command Post and they provided a very pleasant change from the monotony of limited variation of the Arctic ration packs.

As the SITREPs filtered through, it became very apparent that 2 Para's victory was a very hard fought one, with the realities of war hitting home as both the situation and casualties became known. This was the first time that people that we worked with were in a situation where we knew to expect the worse; however, it does not stop the feeling of sadness when individuals that we knew had been killed. There was no animosity felt towards the Argentines, they were 'just' the enemy, who we simply had to beat. Individuals knew what was at stake and we all knew the consequences. We took that news and dealt with it in our own way, but in the end, we had to put it behind us and carry on. In contrast, there was a huge feeling of relief that the BCs and Observation Parties had come through unscathed.

The magnitude of 2 Para's victory hit home when we were to learn of the sheer number of Argentine prisoners taken. Conventional doctrine for mounting any attack was seen as being a 3:1 ratio in favour of the attackers, so to find out that it was 2:1 against was staggering. What was worrying, was the fact that our intelligence had got the numbers so wrong. The other bit of good news was that the northern advance was well underway, with Teal Inlet being taken, having been abandoned by the small garrison there. Some of us questioned both the quality of the Argentine forces and their resolve.

Sunday, 30 May (D+9)

Sunday Day 10. Very quiet stag. Heard that 1400 Argies taken prisoners. World news full of Darwin attack. One Air Warning Red in the late afternoon. Heard that 97 Bty are near & GPO is off tomorrow to recce a position. Morale is still quite high in the Battery but the weather was very cold. Snow on the far hills to the South (Sussex Mts) and frost (heavy) on the ground. The weather is very changeable. Heard some of the tales of the attack on Darwin. Some a little bit hairy. The Bty is being prepared to fly out to a new position. Zombie stag very quiet with lots of nothing happening.

The Brigade was regrouping after 2 Para's attack and it was quiet operationally throughout the day, which gave us time to carry out our general administration. News continued to filter through from the battle, giving us a brief insight as to what went on. One particular incident was to leave us all shocked and angry, namely the death of Lieutenant Jim Barry, who was killed in the act of trying to take the surrender of a group of Argentines. Many said that little, if any, sympathy would now be given to the enemy. Towards the end of the day, we were warned to prepare to fly out to a new position, as yet to be decided, which proved to be a welcome distraction.

Meanwhile, back in England and a secret that I wasn't party to until after my return to the UK, was that Jill was pressed into service as a Visiting Officer for the South West. Jill was the Assistant Adjutant of the Junior Soldiers Battalion, based at Norton Manor Camp, near Taunton and was one of the few female officers based in the region. Her CO, Lieutenant Colonel Terry Taylor 2 Royal Anglian, had taken a call from the MoD who stated that they badly needed a female officer and requested her services.

Visiting Officers were the first point of contact that families had when it came to being informed of either the death, or serious injury of an immediate family member. We were all required to notify who our 'Next of Kin' was on a specific record card, in the event of our own families having to be told if anything happened to us. When required to deliver such a notification, Jill would be taken by her driver to the family's address and, dressed in full Service Dress, would make that fateful 'knock on the door'. The sight of an Army Staff Car pulling up outside one's house and an officer in full dress uniform getting out could only mean one thing and families knew that they were about to receive devastating news. Jill would pass on the facts as known and offer the services of a Padre, before leaving the family to come to terms with their news.

Jill was required to make one such visit to a family of a Private from 2 Para, just after the Battle of Goose Green, but thankfully it was just to notify them that their son had been wounded. As was often the case in these early days, the system kicked in and acted with scant information of the facts, believing that getting the information out was more important than the detail. As such, and in this instance, Jill was sent out with just a surname and an address to deliver the message. When she arrived at the door, the family knew that they were about to be told bad news and once inside Jill told of what she knew. Jill tells of her horror at their response: 'I went inside and began with formalities, by first confirming the identities of the family and that of their son. When I asked, "are you the parents of Private Smith", they paused for a second and then replied, "yes, but which one – we've two sons down there?". The situation was horrific and I didn't know the answer, but after a frantic phone call I was able to clarify which of their sons was involved. The family was just relieved to hear the positive news that their son was alive and didn't dwell on the failure of the Army's Welfare System, in how the news came about.'

Monday, 31 May (D+10)

Mon Day 11. The start of the day on the early shift is very very quiet. Baked potatoes at 0530 with marge. A pleasant change. Worked out that the average age of the Bty is 24.02. At 0820 an enemy low flying plane bombed a target up by Bde HQ. So much for their non-night flying capability. We heard the plane fly over and gave air 'Red'. The BC& CO (4th) visited the position and told us all of the situation and future intentions. (Snowed) Looks like we will be moving to just north of Darwin.

Late at night told we were moving and time to be ready was 1500Z.

With the breakout from the beachhead now starting, preparations were underway in getting the Guns moved forward in time to support the next phase of operations. Events had overtaken the initial Brigade plan's move on Stanley. To that end, Tony Rice and our CO, Lieutenant Colonel Tony Holt, came to the position and briefed us on the revised plan and what to expect. By this stage, the feeling was that as 2 Para had moved on ahead and were beyond our support capability, we should also move forward. Our keenness to move was also due to the feeling of vulnerability from the ever-present air threat. The fact that the beachhead was subject to 'blind' bombing also added to the feeling that we were 'sitting ducks' and that it would only be a matter of time before something untoward happened to us.

The dwindling supplement of baked potatoes continued to be a real morale boost in the Command Post, not only for the fact that they were hot and filling, but that they gave off an unmistakable cooking aroma. They were made even tastier by the acquisition of a tin of margarine. There was also the bonus that cooking them didn't use any hexamine.

Living in such close proximity for so long, the topics of conversation were to say the least, varied, with the Command Post crews finding humour to be had in the vast majority of what we talked about. One such question came about when I was asked how old I was, after a mail run had brought me in a birthday card (my twenty-third). This then prompted the general question of the age of the duty crew, which in turn ran to the whole position. What was a surprise, was that despite the relatively large number of senior Non-Commissioned Officers, in particular the BSM and BQMS, that the average age was only just over twenty-four.

Tuesday, 1 June (D+11)

Tues Day 12. Lay-in till 0730!! Took over stag and 20 mins later an air warning 'Red'. 2 x Mirage from the west. At 0950 we were given the prepare to move at 1st light!! Mad rush to get ready. Did that OK. Bill went forward to recce a new Gun Posn, just north of Darwin. The CO arrived and told us that we were going fwd as a Bde. I took A,C and E Subs out of action + H1 to go forward straight away, but nothing happened. Still at last light there was no hint of a move and it looks favourite for a dawn move tomorrow. Very quiet on stag at night.

I was on duty in the Command Post when a warning order came in, telling us to prepare to move at first light. The irony wasn't lost on us, as dawn was just about to break and it was a mad rush in getting things prepared to go. A helicopter came in and took Bill and Sergeant Taylor off to reconnoitre our planned location, just to the North of Darwin, as Bill remembered: 'It was in an old Argentine position close to a farm. I met Bob Ash there and myself and Sergeant Taylor planned the gun position in some detail before returning.'

Whilst Bill was away, The CO arrived on the position and briefed us on the developing situation and gave orders for the Battery to prepare to move. Thankfully the preparations were all in place and as such, I took A,

C and E Subs, along with HI out of action in readiness for our imminent departure. Bill returned as we were readying ourselves and was soon brought up to speed with the changing situation. In true fashion, we rushed to wait and wait we did! It was clear that by last light that the move was off and that we were to prepare to move out at first light tomorrow. With our own troops now beyond our supporting range, the decision was made to keep the Guns prepared for flying. Thankfully it was a very quiet night for the Commando Brigade.

Wednesday, 2 June (D+12)

Very quiet 1st part of the zombie stag, writing this looking to come off at 0430. Again at 1st light we prepared to move (drizzle). Morale was reasonable at the prospect of going to a GP at Darwin. By late afternoon and waiting all about all day we were told that we would not move until 1st light tomorrow. Situation normal, absolute … up. The lads were upset at not moving, then by a God send a Scout arrived with some mail (3 for me). Very morale boosting. Then 97 Bty advance party arrived with their new BC Maj Burt-Andrews. Simon Friend [GPO 97 Bty] trotted up about ½ hr later followed by the rest of the Bty. 2 Btys on the GP makes for a tight position. An RAF Nav told us that we would probably not go to Darwin, but straight to Fitzroy, just SW of Stanley. Our own Cdo – 3 Bde were not far from Stanley, one Bty coming under CB fire. They located the Argie Bty and another C/S silenced it. A Cdo unit also overran an Argie GP and captured 6 x 105mm Pack How.

The weather was generally grey and misty, with drizzling low cloud and was to scupper any plans for moving 29 Battery forward, putting our move on hold. Needless to say, morale was reasonably high, in the knowledge that we were at last moving forward; however, as the day progressed and we weren't moving it started to dip. The poor weather did, however, provide an element of cover and a sense of security for 97 (Lawson's Company) Field Battery (97 Battery) which, as we were to find out, was on its way to join us. 97 Battery is another of the Regiment's gun batteries and sailed with 4th Field Regiment's Headquarters, as part of 5 Brigade. Thankfully the weather started to break and a Scout helicopter flew in on a morale-boosting mail run, of which I was to receive three letters. 97 Battery's move up saw it follow in the footsteps of the Welsh Guards, which was on its way to Sussex Mountains to take over 2 Para's vacated positions.

Leading their advance party and the first to arrive was Major Dick Burt-Andrews, who had joined the Regiment just after we had sailed from Portsmouth. I had noted in my diary that he was 97 Battery's new BC, but this was not the case; with Dick 'B-A' actually waiting to take command of 88 (Arracan) Field Battery, the Regiment's third Battery who were not deployed, and now augmented our Regimental Headquarters. Wanting to get to grips with the current situation straight away, 'B-A' was brought up to speed by David and Bill. He was followed some thirty minutes later by Lieutenant Simon Frend, 97 Battery's GPO, along with the rest of 97 Battery's main body. It was good to catch up with Simon, and Bill was soon passing on what we had learnt so far.

When each group arrived, they were met with the warmest of welcomes at the edge of the position by Staff Sergeant Mutter and the BQMS, Staff Sergeant McQueenie, who quickly briefed them on the lay of the land. Stories were rapidly exchanged and the realities of where we now find ourselves explained. Simon and 'B-A' described the scene of their walk-in as 'being like the retreat from Moscow', telling some of out of condition Guardsmen sitting by the side of the track, which was littered with discarded equipment, such as helmets, heavy woollen jumpers and rations. There was a general feeling of disbelief, particularly on hearing of the discarded rations along the line of advance, as it was a subject very close to our hearts.

It didn't take the BQMS long to introduce 97 Battery to, as they put it, to the number one sport of the campaign – 'stealing and swapping' and at this, our BQMS excelled! By the end of the day, 97 Battery's main party had arrived and the weather had picked up towards the later part of the afternoon, allowing three guns to be flown in; which were sited on the perimeter's edge, but remained 'out of action', as if parked up off to one side.

It didn't take long for the inter-Battery rivalry to start; however, being 'late joiners', 97 Battery were at a distinct disadvantage, especially after their cruise, as Sergeant Walker remembered: 'There was lots of banter about 97 Battery coming down in the relative luxury of the Queen Elizabeth 2 and the fact they had to wear carpet slippers!'

The position was by now rather crowded and ground rules had to be laid down, to prevent people just wandering around and generally catching up with old friends. An RAF Navigator took time out during the Guns flying in and passed on what he thought to be the plan. He suggested that we were not going to deploy to Darwin as expected, but were more likely to leap-frog onto the Fitzroy area. This was based on the fact that the Commando Brigade's advance had overtaken the plan and the Brigade was finding itself closer to Stanley than first envisaged.

Just before last light, we were also to be joined by the Fire Direction Cell (FDC). The FDC is the Regiment's Fire Direction Centre and is primarily responsible for the coordination of the Regiment's gun batteries during fire missions; however, depending on the tactical situation, it can also take control of all batteries within range.

Similarly to 97 Battery's walk-in, they too followed the now well-trodden path to our position at Head of the Bay House. As it was last light, the position was at 'Stand To' and the BSM was on hand to greet them. The BSM gave them a concise tactical brief: 'This is Bomb Alley, get dug in, no lights after dark – this includes cooking'.

Just as the main party of the FDC made their way onto the position, the Unit Training Office, Captain John Russell, pitched up in the FDC's 1/2 ton Land Rover, with its crew of two. John was an avuncular commissioned Warrant Officer, who had spent the majority of his career as an instructor in gunnery in some form or other and was a true font of knowledge. John's life revolved around training and range work; however, here we were doing it for real and we were a world away from Larkhill and the RSA. Effectively, there was no war role for John, but his vast wealth of experience was put to use and he was to excel as the 'Battle Adjutant'. John's move into taking over the FDC allowed the Regimental Adjutant, Captain Jonathan Bailey, to step out of that role, into one of more an operations and planning one, allowing him to work more closely with the CO.

Later that night we were to receive orders for our impending move forward. These were not for our expected move to Darwin, but as the RAF Navigator had suggested, for a considerable leap forward to the area of Bluff Cove. The grid we were given was Gr 185659, which was an area secured by 2 Para's A Company. We were to have a centre of arc for firing of 1200mils, but were to be prepared to shoot the full circle of 6400mils. To attain the levels of accuracy required in gunnery, mils were used instead of degrees. The length that 1mil subtends at 1000m is 1m and there are 17.7mils per degree, so here 6400 mils equals 360 degrees.

The basic plan was to fly as many guns and ammunition forward, as soon as possible, with helicopters planned to come to us at first light. One sobering fact to be briefed was that we were expected to be in range of the Argentine 155 mm, if they had a tail wind. The radio frequencies, codes and Communications Instruction were briefed, as were the future locations of the Commando Batteries. 7 Battery was to go to Gr 208730, 8 Battery the northeast quarter of grid square 2176 and 79 Battery to grid square 2178. These orders also signalled the point that we were to both rejoin and realign with 4th Field Regiment and effectively 5 Brigade, by the simple statement: 'Adopt Callsign 1 on orders of Callsign 69'.

One of the planning considerations was for a 'split gun' move, due to one of the helicopters, possibly a Wessex, not being able to take the weight of a Light Gun as well as its ancillary equipment. A split gun move is a move of last resort, as it involves separating the barrel from the trail (main frame) and requires a stable and level area to marry them back up again. Equally, it doubles the flying requirement and therefore doubles the risk to losing a gun. Thankfully it never came to fruition.

Chapter 8

Bluff Cove Position

Thursday, 3 June (D+13)
To start with a quiet day with the Battery being ready and stood down for flying.
Then at about 1500 we moved into a Chinook and flew to Bluff Cove, about 22 Km
out of Stanley. A Coy 2 PARA were about 150 to our West. Saw James [Watson].
When we arrived we had a few lifts into the posn and only one gun could get in
before dark. We are on 'Weapons Tight' i.e. self defence as Argies are surrendering
all over!

The morning brought with it the excitement and expectation of the move
and we were more than ready to go, but once again, we were stood down.
Not only was there the general disappointment of our not going, but there
was an unfortunate incident on the position. One of the FDC's Gunners
had a Negligent Discharge from his 9mm sub-machine gun, shooting the
tops off two fingers on his left hand. A call was put in to evacuate him
out as a medical emergency, known universally within military circles
as a CASEVAC, which in turn is afforded the highest priority, and a
passing helicopter was to pick him up within four minutes of the incident
happening.

Then and rather unexpectedly, we were told that we were going to go to
the small settlement at Bluff Cove, as per the plan. The flight to Bluff Cove
saw most of those intended to move forward taken in the one and only
Chinook available, 'BN', in one lift; with Bill's intended flying program
going out the window. We were packed in like the proverbial sardines, with
far more of us loaded on board than seats and it was effectively standing
room only. Once you had placed your bergen behind yourself, you could
'sit' on it and with everybody packed in so tightly, there was no need to be

**The only surviving Chinook, 'BN', brings in the first gun to the new forward gun
position at Bluff Cove, which was dropped off at the top of the exposed ridge line,
just forward of A Company, 2 Para's position, 3 June 1982.**

strapped in, as there was absolutely no room to move. We flew nap-of-the-earth at what appeared to be at a relatively high speed and it felt incredible. 'This was a very sudden move with no notice,' recalled Bill Moore. '2 Para had flown into Bluff cove (viz Brig Wilson's famous phone call, which was actually made by OC B Company, Jonny Crossland, to check whether there were any Argies there.) Originally, Brigadier Wilson had planned an advance to contact to Bluff Cove, which is why we had planned out the gun position near Darwin; but this did not happen. It was a very foggy day and we flew close to the ground, as there was supposed to be a stay behind Argie Blowpipe party somewhere around. In fact this proved a fallacy, as the Gazelle that had been shot down around that time had been fratricide, from a Royal Navy ship. HMS *Cardiff*, I think'.

The initial position had the Battery sited in front of 2 Para's A Company, meaning that geographically we were technically the furthest forward of our own troops. This was casually pointed out by a Private from A Company who wandered over to me, as I was doing a resection to confirm the Battery's location (grid 185659), during the initial set up phase of the deployment. This resection was part of the setting up drill, where I would carry out an independent resection and determine my map solution for the position's centre point, which is then cross-referenced against the GPO's, as a gross error check. On hearing the news, I brought it to Bill's attention, who raised the matter at Command.

Bill clarified the situation with 5 Brigade Headquarters, who agreed that the position should be moved back from our intended position overlooking the settlement, to one just behind A Company, some 5-600m along the ridge to the west. In the time that this took to be clarified, the Chinook had completed a round trip and returned with one gun under-slung, a few rounds of HE, and the Command Post fly-in trailer, along with other Battery members. On hearing the update, Bill went and determined the most suitable position, with myself reconfirming our new location, which we agreed as being grid 17936586, at an altitude of 30m.

Shortly after our arrival and after the initial rush to set up had settled down, we were welcomed by James Watson, who told us that A Company were out of rations. As such, we gave them two days' scales from our reserves, leaving us with just twenty-four hours in hand. Whilst it was good to meet up, there was little time for idle banter, as we busied ourselves for our relatively short move.

Unfortunately, the Chinook had departed and was subsequently re-tasked, ending the Battery's move and, importantly for us, before the gun could be transferred back along the ridge. The only option was for those present to manhandle the gun, the very limited fly in ammunition and the fly-in Command Post trailer over the 'Camp'. The problem now was that it was too dark to move anything over the tussock grass.

Friday, 4 June (D+14)

Friday Day 15. In the morning the BC said we were to move our position down the bottom of the hill. One gun was manhandled 800m! It was really a day for consolidation on the new position. We are on Weapons Tight i.e. only shoot in self defence. Fair all day, but it rained all night.

Thankfully behind the scenes, the decision to deploy us to such an exposed gun position on top of the ridge was being questioned. As such, we were to receive a change to the plan, when the BC contacted us on the radio, ordering us to move some 3-400m south of the revised location, down the slope to the shoreline at Fitz Cove, which was now 800m from where the gun was initially dropped off.

Moving back over the hill to Fitz Cove was far easier said than done. The tussock grass made it incredibly difficult and required all present to move the gun and trailer. Bill sought to layout the gun position, after which he could determine Battery Centre. My focus was on setting up the Command Post, as well as conducting a third resection, which agreed with Bill's calculations. Concurrently, Bill and David would also work out the local defence plan, based on the footprint as determined by Bill.

Whilst we were in this unfortunate state of affairs, we received calls for fire, but were completely impotent and unable to respond. It was frustrating time to say the least, as Bill Moore explained: 'It's also worth remembering that our move was cut off, because Brigade Headquarters wanted to move themselves. We were left with fifty plus men, one gun and no ammunition forward, while 2 Para's forward position was being shelled. We had nothing with which to reply. A poor decision by 5 Brigade Headquarters and not for the first time. We all felt better served by Headquarters 3 Commando Brigade – a far more joined-up and professional organization.'

Saturday, 5 June (D+15)
Jill's B-day!! At around 1530 3 guns were flown in!! Finlay and I made a peat house. The weather in the morning was fine but it dripped during the afternoon. At 1620 we had section ready. (4 guns and 2 guns ammo) Not the best solution but at least it's something. Had a few thoughts home and Jill on her B-day. Only sorry to have missed it, better luck next year!! It's a good sight to see the Guns coming in. We are low on rations and there is no hexi left. Yesterday 3 islanders came past which brings the total to 6! On the stores, I only hope that we get resupplied today. Eventually all 6 guns and ammo arrived. A Sea King brought the CP + trailer with a lot of kit missing. The table arrived hanging on by 1 leg! The 1 tonner arrived & the Sea King blew away the penthouse. Just before last light we adjusted a target (FM 3 guns with C/S I3). All through the night NGFS just offshore bombarded the enemy keeping me awake.

Once the Guns had arrived we started to adjust a collective list of targets, called DFs for D Company 2 Para; however, Bill and the GLCs first had to sort out D Sub, as the majority Bombardier 'Pig' Armstrong's gun stores and equipment were strewn between Head of the Bay House and Bluff Cove. Unfortunately, their kit wasn't as tightly secured as they thought and the lashings had come loose in flight. Consequently, the Section Stores were raided, in order to get D Sub back into action and an important lesson was reinforced. The frustrations for receiving calls that couldn't be answered soon evaporated, as the Guns eventually started firing again. At least we felt that we had achieved something, albeit with only four guns and very limited fly-in stocks of ammunition, effectively enough for just two guns. Eventually the remaining two guns flew in, along with a quantity of ammunition. We were sent the odd harassing fire mission from time to time, but it was relatively quiet. We had a lucky break when the Command Post and trailer flew in, as the load hadn't been correctly secured and some of our equipment was lost overboard in transit, again somewhere between San Carlos Water and Bluff Cove and, like D Sub's missing equipment, was never recovered. What would have made life in the Command Post difficult would have been the loss of the table, but thankfully it was hanging on by one leg, which was snagged in the netting. As it was, one Sea King's downwash blew away the Command Post's 9ft x 9ft tent, better known as 'the penthouse', which thankfully remained undamaged. Helicopter downwash was to prove a major problem for the Guns during resupplies.

Shortly after PADS arrived on the position Lance Bombardier Saxby confirmed our grid, giving us the highest possible survey state. The routine for the Command Post was also set, with H2 running the first shift from 19:00-02:00 hours, with H1 taking over at 02:00 until 09:00 hours. I also noted that our Observation Parties – Callsigns 61 and 62 – were at grids 180661 and 151630 respectively.

Taken from my notebook: (Note, BC is also shorthand for Battery Centre)

Battery Centre: Gr 17927 65426 Alt 20' C/A 1200 mils

	DISPLACEMENTS	
A Sub	5260 mils	70m
B Sub	1220 mils	80m
C Sub	300 mils	70m
D Sub	4340 mils	90m
E Sub	2580 mils	55m
F Sub	BC	BC

Our new location at Bluff Cove was relatively forward and removed from the main body and as such, the decision was made to co-locate the FDC and its Step Up (alternate) with us for security. Initially the FDC was to set up with man pack radios, with their Land Rover Command Post vehicles following on. It wasn't common practice to do this, but needs must. Also redeployed forward and assigned to us, was a detachment from 43 Air Defence Battery's Blowpipe Troop. Blowpipe was a relatively short-ranged, point defence, shoulder launched anti-aircraft missile. It fired a 14.5kg missile, containing a 2.2kg warhead to an effective range of 500m -3500m. The system was relatively new and the technology of the time required the operator to simultaneously track (fly) the missile on to the target, at the same time as tracking the target. We were to discover the system's main short comings, which were that it was very difficult to control at short range and it didn't cope well with high crossing rates; however, its deployment was a marker as to how far forward we actually were.

Considering our position was relatively close to the settlement over the

Gunner Jim Finlay at my 'peat house' shelter, with my kip sheep stretched over the top to weatherproof it, taken from the command post. One of the later guns to join us, B Sub, is setting up on the southern ridge, 5 June 1982.

hill, the islanders kept themselves very much to themselves. When they did venture close by and whilst they kept their distance, the trio we saw gave a cheery wave.

The one certainty I had was that my shell scrape [personal shelter] wasn't going to be far from the main Command Post and I started to identify likely spots. The big problem we faced, was that the centre of the position was in a shallow reentrant, with a wide stream running through the middle, down to the sea shore. Going too far from the northerly bank wasn't an option, due to the very boggy low-lying ground. The Command Post was tucked right up against the bank and I found a suitable spot some twenty-five meters away. My shell scrape was not just an individual one, as my 'room mate' who I was doubled up with was my junior technical assistant, Gunner Jim Finlay. Finlay agreed that the ground looked suitable and we set about the construction of our little peat house. Digging down more than twelve to eighteen inches wasn't an option, due to the high water table and digging any further would just result in your efforts filling with water. The peat clods were stacked around the edge, to raise the height of the side, to the point where you could just move around inside. We managed to find two small bits of broken fence post, which effectively acted as tent poles, and once in place at either end we secured the kip sheet over it. The kip sheet came from our nuclear warfare equipment; it's a very strong, lightweight plastic sheet, designed to be secured across a fire trench's shelter area, to provide the base for the weight of eighteen inches of soil for overhead protection. The wind was unforgiving and our priority was to ensure that the cover was tightly secured. The peaty ground was very soft

A Sea King brings in Bombardier 'Pig' Armstrong's D Sub into the revised position at Fitz Cove (over the hill from Bluff Cove Settlement), clearly showing missing equipment from a loose tarpaulin, before being marshalled into place on the position's rear left, 5 June 1982.

and in reality it didn't take too long to construct and once completed, we moved our kit into the shelter.

The shelter started to come into its own, as the weather worsened, as the day went on. Icy cold rain, driven in on a howling gale made for miserable conditions. The volume of rain helped turn the small stream running through the position into a torrent and the low-lying areas quickly waterlogged. Anything that was left out in the open, and that includes individuals, was thoroughly soaked. Thankfully, Finlay's and my peat house was well sighted and we had taken the time to ensure it was weatherproof, consequently our kit was secure.

During a quiet moment in my peat house I was able to reflect on home and Jill, more so for Jill, as it was her Birthday and as I noted, 'better luck next year!'

It was a different story out on the gun line, with regards to protection from the elements. Normal deployments on training exercises almost always had the gun limbers at hand. the Light Gun's was a 1-Tonne Land Rover, which had plenty of space for the crew and provided an instant

The later arrivals setting up, with B Sub on the ridge and F Sub in the foreground, 5 June 1982.

shelter. All that they had were small low profile canvas tent known as 'Bivvies', which if leaked proved almost impossible to stop. 'We had no vehicles to use as shelter for crew and kit and were just using Bivvies,' Sergeant Walker continues. 'We were wearing the same kit and trying to dry out, with little or no change of clothing and little or no time for personal hygiene. The only way we had of drying our kit out on the Guns was, when possible, to get into your sleeping bag. Steam could be seen coming out of the bag, I am assuming they were drying out!'

The rationing situation was once again dire, with limited amounts of ration packs, but with no hexamine to cook with in stock, save what individuals still had on their person.

This was our first experience of hearing Naval Gunfire Support (NGS) and was the portent of things to come. Unlike our static gun positions, Naval Gunfire required a different approach. Under cover of darkness ships would position themselves inshore and sail between two predetermined coordinates, known as a 'gun line', to provide fire support. Another, but not so subtle difference between us, was the weight of fire brought to bear

Bluff Cove position (2) and Wether Ground position (3). The location marked A was the initial drop-off point for the original gun position at Bluff Cove. When questioned the gun position was moved back to location B. The decision was then made to move down into Fitz Cove at (2). As a result, the first gun that was dropped off at location A, was manhandled in an arc down off the ridge to position (2). This map is a copy of James Watson's original 1:50,000 forward observers map. (Courtesy of James Watson)

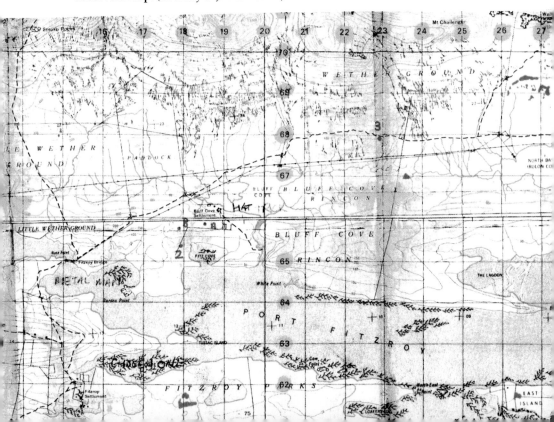

The view from the command post along the central gully's northern bank looking towards the rear of the position, with the command post crew's shelters tucked into the northern bank, 5 to 11 June 1982.

at any one time. We could simultaneously deliver six rounds, in contrast to a ship's single gun, which would take almost a minute to fire the same number of rounds at a sustained rate. The Achilles heel of Naval Gunfire is that any unserviceability with their gun, not least the ship, ends that support. We could in contrast absorb any temporary unserviceability.

The view of the position back at Fitz Cove at low tide from the east (Stanley is behind). The position can be seen to straddle the low-lying reentrant/gully, with the stream running through it. The first to fly in were H1, A, C and E Subs. Left to right on the southern ridge (left) B Sub and E Sub to the rear. On the foreshore is C Sub to the left and A Sub to the right. Directly behind A Sub is the main command post, H1, with F Sub in the middle ground on the right of the gully at Battery Centre and D Sub to the rear right (to the rear left of A Sub, along the northern bank at the rear), 5 June 1982.

Lance Bombardier Nigel Saxby, on the left, and Lance Bombardier Trevor Woodgate, on the right, by their shelter. A further command post shelter is visible on the right hand bank, with D Sub on the more level ground behind, 3 to 10 June 1982.

The metronomic report of the ship's 4.5 inch guns, firing salvo after salvo through the night was the signature of NGS, it could be clearly heard on the wind and it made for a restless night.

Sunday, 6 June (D+16)

Sunday Day 17. From the early hours, as from last light, the NGFS bombarded the enemy. It rained through the night and all of this morning! Still I managed to keep dry in my little peat house. It rained all day and into the night. NGFS bombarded Stanley. The Rats situation is almost a problem and hexi is very low. Morale is still high.

During the night, I was woken up by runner from the Command Post, '"Stand To" – enemy landing craft spotted in the bay about 100m to our front, forward guns laid and loaded in direct fire role'. The runner turned out to be Bombardier Marsh, who'd previously woken Bill Moore. It was pitch black and on arriving at the Command Post Bill briefed that the position was to 'Stand To', that the seaward guns were in the direct fire role and were monitoring the passage of the landing craft. A Sub under Sergeant Morgan was observing the craft and had alerted the GLC, Sergeant Irvine, who immediately brought A Sub into the direct fire role. Bill Moore then ordered D and E Subs to do the same. Radio communications were established with our BC, Tony Rice, who at the last safe moment confirmed that they were in

The crew of H2. Front row, left to right, Gunner Tony Horn and Lance Bombardier Dave Handley. Middle row, left to right, Warrant Officer 2 Trevor Banton, Sergeant John Maxwell, Bombardier Keith Armstrong, Gunner Dave Mackey. At the rear is Gunner Mick Botterill. One of the command post's 84mm Carl Gustav anti-tank weapon, which were never used, is in the foreground, 5 to 11 June 1982.

fact friendly forces and a Company of Scots Guards. It transpired that the 2nd Battalion Scots Guards were twenty-four hours ahead of schedule, but nobody thought to pass that message on, as Bill Moore related: 'The Scots Guards (2SG) had moved round by sea to conduct a relief in place with 2 Para. Nobody had told us they were coming. Nobody had told the Royal Navy either, who opened fire on them during their trip. It was poor coordination all round. In 2009 I was in Baghdad and was talking to a Lieutenant Colonel who was, in 1982, a platoon commander in the Scots Guards. He had no idea that they were nearly attacked as they approached Bluff Cove.'

When I first went to the Command Post in the morning, I noticed a 'steaming' area of heather close by, which on closer examination turned out to be a five-man Naval Gunfire Forward Observation party from 148 (Meiktila) Commando Forward Observation Battery Royal Artillery (148 Cdo Bty), led by Captain Kevin Arnold, who kept themselves very much to themselves. They had been allowed a period of 'rest' and took up residence in our position, which offered them relative sanctuary.

During the day, I went around the position and happened upon one of the gun crew at the rear of the position, try to improvise and overcome the chronic lack of hexamine. The normal scaling of hexamine to 24 Hour Ration pack is one box per twenty-four-hour pack, for temperate (tinned) rations; however, we were being fed 24 Hour Arctic Ration acks, which were almost exclusively freeze dried for the main meal elements. As a direct factor of having to boil so much water, arctic rations were normally double scaled with hexamine. The unfortunate reality was that hexamine didn't always follow on with deliveries of ration packs and it was not uncommon to only have upwards of just half a box per day, towards the end of the resupply period. One enterprising Gunner sought to overcome his shortage of hexamine. He had dug an ammunition box into the peat and placed two metal trip flare posts over it, on which he placed his mess tin, complete with his main meal, which he was ready to cook. Directly underneath, he had fashioned a pile of cordite, which had been removed from one of the disused charge bags. Running from this small mound of cordite was a few strands of the explosive, which were to act as a taper. We all kept back as he threw a match onto the taper, which along with the pile of cordite immediately flashed over with a blinding light and tremendous heat. On looking inside all that was left was the mess tin's handle and attachment plate, with the remains of what hadn't vaporised as a small amount of molten metal in the bottom. Of course he looked crestfallen.

Walking around the position one could see that morale was high, despite what the weather was throwing at us. I noted that despite the rain, our peat house remained weatherproof. Both the weather and the shortage of rations, made all the worse by the chronic lack of hexamine, tested one and all.

Gunner Kirvell reflects after the war, on not only on how we fared, but on the often dire rationing situation, referencing the events of the 25th May and the 'dustbin stew': 'Some of my memories of being on the Island, apart from the cold, constantly being wet, having to ration our 24 Hour Arctic Rations packs, after not receiving rations for over a week and only ever getting the same Arctic Ration pack for weeks.'

One can either laugh or cry and crying wasn't an option. This was Northern humour at its best.

The guns in action, with F Sub in the foreground and B Sub behind. The low brown semi-circular 'wall' behind the F Sub is not for protection, but in fact the ready ammunition stored on the platform, 5 to 11 June 1982.

Monday, 7 June (D+17)

B-day, lying-in. The sun came out and it has been a great day for personal admin. Had a strip wash to the waist & a shave!! Came on stag at 1230 and did sod all till 1730 the a FM 1 Gun. Very quiet. Received mail at the position. 1 B-day card from H & V and 2 letters from Jill, 1 of which was a card. Jill's letter says she has finally got some of my mail. Very heart warming and some good news. The CO – 4th came round and it looks like the attack on Stanley may go in on Friday as a 2 Bde attack, 3Cdo in the north and 5 Bde to the south. Lots of ammo has arrived just down the coast. All quiet till the early hours.

The weather over these last few days had been foul, with its driving rain, some of it quite heavy in the strong winds, which in turn made the wind chill in wet clothing a challenge.

The chronic shortage of hexamine made it nigh on impossible to get the full calorific value from the 24 Hour Arctic ration packs, as most of the meal's hot content is based around dehydrated ingredients. I had planned to celebrate my birthday by keeping back a tablet of hexamine, with the express intention of having a large mug of chocolate porridge.

By standards it was a relatively balmy morning and I elected to take the opportunity to conduct some much-needed personal administration. Armed with my wash kit, I went over to the stream that ran through the gun position and stripped of my top clothing and braced myself for the icy water. To say that it was bracing would be an understatement, but needs must. I was just about to fill my mug with the running water, when I noticed that it was teeming with flukes, presumably from the sheep. The temptation was to double up with the water purification tablets ('puritabs'), but that would have left such a chlorinated taste in the water it didn't need much to dismiss that thought. Having seen the size of the flukes, my only concern was that the standard single tablet would be up to the task.

Whilst I was getting dressed, a Gazelle helicopter flew into the position and landed right by me. The Observer in the left-hand seat beckoned me over to approach his door, where on getting there, he quickly opened the small sliding window and thrust a blue mail bag into my hand. Almost as soon as he passed it over they were off and I wandered over to the Command Post for them to distribute the mail, as I went back and sorted myself out. Halfway back to my wash site I was called back as there were letters for me. To get birthday cards, some 8,000 miles away, on the day and in a war zone was a great boost to morale.

At the 'O' Group later, we were given an insight as to the possible plan, in preparation for the expected assault on Stanley. The following is a summary taken from my notebook:

'1 Gazelle has been shot down, killing the pilot and the OC of the Signals Squadron, by a stay behind Argentinian Blowpipe detachment. [We were to find out some time later the true facts where, in reality, a Sea Dart missile from HMS *Cardiff*, in the early hours of the 6th June had shot the helicopter down, killing all 4 on board.]

'2 Para were to redeploy a short distance to Fitzroy, with the Scots

Captain David Gibbins and Staff Sergeant John McQueenie were away from the position and on a foraging mission in the forward administration area when this was taken. Over the ridge behind the position to the west, some 3,000m away, lay a central ammunition dump and the waters of Fitzroy, with the LSL *Sir Galahad* **at anchor, immediately prior to the air attack. The attacks on** *Galahad* **and** *Tristram* **were incorrectly reported as being at Bluff Cove in the initial press report and to prevent confusion were never corrected to the true location, which was just outside of Fitzroy's Harbour, 8 June 1982.** (Courtesy of David Gibbins)

Guards centred at Bluff Cove and the Welsh Guards to grid square 2123. Currently Fitzroy is being held by the 1/7 Gurkha Rifles. 42 Commando were redeploying to Mount Kent, with 3 Para moving to Mount Longon, or possibly to Tumbledown Mountain. 5 Brigade will advance on a narrow front, with boundaries only being 2km apart. Should 3 Para not make Tumbledown, then 2 Para or 5 Brigade will push forward.

'29 Battery – We were marked to move forward to grid square 2968, with the comment that we could even move forward by road!

'97 Battery – It was marked to move a little further to the East of us to grid square 3269. Our centre of arc was to be 1200 mils. To support the operation, 4,000 rounds of artillery ammunition was being moved around by the LSL *Sir Tristram*. We could also expect both rations and hexamine in the near future. Prior to the attacks, we could get an ammunition preparation order, as ammunition expenditure is expected to be high. Finally, and from our CO (4 Field Regiment), that the attacks due on Stanley on Wednesday, were now due to go in on Friday'.

Tuesday, 8 June (D+18)

At 0157 C/S 22 spotted suspected enemy, at a target from C/S 29's FP [Fire Plan 'Lucky Strike']. (Time scale 072000Z – 101200Z.) C/S 29 loaded and laid us on that target. What I did was just that + conv [converge]. At 0615 he gave us 'end of mission – wait out'. All that time at Stand To. It rained during the night but the morning is OK. Windy but OK!! (Yesterday every type of helo arrived on the posn less for a Puma.) All quiet till 1705 when 4 Skyhawks flew past our location and attacked 2 LSL's just to the south of Fitzroy. The Sir Tristram *was hit and the fire put out but the* Sir Galahad *was still burning and had to be abandoned. Casualties were reported. High altitude aircraft were spotted and explosions were heard from the south. This could be high alt bombing or the LSL's ammo. Various high altitude planes caused 'Air Raid Red' At 1920 4 Skyhawks flew near (very) near our position. The Inf on the hill engaged with SA fire and eventually 1 hit claimed. At 1950 4 Skyhawks attacked again very close just past the edge of the perimeter and lots of SA fire went up. No hits claimed.*

One Fire Plan, 'Lucky Strike', stood out from the rest, not for its complexity or weight of fire, but for its sheet time scale and seemingly random target list, which was almost three days in duration. This one came about due to forward patrols picking up likely targets on the southern edge of the Argentine main defensive line and, as such, we were required to be prepared to engage any target of opportunity, as detailed in the Plan without delay.

Fire Plans are a major evolution within the Gunner world, as the plan revolves around a choreographed battle plan for all supporting fire, be it artillery, mortars, ships and air. The Plan assigns Batteries to targets along a known timeline, for which preparation is the key. It's formal nature and the significance it has within the battle plan, means it's communicated officer to officer over the main radio net and getting it wrong goes beyond the Pale. Every effort is made by both the CPO in preparing the firing solutions, along with the Guns, in making ready the ammunition scales, as detailed by the various target methods. Once prepared, it's more of a waiting game, with Batteries effectively given over to the plan as a priority. Once a plan is started, the Guns are laid and loaded on the first target, either waiting for a set time to fire, or on the orders of the fire plan's originator. Here we were waiting to be told, due to the time scale, but it still meant that the crews had to be ready to respond without hesitation. This in turn plays havoc with any personal administration, and or, rest.

In the early hours, one of the Forward Observation Parties spotted a likely target and I immediately brought the position to readiness, gave out the orders and the Guns replied 'Ready' in quick time. The expectation was that we were to fire straight away, however, time seemed to just stand still. Moments blended into seconds and seconds merged into minutes and still nothing happened. I could sense the confusion amongst the Number 1's and tried to give an update, equally, we asked the Forward Observer for his intentions, but were told just to 'wait out'. Eventually, after four hours stood to, we were given 'End of Mission', without any form of explanation or thought as to what we had been through, needless to say, the Guns weren't impressed.

At 17:05 Zulu, just prior to the initial wave of Skyhawks, I was outside the Command Post when I picked up on the sound of the incoming aircraft. After a few seconds, I was certain of what I'd heard and went into the penthouse tent and ordered that 'Air Raid Warning Red' be sent out over the position, as well as on the Command radio net. I noted in my diary that the initial wave consisted of four Skyhawks, in two pairs, with the latter pair following on very closely after the first; however, records show that there were actually five aircraft in this first wave. I can only assume that one was out of my line of sight.

The response from the position to the first wave was limited, with some of the Gun Sub's opening-up with their LMGs, without any apparent success. This was mainly due to the speed that they came in at and the very short window of opportunity to engage them, as they were almost on top of us. The Air Defence Blowpipe Detachment now co-located with us, joined the fray and engaged the incoming aircraft, also without success. Firing at the second pair, the first missile misfired and the second missile flew at the wave, but carried straight on uncontrollably.

The Light Machine Gun (LMG) was our main small arms defensive weapon and looked very similar to the old Second World War British Army Bren Gun. It fired a 7.62mm round, from a thirty-round magazine, at an approximate rate of 500 rounds per minute and each gun sub had one. However, we were not alone in trying to engage the attacking aircraft, with a Company from the Scots Guards, dug in just over the hill by the settlement, now alerted, providing sporadic small arms fire. The aircraft must have been aware that they were being fired at, as they dodged and weaved, trying to make themselves a difficult target as they passed us by, before swinging out to begin their bombing run. When standing high on the bank at our position, one could see the upper masts of the ships superstructure out at anchor at Fitzroy, over the low hill to our west and it was clear that they were the intended target. The first three Skyhawks lined up on *Sir Galahad*, with the first plane hitting with two of its three bombs, the second aircraft missed and the third struck with one bomb. On seeing that the first strike had hit *Galahad*, the second pair turned to *Sir Tristram*, hitting home. We could clearly hear both the small arms fire coming from the area of the anchorage, as well as the loud reports of the exploding bombs. What was also clearly visible against the clear blue sky were the palls of thick black smoke coming from the burning ships.

At 19:20 Zulu a second wave of four flew by, but a little further to the north, and by this time the Scots Guards were more prepared for any incoming air attacks and it appeared that the entire Company joined in. When this second wave flew by, the northern Gun Subs were alert to the attack and opened up, as did the Blowpipe Detachment. The third missile they fired came out of the launch tube and into the ground after approximately 50m to some alarm, with the last missile having a very close pass to one of the Skyhawks. The lucky pilot just managed to out-turn the missile, which we could see 'skidding' through the sky very close to his tail, because of his proximity and crossing rate. Whilst the effectiveness of the weapon was questionable, what was not in doubt was the calibre of the firing detachment. Where we were all taking cover, the detachment stood up in plain view, to engage the enemy.

In contrast, the Scots Guards had the far heavier General Purpose Machine Gun (GPMG) which was issues down to Section level. The GPMG fired the same 7.62mm round, but was belt fed and had a cyclic rate of fire of 750 rounds per minute. It was generally effective out to 800m, but

The LSL *Sir Galahad* seconds after being hit during the initial Argentine air attack at Fitzroy. The photograph was taken from the area of the ammunition dump, 8 June 1982. (Courtesy of David Gibbins)

was capable of firing out to 1,800m in a sustained fire role. Importantly, the belt-fed ammunition was arranged that one in four bullets was a tracer round. Tracer rounds had a small amount of pyrotechnic charge in their base, which was ignited in the firing action. The pyrotechnic composition burns very brightly, making the projectile trajectory visible to the naked eye; which enables the gunner to make aiming corrections without observing the impact of the rounds fired and without using the sights of the weapon, which was something we couldn't do with the LMGs. The Scots Guards put up a 'wall of lead' and we were able to see them close-in on the low flying aircraft. The individual fire of the GPMGs could be seen to converge, similar to the tip of a cone, just behind the target aircraft's tail. Unfortunately, the jets' crossing rate was so high, that almost all the rounds were seen to pass just behind; however, it was an incredible sight, seeing their collective response coming to bear. This second wave pressed home their attack, but there was no reported further damage to the ships. After the attack, one aircraft was claimed as a hit, although no one person could hope to claim it. It later came to light, that all four of these aircraft were reported to be damaged and only just made it back to the mainland.

The third and final attacking wave of four came in shortly after at 19:50 Zulu, although engaged, there were no apparent hits seen during this last engagement; however, they didn't continue the attack on the LSLs and flew on to find another target.

At the time of the air attack on LSLs *Sir Galahad* and *Sir Tristram*, the BK and BQMS were over the hill at Fitzroy, near the beach, on a foraging mission, trying to organise helicopter resupply of both ammunition and rations for the Gun Position. They were alerted to the incoming aircraft by the fire that went up from the area of our position; and were to witness the tragic events of the air attacks on the two LSLs unfold before them, which David Gibbins later described: 'Seeing the attacking planes we opened fire as a warning of impending attack, but were then to witness the ensuring fires and gallant rescue attempts especially of those helicopters that hovered so close to the inferno to winch survivors up. As lifeboats came ashore we assisted in organising transport and first aid for these badly burned soldiers and Chinese workers. Eventually, we were not able to utilise organised helicopter resupply support due to their re-tasking on CASEVAC duties. With darkness falling, we received the current password to get us back on foot through the Gurkha defensive lines, on route to the Gun Position. After slow and wet progress we found ourselves challenged by the sounds of cocking rifles and a request for password. We gave it, but it wasn't recognised by the sentry who was getting jittery! Then thank goodness I heard a British Officer hail us a little less formally and escort us through the position. We arrived back to share with the Gun Position what had occurred and reflected on the terrible losses that had occurred.'

Sergeant Walker sums up the feeling on the position, having witnessed events at relatively close quarters, compared to witnessing events unfold whilst at Head of the Bay House further up the anchorage: 'Seeing the Sir *Tristram* and *Galahad* being hit, so close to our position, this is really when reality kicked in. Our Battery went down to help the Welsh Guards off the ship – it was horrendous for them.'

The BK and BQMS eventually arrived back on the position later that night, both extremely subdued men. What also filtered through, having been overlooked during the attack, was that we had fellow members from the Regiment, namely two Forward Observation Parties from 97 Battery, on board *Galahad* during the attack. Thankfully, all members from both these

This was taken just above the beach in the small crescent cove, some 1,000m south-east of Fitzroy. Rescue helicopters rush to assist as the fire rages on board, as those watching moved down to the water's edge to await casualties, 8 June 1982.
(Courtesy of David Gibbins)

**This is the Artillery Fire Plan
Pro forma for Fire Plan Lucky
Strike, as taken down by
Lieutenant Bill Moore. Fire Plans
are strictly coordinated and
choreographed fire control orders
and normally originate with
the Battery Commander. They
are formally passed down from
officer to officer and invariable
require a considerable amount of
preparation, 8 June 1982.**

Observation Parties were safely
accounted for and knowing
of the loss of lives and the
expected casualty list, we were
greatly relieved knowing that
they were safe.

Wednesday, 9 June (D+19)
*Sitrep on yesterday. 6 en planes
down, they hit 3 ships + 2 LCUs.
At least 50 killed and many
limbless. A lot of stores went
down. Quiet day getting more
ammo and stores in by helo.
At about 1830 we had a FM
Regiment (2 Btys) on a suspected
en coy posn. Opening orders 10 rds FFE, with small adjustment
we were firing 5 rds FFE with no problems PD & VT. A total of 152 rds in 1
fire mission. C/S 29 said that we were on tgt, 'good shooting' and 'it looked like
extensive casualties, well done!' C/S 3 re-engaged later but that was all. A DF list
was sent down, we are ready at night but now it's just a case of waiting.*

During the day, we were to receive a sobering update on yesterday's attack.
We were told that out of the total number of attacking, that six Argentinian
planes had been shot down. We knew at first hand that both *Galahad* and
Tristram had been hit, but didn't have any knowledge as to what extent. The
suggestion from what we could see, was that *Galahad* was extensively
damaged and still smouldering; however, that the fire on Tristram had been
put out. What we didn't know until the sitrep came through, was that HMS
Plymouth had also been attacked and bombed, with thankfully all four hits
failing to detonate; also, that of the 2 LCUs in question, from the Landing
Ship HMS *Fearless*, that one had been sunk and one badly damaged. Records
were to show later that a total of fifty-six personnel were killed in the attack:
Sir Galahad – forty-eight, *Sir Tristram* – two and HMS *Fearless*'s LCUs – six.

As the day went on, a steady stream of ammunition and stores were flown
into the position, which punctuated an otherwise relatively quiet afternoon.

The resupply had unavoidable consequences, primarily brought on by the helicopter's downdraft, as they dropped off their loads at the Guns. These winds were of hurricane force strength and anything not fully secured down was liable to be sent flying, to Sergeant Walker's annoyance: 'The helicopter's down draft was a huge problem, we were having to drop cam nets and the noise affected communications between the crew and the Command Post.'

This was all to change at approximately 18:30 Zulu, when my Command Post took in the first of the multi Battery missions. The call was from Callsign 29 for a 'Fire Mission Regiment', with a suspected Argentine company position as the target, to which I immediately ordered 'Fire Mission Regiment' out over the gun tannoys. The Guns knew by the very fact that I'd called 'Regiment' instead of 'Battery' that the stakes had been raised and the air was electric. The opening ammunition order of ten rounds per gun for the initial salvo was passed on as soon as it came in. The Guns would normally have five rounds at immediate readiness and getting further rounds prepared fell on the Ammunition Numbers (Number 5s) and Covers (Number 6s). We were the first to report 'ready' which 'won' the adjustment and get the opening rounds in the air. Small corrections followed with 29 Battery's guns in the lead, with five rounds per gun salvos being the standard rate. We fired a mixture of point detonating HE and airburst MT, with the emphasis on standard HE. Standing at the back of the penthouse and watching the gun's fire, at a rate such that nobody had ever seen before, was a remarkable sight. The noise of the Guns and the activity of the crews was intense, fuelled by the Gun Subs, each in their own race to come first. We fired a total of 152 rounds in that single mission, which unbeknown to us, was a portent of things to come. Callsign 29 reported that we were on target and 'good shooting … it looked like extensive casualties, well done.' which I passed onto the Guns. 29 Commando Regiment's Callsign 3 was to re-engage this later on, but for us it remained quiet.

A DF target list was sent down, for which the firing solutions were calculated and the ammunition made available. The GLCs had not only to ensure that the Guns had adequate stocks, but also had to deal with the growing pile of salvage, which grew exponentially as the last mission progressed.

Later, Bill was to receive orders to move the Battery forward to a new position closer to Stanley, in preparation for the ensuing final battles. The gun position was selected from a map appreciation, in the southern shadow of Mount Challenger some 6,000 meters away, on the lower slopes of Wether Ground. To the east, a small ridge ran across the front and to the south lay a very wide and exposed open valley bottom. We were to find running through the centre of the position that there was a hardcore track. This track ran from Stanley and was intended to connect to the settlements of Bluff Cove and Fitzroy, but ended some 2km back behind our intended position.

The plan was a simple one, borne out from the lessons learned from the two previous moves. The intention was to move the Battery as two troops, allowing for a foothold always to be kept on the ground. I was to go forward with a troop of three guns and H1, set up and then provide the foothold for the remainder of the Battery to follow on in turn. At orders that night Bill set out his plan: 'Stand To' in the morning was to be cancelled, although the LMG trenches were to be manned, with everybody working through, to prepare for flying stations. Each detachment was to ensure that they were suitably scaled with water and rations; with each having one full jerry can of water and/or a combination of individual or ten-man ration boxes. Importantly, that all kit was to be securely tied down, having witnessed the damage that the helicopter's downwash can do.

Bill briefed that the battle plan was for 45 Commando to take Two Sisters tomorrow, or the next night with Tumbledown and Mount William to follow as later objectives. The Gurkhas were expecting to move forward to the Mount Harriet area. Bill pointed out that our new position, in grid square '2267' was quite exposed and probably under enemy observation. Also, that we were to be the furthest forward of our own troops, conventionally speaking, and that the expectation was that the '23' Easting was at the limit of the Argentinian 155 mm guns on the outskirts of Stanley.

We were all also to be ready by last light, in preparation for a move, which could happen at any time after dawn. We were also to take with us both the Blowpipe Detachment and the FDC, that had blistered onto our position. This new location was a clear area, with the Welsh Guards behind us; however, being so far forward, all the LMGs would go forward for protection.

The planned flying program was as follows:

Serial 1 – GPO and Sergeant Taylor (Gazelle)
Serial 2 – Sea King 1 Clearance Party (15) Myself, BSM, Lance Bombardier Saxby, 3 Technical Assistants from H1, Signallers from H1, LMG gunners from D, E and F Subs, the Covers from A and B Subs and Staff Sergeant Mutter.
Serial 3 – Sea King 2 Clearance Party (15) The Covers from C, D and F Subs, the remainder of H1, A Sub's standard detachment, Gunner Morris (B Sub), Sergeant Irvine and the BQMS (to be confirmed).
Serial 4 – PADS Vehicle.
Serial 5 – CP Trailer.
Serial 6 – A Sub's gun.
Serial 7 – A Sub ammunition.
Serial 8 – B Sub's standard detachment, 6 from C Sub and half of H2's Command Post crew.
Serial 9 – B Sub's gun.
Serial 10 – B Sub's ammunition.
Serial 11 – The remainder of H2, Sergeant Maxwell, Corporal Giles and Sergeant Jones, Gunner Hadjicostas and members of d and E Subs.
Serial 12 – C Sub's gun.
Serial 13 – C Sub's ammunition.

Gunner Kemp was nominated as a possibility for the last serial. One person from H1 signallers was to take the 344 radio. The Command Net frequency was 20.028, with Command Spare1 – 3.0335 and Spare 2 – 5.071 respectively.

Chapter 9

Wether Ground – The Last Position

Thursday, 10 June (D+20)
At 0200 woken to find the DF list done and just waiting for the inf to advance. Later on in the adv was cancelled, so the early hours were very quiet. At 1st light we were ready to move. After much waiting and much confusion, half the Bty flew out just before last light and set up 6 km nearer to Stanley. Not far now. The posn is very good really and it's on a road, not tarmac though. Throughout the late afternoon, an Argie 155mm shelled the valley just down the slope. It's funny to hear an en gun fire, take cover, hear the shell whistle in and watch for it to explode just down the slope. They tried to range in near us but they missed. 97 did a lot of firing and so did NGFS. The 1/7 GR are all around mortar base is just down at the rear of the position.

Unbeknown to us, arrangements were being made for David's abstraction, from his normal capacity as BK. He was ordered to the front early in the day, leaving us to join 2 Para, to replace their incumbent attached Forward Air Controller (FAC), an RAF Regiment Squadron Leader, who physically had reached his limit. Whilst David was a Forward Observation Officer in his own right, he was also a trained FAC and It was a straight one for one swap, with David taking over his small team of the Tactical Air Control Party. David was helicoptered to 5 Brigade Headquarters to receive the latest tasking codes, before flying off to be dropped off with 2 Para, who set off that night to act as reserve for 3 Para's Mount Longdon attack. David

The final forward position at Wether Ground, some six kilometres from Bluff Cove towards Stanley, taken from the area of the command post by the road looking north. The track runs out some 2,000m behind the position. Troops can be seen in file crossing the skyline, with Mount Challenger in the background, 10 to 13 June 1982.

This photograph shows C Sub in action, with the next round ready to be loaded. The 'white' extension to the shell case shows that the Fire Mission is using Charge Super. Note the height of the bowed trail and rear towing eye, which will be explained on page 178, and was mentioned earlier on page 92.

was to remain with 2 Para until the end of hostilities, getting involved with 2 Para's support on Mount Longdon and the Battle of Wireless Ridge. It was during the Battle of Wireless Ridge that David's skill was put into practice, controlling the Harriers, striking at the heart of the Argentine defences.

David Gibbins wrote of this: 'Namely the 105(mm) Battery situated very

C Sub team photograph taken between missions. The person to the left of the gun, with his back to the camera, has not been identified. The faces to the right are, left to right: Gunner Martin Straughan, Sergeant Steve Sprotson (sitting with tea in hand), Gunner Steve Thompson, Gunner Frank Muir and Gunner Richard 'Kaff' Tottle. Looking left are the two low detachment's bivvies. To the right in the foreground are empty shell cases, with the immediate prepared ammunition by the side and the ready ammunition prepared. Behind the camouflage net in the open is the growing mountain of salvage, from the seemingly endless supply of ammunition, 10 to 13 June 1982. (Courtesy of Steve Sprotson)

conveniently close to a marked up Red Cross First Aid Post. This made an excellent marker for Harrier attacks down the main valley into Stanley. Once I was in position I was informed that I was the only established FAC with an overview of Stanley and all available air was available to me! Along with John Greenhalgh and his Scouts firing anti-tank missiles, we inflicted significant casualties on enemy forces retreating towards Stanley.'

The sequence for the move went initially as planned: The GPO and TARA Sgt (Bill and Sergeant Taylor) were picked up by Gazelle at 11:38 Zulu and flew over the location and conducted the visual inspection of the ground, just as was intended for the initial landings. It was during their foot recce that the harassing fire from an Argentinian 155mm field gun started. Whilst the rounds were not landing too close, Bill did comment afterwards that it concentrated the mind. If the position proved suitable,

The standard number of rounds prepared behind C Sub. The rounds are out in the open, with the cartridge cases remaining in their protective black plastic cases, as seen in the blurred left-hand corner of the photograph. Again, note the height of the trail above ground, 10 to 13 June 1982. (Courtesy of Steve Sprotson)

a smoke grenade would be dropped to show the proposed centre of the position, before departing the area, whereby the clearing advance party led by myself would land in two Sea Kings. Again, we were to be ready to fight for the ground, secure it and prepare for the arrival of the Guns.

A short while after I had landed with the clearing patrol and secured the area, Bill and Sergeant Taylor flew back in and set up the layout of the position and we waited for the troop, namely the three guns, my Command Post, H1, the PADs vehicle and the associated personnel, to arrive. Whilst the PADs vehicle was being set up by Lance Bombardier Saxby, I completed my map survey and passed on my grid to Bill, for him to cross-reference against his plot. Agreeing in principle and certainly more than good enough to work with, Bill then waited for confirmation from Lance Bombardier Saxby and PADs, who confirmed it as being at Gr 22956795, Alt 100 feet. Luckily we were not rushed, as there was sufficient time to complete this before the troop of guns arrived and were set up. The Command Post came next and was quickly set up, allowing me to work from the previously prepared flying trailer. The table leg that snagged on the underslung load netting during the previous move was damaged, which resulted in one of the junior technical assistants having to hold the table up, until it was repaired. The plan continued in earnest, with the support helicopters ferrying in the troop et al, in what seemed an endless stream of helicopter sorties, which was in part, mainly down to the very short 6km transit distance. At some stage in proceedings, Bill hitched a ride back on a returning helicopter, to brief the rear position on their impending move, leaving me in charge of the forward section. Also to fly in was the FDC, who set up a short distance behind the position to the west, in a small and shallow hollow.

Throughout the move forward, the rear section was taking calls for

An image showing C Sub in the act of firing. The gun is at full recoil, suggesting that it was fired at Charge Super and out to maximum range, which took a heavy toll on the guns. The blurred image paints the picture of the incredible forces present, not only of the physical force to take the breech so far back in its recoil run, but also of the over pressure and deafening noise. Any lapse in concentration by those crew members inside the trails during firing, would have certainly had tragic consequences. Firing at the angle of elevation seen here, coupled with the soft ground, rather than recoiling in 'free air', meant that the breech hit the peaty surface, 10 to 13 June 1982. (Courtesy of Steve Sprotson)

fire, which tested the helicopter crews flexibility during fire missions. The realisation was that with last light looming, that there would be insufficient time to move the remaining troop forward, so Bill left Warrant Officer 2 Banton in command of the rear troop, consisting of H2 and D, E and F Subs, before hitching a ride on one of the last serials going forward.

Bill Moore: 'The gun position was about 2km in front of the Welsh Guards. During our recce, Sergeant Taylor and I were shelled by the Argentinean 155 [mm] that we came to know and love so well! We were sent there to have the chance of shelling Port Stanley airfield where Argie C130 resupply flights were continuing during the hours of darkness. You may recall that were it not for the intervention of Tony Rice we would have flown some 6kms further forward – right next to an Argie company position – as we later established'.

By now, the Battery was well-versed in moving by helicopter. Our role training back home involved helicopter operations, but that was limited due to both availability and nature of the training and it was far from being a comprehensive exercise. The slightest error in rigging either the Guns or equipment for flying was harshly punished, commonly with the loss of stores or some degree of damage.

Sergeant Walker: 'We were flying to every position by helicopter with underslung loads, being the senior Gun Number 1, I had considerable experience for which I was to become grateful for.'

The incoming Argentine harassing fire seen during the afternoon was more random than specifically targeted, with the rounds landing just off to the side of our location and further on down the valley behind us. Far from being dismissive of the situation, we were witnessing the effects of what an artillery round can have at first hand and it was quite sobering, with Sergeant Walker telling of 'shrapnel pinging off the cam net around us.'

The effectiveness of artillery fire is perfectly demonstrated back on Salisbury Plain's impact area, not only to the Gunner community, but to a number of the Army's wider training courses. Situated on the southern boundary, just within the artillery live firing danger area, lies a partially buried forward observation bunker called The Bombard OP (Observation Post), where shell fire is deliberately brought to bear in the area to its immediate front.

The bunker is long and narrow, with a heavily-armoured front wall, with numerous narrow viewing slits running along its length, where the viewer can see the heavily-cratered ground in front, albeit behind inches of ballistically-tolerant glass. As the incoming fire comes in from behind, the bunker is further protected, being cocooned in a deep layer of chalky soil both around and on top of it. Once in, blast doors are closed and the bunker is locked down. Lying in front of the bunker are the rent carcasses of old armoured fighting vehicles used as targets. Once range safety has confirmed all's safe then the demonstration can start.

To begin with, rounds are brought into the targets on the outer edge, some 100m away and just before they impact, notice is given to focus and observe the fall of shot. Seeing a 35lb high explosive shell go off in such close proximity is impressive to say the least, but to see six is an awesome sight. One can see and feel the blinding explosions in all their devastating raw power and hear the shrapnel ricochet off the bunker's front wall. The demonstration continues with the shell fire gradually creeping towards the bunker, until it is almost on top of it. By this stage, not only is the bunker peppered by shrapnel, but also from rocks and stones thrown up by the exploding shells, with the noise reaching a deafening crescendo and the explosions seemingly even more forceful. The Gunners classify impacting rounds within 50m as 'danger close', where there's significant risk to friend and foe alike. By the end of the demonstration the impacting rounds are closer still and you feel like you're in the jaws of hell, to be outside would result in certain death.

We now were out in the open and a world away from The Bombard and far from being dismissive of the situation, we were witnessing the effects of what an artillery round, almost three times the size of ours can have at first hand and to say it was quite sobering would be a massive understatement.

News filtered up to the position of one lucky escape, which was that of the FDC, who during the intermittent enemy counter-battery shelling, experienced a 155mm round land between the two Command Post vehicles some 30m away from the FDC, in the only soft 'peaty' ground. Had it landed only a few meters from its original impact point and on the rocky surface, the results would have been catastrophic; thankfully they were only plastered in peaty mud.

Unbeknown to us, the Gurkhas had been sent forward by 5 Brigade Headquarters, with orders to protect our location whilst the build-up preparations continued. The reality was that we were so far forward, that we were vulnerable to being counter-attacked and as we constituted twenty percent of the field artillery's capability, Brigade were required to mitigate that risk.

Back at Bluff Cove, Mike Seear, a Gurkha Officer, was shortly about to leave and move up with the battalion to join us. This extract from his book tells of the march from Bluff Cove forward to our forward gun position below Mount Challenger. The Gurkhas were watching Argentine 155mm rounds land further up ahead. It gives an indication both of what they were to expect when they moved up, as well as what we were going through:

'I squinted through my binoculars. Enemy shall fire was exploding on a crest line and their dark pillars of peat and smoke rose with surprising height. One minute later, puffs of smoke and thuds indicated where 4 Field Regiment's 29 (Corunna) Field Battery's gun position, which we have been tasked to protect, was being established at Wether Ground.

'The results of this Royal Artillery fire were observed by a Gurkha reconnaissance patrol. More explosions occurred near 29 Battery. They were enormous.'

I was on duty in the Command Post, during what was a relatively quiet night and it seemed like the early hours, when after muffled voices were heard outside, a helmeted camouflaged head popped through the tent flap.

'Hello – I was wondering if you could help me?' it said in a rather upbeat tone.

'Who are you?' I replied.

'CO 1st/7th Gurkhas. Who are you?'

'CPO 29 Battery and this is my gun position'.

'Excellent, so you'll know the lie of the land and can hopefully help. We've been sent up here to set up a defensive position, where do you recommend?' continued the CO in the same upbeat manner.

'Sorry Colonel, I had no idea. May I suggest that you put them all round us?'

'Can't do that I'm afraid. What's the ground like round here?'

At that point we went outside and whilst frosty, it was quite calm and with clear skies above, the ambient starlight, dominated by the Southern Cross, gave enough for us to see the lay of the land. I explained the topography and that shells had been landing in the valley just to our south. Soon after leaving the Command Post, the CO, Lieutenant Colonel David Morgan, and I were joined by Bill Moore, who then took the lead in helping the CO with his request. Bill painted the picture, as you could just make out the lay of the land in the darkness, that we were well-sited on a reverse slope, a few hundred meters from the ridge-line straddling the road, with flattish ground immediately to the north, before it rose quite steeply to the mountains beyond. As Bill Moore reflected, 'When you meet members of the Battery even now, all they talk about is how the ridge saved them.'

The CO made a quick assessment and informed us that he was going to set up his positions on the ground 100m or so beyond our northern edge up to the ridge-line, he then thanked us for our help and disappeared off into the night. 'In fact they moved onto the ridge just in front of us,' continued Bill Moore, and proceeded to brew up, still in the dark, which exacted a response from the Argentine 155mm.'

I stayed out on the road and with the ambient light from the stars providing as much illumination as a full moon, watched this seemingly endless snake of men pass by the Command Post. What was amusing to note, was that roughly every thirty men a considerably taller shape carrying only belt order and a weapon walked past, this was the Officer, followed by a mountain of kit, which turned out to be his 'Sherpa'.

Mike Seear continued his narrative: 'For the remainder of us there would be another hour's tab along 2km of track before arriving at the semi-prepared gun position of 29 Battery. It was 22:30 hours as the silhouettes of three 105mm Light Guns resting under camouflage netting became visible.'

Friday, 11 June (D+21)

After a very quiet early hours, the Battery started to fly in by mid afternoon. Early on we were told that the push starts tonight. 2000 rds HE approx were flown to the position for tonight's operations. 3 Cdo Bde to the N and 5 Inf Bde to the S. We also fired on quite a few en posns causing quite a few casualties. [The Battery fired in support of 3PARAs attack on Mount Longdon.] [Bill Moore: 'We were kept back, initially, owing to our survey state (when in fact it was probably more accurate than the other Batteries) and joined the party late on.'] The Batteries are all now with the Cdos, making a total of 5 Gun Btys. The en have 3 Pack 105mm Btys + 2 x 155mm + 1 x 105mm. [Bill Moore: 'they had had Pack How's and 3 x 155mm.'] Also tgts were adjt for the operations by me. All day we have been under a single 155mm CB gun. He always misses by a few 100m, but his VT is over the top of the posn. Morale is v high with the thought of all that firing on the Argies. Now with everything done it's just waiting. The Welsh Gds have moved passed us and various other units have filtered past us all day. The Bty now have chalked up a few en casualties. Mail also arrived today, 4 B-day cards and 4 letters (1 from Jill – v imp). There are 1000s tps going past, it's a heart-warming sight. We are the furthest forward Gun Bty.

The early hours were thankfully quiet, allowing some rest by half detachments and we were ready from first light to receive the remainder of the Battery to fly up and join us. The Guns eventually flew-in mid-afternoon, along with a resupply of ammunition, in preparation to the operation that night.

Bill had already designated where the joining gun platforms were to be sited, which allowed for the survey and displacements to be prepared in advance; the details of which were:

Battery Centre: Gr 22956795		Alt 100'	C/A 1400 mils
	DISPLACEMENTS		
A Sub	1280 mils	70m	
B Sub	380 mils	60m	
C Sub	2440 mils	75m	
D Sub	3360 mils	95m	
E Sub	5300 mils	60m	
F Sub	4120 mils	110m	

The Argentine Observation Posts clearly had an understanding what was going on at our new location. They had seen a considerable number of helicopters, with under-slung loads, fly up the valley to a point just out of their view behind the ridge, only to reappear moments later 'empty'. It was this that provided the catalyst for the harassing 155mm fire.

The report of a 155mm firing is both distinctive and loud, the sound of which carried on the strong prevailing westerly wind. Having an idea as to where it was located, we were able to calculate the approximate time of flight for the incoming rounds. Towards the end of that time, the distinctive whistle of the shell is the portent of its imminent impact, coupled with the lottery of where it would land. It was however, normally sufficient time to allow you to find some form of cover at hand, or at least lay down. The incoming 155mm rounds were a mixture or both ground and air burst, the latter was clearly mechanical time fuses, which was evident by the erratic nature of the explosions above. It was the airbursts that were to catch us out, as the length of time that you heard the whistle for was very short. As a warning, the cry of 'In coming' was given and that was one's cue to take cover.

I witnessed a lucky escape, by a few Gurkha soldiers having their breakfast shortly after first light. At the time, Bill and I were 'surprised' to see the Gurkhas light their hexamine stoves before dawn broke and the sight of these little fires was just the cue for the Argentine Forward Observers to hone in on.

In the inky darkness of the Falklands, light discipline is vital and we were surprised to see them appear casual about it. As it happened, they were about to learn a harsh lesson. A 155mm round landed on the crest of the ridge, just the east of their platoon's collection of little peat 'sangars', adjacent to our position. A considerable number of heads popped up over the top of these sangars, looking to comprehend what had just happened. They all soon disappeared from view and back to the task in hand, presumably dismissing it as an isolated occasion. A few minutes later, a second round landed approximately half the distance from the original fall of shot, towards the leading platoon's sangar. This again caused the occupants to take note, with those in the closer sangar clearly working out that the rounds were being adjusted towards them.

Not taking any chances, they 'vacated' their sangar and took up residence in the next sangar to the rear. Once again, a few minutes later, a round came in and landed almost inside their recently vacated former 'home', appearing to destroy it and all their possessions. One Gurkha soldier was seen to be left with the clothes he was wearing and the cup that he was holding.

The Battery was also very fortunate, in that the fall of shot from the 155mm saw rounds land all around, but without landing within the perimeter of the position, or the time fuses going off directly overhead. The location of the Guns could not have been better placed behind the protection offered by that little ridge.

There were a few occasions where shrapnel landed and caused damage. One airburst caught out Gunner Oteh in the open, who had been returned to the position from the BC's Party due to trench foot, where a large fragment caught him square in the back, flooring him with the impact. Oteh immediately stood up thinking that he'd been hit by a stone, thrown by a member of one of the Gun Detachments and spoiled for a fight. He was quickly attended to, as he was seen to go down, whereupon it became very evident as to the cause of his fall. A rather large piece of shrapnel had caught him square in the back, tearing his outer clothing, which was now lying next to him on the gravel road. The razor-sharp shard had luckily struck him flat on, knocking the wind out of him, with its energy being absorbed by the many layers of clothing he wore.

The same airburst saw a piece of shrapnel go through the top of my kip sheet covering mine and Finlay's peat sangar. On discovering the damage there was a definite feeling of 'oh shit', as by chance we were on duty and not resting inside, it made us realise just how much of a lottery incoming rounds were; as when you're asleep, or trying to in your sleeping bag and a round goes off, there's absolutely no time to react.

I dug out the offending piece of shrapnel as a keepsake, wrapped it up and put it in my bergen. The fact that I had to dig it out of the peat indicated that this could have resulted in an unfortunate outcome. Indeed, we had members on the position who were struck by shrapnel on several occasions, but thankfully there were no casualties, only shredded clothing.

Being showered by shrapnel, the effects of which being amplified by hearing it pinging off the rocks showed just how vulnerable we were. The desire to take cover under such circumstances is perfectly natural and understandable; however, during a Fire Mission and in action, when rounds come in, it's something that has to be overcome. There's no hiding place on the gun line and neither was there in the Command Post, you stood your post like thousands of Gunners before you. Being cooped up in a tent made that feeling of vulnerability more intense and the thought of a thin canvas covering offers zero confidence.

Sergeant Walker describes how, as a Number 1, that the Guns saw events from their perspective: 'The rounds were landing 100 meters in front, behind and to the left and right. But they couldn't bring it together. If they had we would have been wiped out. We were there thinking the next one could be us and some people's reactions were worse than others. You could see the fear on some of the younger lads faces, but you had to keep doing your job and firing the gun.'

B Sub's Gunner Kirvell, who like most, saw humour at the darkest of times, both recounts and reflects on his experience of coming under fire: 'I can say that in all my time during the war I didn't get scared and that's not me being macho, but I just never gave it much thought about what was happening at the dangerous times, which were numerous; like when the Battery's gun position came under enemy fire and we had to conduct counter-battery fire. On our Gun Sub we just sort of laughed at funny things, that happened when you're in danger. Like not being able to jump in the trench whilst being shelled, because you had to fire the gun back at them. Mind you, we had stopped digging trenches, as they only filled with water and also we didn't see the point when you couldn't use them, due to having to carry out fire missions under fire. But then also laughing at remembering seeing three of us trying to hide behind the gun's breach block, as shrapnel pinged off the cam net; also, remembering one of the crew going mad because he thought we throwing stones at him!

'It's funny but I only try and remember the good times of it all; the Falklands War and my other subsequent deployments during my time in the Army and that was my Dad's final piece of good advice – he only tried remembering the good time of his experiences during the Second World War.'

One constant thread of humour on the position revolved around the BSM and his unyielding desire to be an RSM. Because of the incoming fire, Bernie Winch never seemed to be too far away from the irrigation ditch that ran alongside the track, which bisected the position –just in case. The Gunners found this most amusing, but not nearly as much as the BQMS, Staff Sergeant McQueenie.

One unforeseen bonus for having been under shellfire was the hole in the ground it left. These craters proved to be ideal latrines, which saved one from the ubiquitous 'shovel recce' and provided an element of security, as one is hidden from view. Christening the craters was the prize.

The realities of helicopter availability and their priorities wasn't lost on the Gurkhas, as Mike Seear commented as he watched our resupply, from the forward ammunition dump at Fitzroy to our position: 'A Wessex brought in the Tactical Headquarters. Their priority task was the move forward of 29 Battery's remaining three Light Guns and shells. That was the reason why we had not received any logistic resupply. Helicopter priority had gone to the Gunners because their insatiable consumption of ammunition in providing harassing and counter-battery fire and supporting fire to patrolling sub-units'.

Mike Seear continues to emphasise the point of just how much effort goes into moving a gun battery, by citing that it takes some forty-five Sea King lifts to move just the bare minimum of men, equipment and ammunition; which was very much the reason as to why helicopters were not available for troop movements. His frustration is noted, 'For example, three days were needed for 29 Battery to be moved from San Carlos. It arrived at Bluff Cove on the 5 June, but even now, six days later, their last three guns was still being flown up to Wether Ground'.

The hard facts of having an extended supply line, which was almost exclusively reliant on helicopter support and made even more tenuous by their availability, is that something has got to give. In general, helicopters took ammunition and supplies forward, of which the Gunners were at the forefront of that effort, and brought casualties back. The root cause of the general lack of availability however, was the loss of the container ship *Atlantic Conveyor* and its cargo of support helicopters.

It was during a lull in proceedings and not being due in the Command Post, that I wandered down the track to visit the FDC and catch up with John Russell. We shared a mug of tea and John recounted their extremely close shave, showing me the crater made by the 155mm. Having seen rounds come in at first hand, what they went through and how they came out of it unscathed was remarkable.

On my way back to the Command Post, I stopped off at B Sub and joined Sergeant Walker and his team, by helping them to clean up the mountain of salvage that was building. This problem was felt by all the crews and keeping on top of it was not easy, made all the worse by the increasing firing rate.

The gun's camouflage netting was designed to conceal the gun, its crew and the limited 'peacetime' scales of ammunition. Here, the ammunition stocks behind each gun meant that space was at a premium, but the problem was that of the growing pile of waste, not least the empty brass shell cases. While I was helping out, a Fire Mission came in and I was able to witness proceedings from their perspective. Whilst familiar and practiced with each individual role on a gun crew, they were operating as an incredibly slick unit and I was aware of unduly interfering with their cohesion. As such, I helped at the rear preparing and getting ready the ammunition orders. It was whilst there that Sergeant Walker offered me the opportunity to fire his gun as the layer. It was during a Fire Mission, in between repeated 'Fire For Effects'. The hard work was done by the Number 3, during the initial response, where all I had to do was slot in to his seat, confirm the lay and pull the firing lever on Walker's command. After further clearing up, I left thanking Walker for the opportunity and he in turn thanked me for my efforts; but before I left, I picked up the empty shell case of the round that I fired, as a memento and put it into my bergen. When I finally made it back to the Command Post, I recounted what I'd seen at the FDC, as well as of my efforts in firing B Sub.

Mike Seear describes the events of the Gurkhas coming under 155 mm fire: 'They were watching the incoming rounds land near the Company position below them just above the Gunners. They put in a call to Brigade telling that they were "now under heavy shelling!" 'Below us the three light guns of 29 Battery returned counter battery fire.'

This was not the case. In fact, it wasn't counter-battery fire, but was just a 'normal' fire mission, it just happened to be as we were being shelled, so it must have looked as if it was counter-battery from afar. Counter-battery fire to a Gunner is effectively going 'toe to toe' with your enemy and is felt almost as a personal affront. Whilst the response from the position in any fire mission was nothing less than total commitment, there was a palpable feeling of everyone adding something extra into the fray when the Argentine rounds came in, as we returned fire with interest. What would not have been apparent from afar, was that the Guns and Command Post were manned whilst under this incoming enemy fire and that in being out in the open that there's no hiding place.

The unfortunate thing for us was that the 155mm shelling us was out of our range; however, some of the Argentine 105mm Pack Howitzer Batteries were well within our range, but unfortunately for them, we were out of their range to us. Unlike the harassing fire from the 155mm, we were to exact a devastating response against the Pack Howitzers, borne out by the end of mission reports citing the damage and destruction inflicted as a result of our efforts. As I passed these results out over the gun tannoys, you could hear the odd cheer. There was no sense of hatred or animosity, more of a feeling of it being a matter of fact – us or them – what was clear though was a general feeling of superiority as we fired upon them.

Mike Seear: 'Current life what not amusing, and nor were we the only attacked unit, because enemy shells had gouged out large furrows of peat near 29 Battery. Their seven-man gun detachments were lucky to escape injury and, like the Gurkhas, had combat kit torn by shrapnel …

'Despite the shelling, 29 Battery continued to receive their underslung helicopter loads of ammunition and the other three Light Guns. This first round of enemy shelling was ended by the Gunners returning what we assumed to be several salvos of counter battery fire'.

The orders we received detailed the plan of action. John Russell as the

FDC's Battle Adjutant had been to CO 29 Commando Regiment's 'O' Group and had returned to brief Bill; the summary of which is taken from my notebook and is given here:

The opening statement 'The push is on' set the tone of the 'O' Group. At midnight, operations were to commence with silent attacks by 3 Para and 42 Commando, Mount Longdon and Mount Harriet respectively. 45 Commando would follow with a two-phase assault on the Two Sisters, with the Welsh Guards and 2 Para being held in reserve. Depending on the success of the operation, the attack may push forward to exploit Tumbledown and Mount William. Specifically, in the Command Post, the detail of the realignment of the gun batteries was established. 3 Para were allocated BC 79 Battery, callsign '79', supported by 79 Battery's guns who would take the callsign, '3'. Similarly, 45 Commando had BC 7 Battery, callsign '19', but were to be supported by 8 Battery, callsign '2'. 42 Commando was allocated one of the BCs – callsign '39' – and had 7 Battery, callsign '1' in support.

The Welsh Guards were to be supported by 97 Battery, as a complete entity, with ourselves linking back up with 2 Para, with BC 29 Battery now taking on the callsign 'Golf 19' and ourselves the callsign 'Golf 1'. The phonetic alphabet's 'G' for 'Golf' suffix now denoting our separation from 29 Commando Regiment back to 4th Field Regiment, along Brigade lines.

There were to be four target lists, with BC 8 Battery, callsign '29', acting as 'Anchor OP', essentially the forward controlling authority. Of the four target lists, 3 Para had '3rd Step', 42 Commando had 'Manx Maid', 45 Commando had 'Iron Lady' and any exploitation forward to come under the target list 'Deck Crew'. To prevent any confusion, all targets were to be prefixed 'ZU' (Zulu Uniform). Each Battery was to inform the FDC if stocks of HE were to fall below 150 rounds per gun. Equally we were to monitor the ammunition stocks for all the non-standard natures, such as smoke and illumination rounds. We were also informed that we would be supplied with 2,000 rounds of HE by tonight. The signals instructions detailed both the structure of the radio network, along with the frequencies to be used and their timeline.

With regards to the Fire Plan, there would be little in the way of firing any confirmatory 'check rounds', also that there would be no structured time serials, as the battle plan was expected to be fluid, with all targets therefore being 'on call' – effectively being 'as and when'. Should there be a requirement to thicken up the fire, we were to be allocated, along with 97 Battery; however, 97 Battery would need to have the capability to fire throughout the arc 600-1600mils.

The stage was set and we all knew exactly who was supporting who by callsign, we had the artillery's battle plan in the form of the various Fire Plans and specific instructions, target lists were calculated and the ammunition needed to support it prepared.

The timings for the operation detailed the time each for unit to cross their respective start line; with 3 Para going over it at 23:59 hours tonight, 42 Commando would follow at 00:30 hours, with 45 Commando crossing over for Phase 1 of the operation at 01:00 hours and at 03:00 hours for Phase

3. Backing up the attack would be eighteen sorties of close air support. The attack would begin as per the times just given, with units crossing the start line, with radio silence in place until first contact.

The administrative element covered the service and support aspects of the plan. The main echelon would remain in Ajax Bay, with 3 Commando Brigade's administrative echelon based at Teal Inlet and 5 Brigade's at Fitzroy. Afterwards, all Quartermaster forces will be concentrated at Fitzroy. With regards to medical support, the Regimental Aid Post was also detailed to be sited at Fitzroy. Passwords were given as a double-phonetic letter challenge and response i.e. 'Kilo Kilo and Charlie Charlie (KK-CC)', along with their period of validity. It was impressed that everybody was to be well-fed by last light, as a busy night was expected. To that end, that there was to be an issue of rations, particularly the 'Ten Man' pack, with the priority of the limited supply going to the Guns. These Ten Man ration packs were large boxes containing the rations for ten men for twenty-four hours. In contrast to the predominantly freeze dried Artic style rations, the Ten Man packs were the Temperate type and came in tinned form. This meant that the Gun Subs could 'centrally' heat their meal by detachments, which greatly reduced the amount of hexamine required to warm them through. It also ensured that every one of them ate well.

We were made aware that there was a minefield in grid square 2870, some 5kms away, along with the fact that we may be here for some time.

For ease of explanation, the following is the extract taken during the orders, detailing the state of the Guns, their servicing requirements and their initial ammunition stocks:

		Service	*platform*
	1	✔	✔
He 200	*2*	✔	✔
Smk 10	*3*	*elevating gear at end*	✔
Illum 10			
Carts N to cover	*4*		*needs to*
----- Super 30	*5*		*No* ✔
60 L27	*6*	✔	✔

HE L27 20

Priority of Service
D - E – F

The orders ended with the comforting advice regarding the harassing counter-battery fire, which was 'keep down!', with the final words relating to a rations issue at 17:00 hours.

By last light the helicopters had dropped the 2,000-round ammunition resupply about 4-500m outside the position. Every person that could be spared went down to the newly-formed ammunition dump. Whilst the distance was short, the tussock grass and terrain made it hard going, made all the riskier by ensuring that it was done in daylight. By this time there were at least 200 rounds behind each gun and the crews were getting a last meal before the long night's firing ahead.

It was during our time at this gun position, that the Dobbins' and Kilmartins' teams came to the location with limited supplies of mutton and freshly made bread, which were handed out to the gun crews.

Saturday, 12 June (D+22)

Sat Day 23. At 0001 H Hour and the adv started. All through the night all the Btys fired, most of the time (fired at once) on tgts around the Two Sisters. By 1st light they had gone half way to Stanley and taken Two Sisters and consolidated. We incurred some casualties but no figures yet. The en were in numbers however many casualties + prisoners. At 1000 I took over again and fired most of the early afternoon, on tgts like troops in open (many cas), CB (dets leaving guns) – twice, an aeroplane and 3 helos – 2 damaged and the admin area burning and the ammo dump exploding. Casualties also. Basically a good day's shooting. Quietened down by night. Again we were under CB and that 155 was silenced. All through the night NGFS shelled around Stanley. We were 17500m from Government House. Tonight the push started again, so we will have to wait, probably to be busy again. Again re-supply to bring us to over 2000 rds HE.

Whilst the advance started at 00:01 hours, we weren't used until approximately 04:00 hours, when we started a fire mission that was to last several hours. The bulk of our fire went to support 3 Para and the BC and his Forward Observer from 41 Observation Battery; with the coincidental fact that 41 Battery's BC, Major John Patrick, was our previous BC before Tony Rice and knew 29 Battery intimately. 41 Observation Battery was formed only weeks earlier, on 22 April in Aldershot, as purely an Observation Battery, in order to provide 3 Para with dedicated Gunner Forward Observation Parties in support. 41 Observation Battery closed the capability gap of there being five fighting units, each requiring forward observers which was now met, but only four gun batteries available.

The light snow flurries during the night gave way to a clear bright but cold day and it was perfect flying weather, as noted by Mike Seear: 'After first light and stand-down, the helicopters began resupplying ammunition to 29 Battery's gun position. Their work rate (helicopters) was intense, for in forty-eight hours, they had flown forward 5,000 rounds. … More Light Guns flying past underslung from the Sea Kings indicated that 4 Field Regiment's 97 (Lawson's Company) Field Battery was being leap-frogged over 29 Battery to a gun position south of the recently taken Mount Harriet.'

It came as no surprise that the intense fly-in program for the resupply had once again alerted the Argentine forward observers, who worked out that something was afoot and the harassing 155mm gun started again. As previously alluded to, from an Artilleryman's perspective, this was continuing to be both frustrating and 'tiresome,' that we were in range for the Argentinian 155mm, but that it was out of range to our 105mm Light Guns. However, once again, we were able to exact that frustration by conducting counter-battery fire on one of the Argentine 105 Pack Howitzer position. As before, unlike the inaccurate harassing fire from the 155mm, ours continued to fall directly on target.

Both myself and my crew were also to be heavily involved in the early afternoon, with targets ranging from troops in the open, parked aircraft and helicopters, to an administrative area, with reports of an ammunition dump exploding. Thankfully, towards the end of the afternoon, the harassing 155mm was silenced by a Harrier, which had been called in by David in his new role with the Tactical Forward Air Party, who was by this time fully embedded with 2 Para.

Whilst on duty in the Command Post, I had a classic call of nature and during a brief lull in firing popped out. At that time, Bill was making his rounds and provided the necessary overwatch to allow me to leave, while I went outside. No sooner had I left that a Fire Mission came in and I made all haste to get back in. When I went in, Bill was, with the help of Bombardier Marsh, completing the firing solution and I stood by his side, anticipating to take over. The feeling prevailing amongst us was that we were getting the upper hand on the Argentines and that the fighting may soon be over. Bill had spent all his time out amongst the Guns and apart from the first day of firing back at Head of The Bay House, hadn't spent much time in the Command Post.

To that end, Bill hadn't actually controlled a mission and sensing that time was running out, was rather keen to do so. Bill turned and asked if he could carry on and I had no reason not to agree. The reality of the moment was that Bill was the GPO and his word was final, so to be asked was a mark of how far we had come. It was an acknowledgment that it was me that had all the experience as CPO. Not forgetting that I had been out and helped, albeit briefly, on Sergeant Walker's crew during a mission, It seemed more than fair for Bill to work the Command Post and 'complete the set'.

I continued to stay in the background monitoring progress, with Bill passing out the orders to the Guns. There was no fire control order in place, so as the first gun reported ready, Bill should have ordered it to fire; however, this was Bill's first mission and like I did on the first mission of the war, he paused, as if to wait for 'Safety' to give range clearance, as per the range routine at the RSA. Realising the situation, I leant forward and quietly said 'Bill, there's no Safety, fire the Guns.' Bill immediately responded, gave the order and went on to complete the mission, with an almost tangible feeling of relief at its end. I took the opportunity to offer him the rest of the duty, but Bill declined with thanks and went back out onto the position.

We fired almost continuously until mid-afternoon, expending around 1,000 rounds of predominantly HE. The excessively high rate of fire was taking its toll on the Guns' recoil systems and at one stage we only had two guns capable of firing, as Joe Walker complained: 'Maintenance of my gun and equipment during sustained fire missions was a huge problem,' which was equally felt amongst the other Number 1s, along with the GLCs and GPO.

It was here that Corporal Giles, our REME Gun Fitter, worked miracles in getting all guns back into action. The amount of firing that we had just completed was to cause a mountain of salvage behind each gun. Everybody joined in to help clean it up and it took well over three hours just to move some 10-20m back to their original platform's position.

One major problem faced by the Guns was the ground that they were sited on and this turned out to be a significant problem through the war. Often, the only relatively flat ground suitable for the gun platform was on an area of deep peat. It was not a problem at the first position, as the farmstead was on relatively firmer ground and the platform's serrated 'teeth' held the gun's positions. However, as we moved forward and over time, during the periods of intense firing, the Guns would move/slide back, because of the recoil, many metres from their initial platform position. The elevation of the gun barrels compounded the problem, by also driving the Guns down and back into the peat. Gun detachments were faced with having to dig out their guns, which often sank up to their trails (fixed towing arms). The long six-foot pole attached to the rear of the gun, used by the Number 1s to coarsely traverse the Guns, sits up some three feet at the tip, would end up touching the surface. The matter was exacerbated by the high charges being fired. Eventually there came a point when the gun's sights could no longer 'lay' on its prism, requiring the gun to be taken out of action and manhandled back into position, which required every 'spare' individual to help.

Six-foot angle irons were driven down between the platforms, in an attempt to prevent the rearward movement, with some success, but it only delayed the inevitable. It posed a challenge not only to Bill Moore as GPO, but to the GLCs as well. With all the Guns being subject to this problem, having more than one gun out of action at any one time wasn't an option and considerable effort was expended to ensure that it didn't happen.

The hard work was not over, as more ammunition was flown in and again we were brought up to a scaling of 2,000 rounds of HE.

Sunday, 13 June (D+23)

Sunday Day 24. A very quiet evening and the 1st early hours. The Sitrep that came through from yesterday read: 'To All stations from 0C' – 'We have had had a very successful 24hrs. All our objectives are firm. Our casualties are relatively light. We have taken about 450 prisoners either at my location or on their way here. For us the Arty, the day has been a great success, engaging tgts such as Coy HQs, Helos, Admin Areas etc … good shooting, well done.' Quite quiet day spent adjusting targets for tonight's push. Scots Gds are to take Tumbledown Mt. When that's done the 1/7 GR will take Mt William. We were up-scaled with ammo and prepared for tonight. Harriers have been flying over the posn at about 50' and attacking Stanley. Mail from home (including 2 from Jill and one with 8 cards in it). Weather is very cold. Last night in the shade it was -3 °C, so with the wind chill it is a lot lower. The attack went in on time. The Guards on Tumbledown are being held up by snipers and the large amount of firing hasn't happened. It's getting very quiet!!

During the morning, Bill was summoned, along with the all the other GPOs, to attend our CO, Lieutenant Colonel Holt's 'O' Group, leaving me temporarily in charge. They were to receive a very detailed briefing on the next phase of the advance. 29 Battery was to be placed at Priority Call to the Scots Guards and then to 1/7 Gurkha Rifles, for the battles of Tumbledown and Mount William respectively. The CO ordered a minimum of 250 rounds of HE on each gun platform and Bill radioed the ammunition preparation order through to me, to which I had well in hand by his return. As soon as Bill returned he called an 'O' Group and passed what he knew on. We spent most of the day adjusting targets and, having been exposed to the reality of firing at a high rate, considerable preparation went in for tonight's main attacks.

The sight of the Harriers flying over the position was an incredible sight. Up until that moment, we hadn't seen much of our fighter assets at first hand and to see one doing 300 knots at fifty feet, fully armed and heading towards Stanley was a huge boost to morale.

We commenced firing at 01:00 hours on Fire Plan JOHNNY ROOK in support of the Scots Guards, but the situation on Tumbledown was about to unravel. The Fire Pan gave way to the odd sporadic round onto the Scots Guards objective, with the sole purpose of helping the infantry orientate themselves in the dark.

Bill Moore wrote to me of this: 'You may remember the nausea on Tumbledown. The Scots Guards had planned a silent night attack. 2 Para had learned from Goose Green that such things only work if you can guarantee surprise. Having five-gun batteries adjust every target during daylight, even the Argies realised something was up. The Argies allowed the Scots Guards to get within 200m of their position when they opened up. We could not support them as the enemy were too close. The Forward Observer – Willy Nicholl – also became detached from the Company Commander (John Kiszley) and we had a difficult conversation with the Forward Observer, as he tried to thread the eye of a needle with both illum and HE to regain the initiative. I remember him saying it well "I don't know where I am, I don't know where my company commander is and I am not sure where the enemy are". The Gunners later awarded Willy a prize for his actions.

'You will also remember it was a bitterly cold night. As you say, all the cam nets had been shot away or destroyed by repeated helicopter resupply flights and it was blowing a blizzard. During lulls in the firing, Gunners were sitting on the Guns in soaking wet sleeping bags, in an attempt to keep warm'.

The reason for the Gunners sitting on the trails, was that Willy Nicholl's Fire Mission was over four hours duration, in which there was very little actual firing. We were ready to respond, but as the Mission was on-going, the Gunners could not leave their posts. In retrospect, with five gun batteries in support, the Argentine positions on Tumbledown should have been saturated in HE well before the Scots Guards went in. I remember offering up support, including illumination missions, but nothing came of it. As a result of the chaos, the Argentines let the Guards get close to their positions before opening with deadly sniper fire. As such, we were forced down the line of Danger Close missions, which by their very nature is a time-consuming and potentially costly process. When firing Danger Close, rounds land very close to our own advancing infantry, in the region of 50m and it's a calculated risk regarding taking casualties, which was a hard but necessary decision to take, in order to maintain momentum whilst pressing home the attack. It can conversely be used in defence, where fire is called down almost onto one's own position, should the enemy be on top of you, but thankfully we were always on the front foot.

Monday, 14 June (D+24)

At about 0600 they finally took Tumbledown (2SG). The attack was held up by en snipers. At 1st light I started to engage tgts near Sapper Hill & Mt William. Also CB north of Stanley. The enemy after sustained harassing fire this morning were retreating and in disarray. Last night (Tumbledown) many en dead + casualties, 450 prisoners. Few own cas. Harassing en positions around Stanley. At 1520 we were told that all Arty fire was to stop. The en on Sapper Hill are out of trenches with hands in the air. Airstrike with 2 Harriers was cancelled (tgt 4 x Pucara + Guns (105)). NEGOTIATIONS ARE GOING ON. At 1525 the en (info 0) had given up and the Paras were marching through Stanley! Morale could not be higher. It was then said that British troops had not gone further than the outside of Stanley. On the 1000 O'clock news it said that Argies had surrendered and a cease fire was on. Also over the net it said be prepared for a move (to buildings), but where! A very cold night, just like it has been for the last 4 days. Snow, high winds, rain and hail also below 0 °C temps.

Eventually, with virtually a blizzard blowing, and after five hours from beginning their attack, the initial Guards objectives on Tumbledown were taken. The Scots Guards then swept forward to East Ridge with us giving supporting fire.

Concurrently and throughout the night of the 13th and up until just after first light, we had also been heavily involved in supporting 2 Para's attack on Wireless Ridge, which involved the heaviest concentration of Gunner firepower seen so far. Hearing the call for fire – 'Fire Mission 5 Batteries' over the radio reinforced to the position that we were well and truly in the thick of it. During the battle, some 6,000 rounds were expended, or some 200 rounds per gun during that battle alone.

At first light, I started to engage targets near Sapper Hill and Mount William, with counter-battery fire on a 105mm Pack Howitzer Battery, just to the north of Stanley (I was to visit this position with Bob Ash after the surrender).

At this point the Scots Guards halted and passed control over to the Gurkhas, for their attack on Mount William. Due to the delay, the Gurkhas were forced to remain in their forming-up position all this time in the snow and I'd imagine were rather keen to press on. As the Gurkhas approached Mount William, they were greeted with the sight of Argentines standing up to surrender, or fleeing back to Stanley. The main Artillery effort was then switched to disrupting their rear areas as the Brigade attack pressed on.

With the Argentines having given up on Mount William, at 14:30 hours the focus of the advance was turned on to Sapper Hill, with us supporting that effort. When this news broke across the command radio net of enemy troops surrendering en mass, we were instructed only to fire in self-defence. It was Sergeant Morgan and A Sub who were to fire the last round of our campaign, which was in a way fitting, as it was A Sub that fired first artillery round of the war.

At 15:20 hours orders were received to stop all artillery fire and five

The position at Wether Ground just after the ceasefire. It shows A Sub, just to the right of the hardcore road that bisects the position, minus its camouflage net and crew clearing up just forward of the command post, the crews bivvies then clearly visible. Elements of both H1 and H2 crews are seen standing by the main command post shelter; constructed from empty ammunition boxes, it was palatial compared to the low-profile poncho-covered two man shelters. The central poncho hood required a 'tent' pole to keep the roof rigid. The men in the picture, dated 14 June 1982, are Gunner Jim Finlay (left), Sergeant John Maxwell (rear right), Bombardier Malcolm Hagan (rear left), Gunner Mick Botterill (back turned), Bombardier Phil Marsh (dark glasses front left), Lance Bombardier Gregory 'Cozy' Powell (second from the right), and Lance Bombardier Nigel Saxby (bottom right).

minutes later, we were to receive the welcome news that 'NEGOTIATIONS ARE GOING ON'. In the space of approximately one hour, from the taking of Tumbledown, to the total collapse of the Argentine defences a cease-fire was announced, with the Paras marching through Stanley.

We were both cold and exhausted in equal measure, but morale couldn't have been higher. With conditions being as brutal as they were, the priority was to get everybody in as much shelter as possible, along with getting something hot inside them. It didn't take long before groups started to construct shelters out of empty ammunition boxes, utilising empty pallets with ponchos stretched over them as roofs. It wasn't much but it was all we had and importantly it did the trick. We had fired so many rounds that there were plenty of empty boxes to go around and some of the constructions were quite palatial. After the war, much was made of the Guns being down to their last few rounds. Whilst one of the Batteries may have run perilously low, this was far from the truth, as we still had hundreds of rounds on the position. Our relatively low lying position help the helicopters bring in our resupplies, particularly when the cloud base was low.

Throughout the campaign, we were able to tune in our HF radios to the BBC World Service. Whereas all external news was welcomed, the most sought after were the World Cup football scores, which started on the 13 June. The surreal part of this was that during lulls in Fire Missions, football scores were pasted out over the gun tannoys, which on occasions raised more of a cheer than mission results. Bombardier Hagan had truly mastered the art of the 'thrown wire' antennae. He literally just attached a long length of cable to the aerial socket and threw the weighted other end as far

This was taken shortly after the ceasefire, some of the command post crew attending to their admin. The command post's camouflage net is just visible to the left, 14 June 1982.

as the cable allowed. On one occasion towards the end of hostilities, one of the signallers, who I recall as being Bombardier Hagan, not only to his own amazement, established a very brief two-way call, with an HF radio enthusiast back in the UK. A telephone number was given with a message saying all were well.

Whilst these real-time news updates from our HF radios were very well received, the most important thing for maintaining morale was the regular arrival of mail. Having a letter from home gives a tangible feeling to what's written within and that can't be underestimated. The fact that we received mail on the battlefield was one of those seemingly less important priorities, but it was a key factor in keeping up one's sprits. One or two individuals were to receive bills through the postal system, but the mere fact that they had received mail of any kind raised a smile.

By the last day's firing, the incessant high winds, compounded by the helicopter's downwash and the number of rounds fired at Charge Super, most of the Guns' camouflage netting was shredded beyond use.

Gunner Jim Finlay walking down through the position, 14 June 1982.

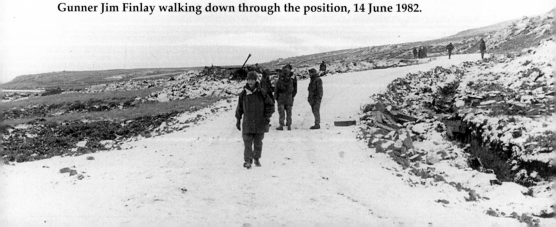

Chapter 10

Surrender: The Immediate Aftermath

Tuesday 15 June (Day 26)
After a long safe night's sleep and a cold awakening, we were told to be ready to move tomorrow. Bill said that the Argies had broken into the HF net and said that we might have taken the Falklands for now, but they may take it later! 97 have a war artist at their location – what for? & the CO may not even visit this location. The wind is terrible. It drops the temp by so much. I can't emphasise how bad the weather is. At 1520 I heard from 0 that the World Service said the Argies surrendered after the Arty fire on their rear areas – H1 in action! (in the morning). World news said that Maggie stood up in the House and told of the Battle of the Falklands. She was cheered. 15,000 Argies surrendered, 10,000 in Stanley, 2000 in West Island and around 1800-2000 previously in Darwin. News reporters said that the Argies were dejected and seemed relieved that it was all over. The ceasefire is an end to hostilities that are on the island & 15 km to sea, however mainland Argentina said that it was just a battle and not a war. Riots outside the Presidential Palace demanding down with the Junta. It looks like we will go back with 5 Bde and move to Fitzroy and join up as a Regiment. 2 Bns on LSLs and the rest in tented camps around. The fuel pumps for the Avgas for the helicopters has broken, so air

Taken from the command post, this photograph shows A Sub to the right of the road, which sweeps up and over the low ridge to the east and Stanley. It was this ridge and its proximity to us that saved us during the harassing fire from the Argentine 155 mm. Coming down the road towards us is a small party of PoWs under escort, some of whom are wounded. They stopped just in front of Sergeant Kenny Morgan's A Sub to await collection, 15 June 1982.

movement has almost stopped. It will take approx 6 days to ferry prisoners to the mainland and 2 days to leave this loc. 3 Bde looks like it will move 1st. Arctic tents arrived to make the stay a little more durable.

Trying to catch any sleep during a fire mission is almost impossible and we had been in action for most of the last forty-eight hours, needless to say that the long night's sleep was very much needed. Yesterday's euphoria was very much subdued due to the conditions. The cold weather was made all the worse by the strong winds, which tried to sap one's resolve, as I noted in my diary – 'I can't emphasise how bad the weather is'. News started to filter through, not only from the World Service, but from within the Regiment. Two bits of news to travel along the Regimental grapevine were met with a hint of disbelief; firstly, that 97 Battery had a war artist on their position, which was almost universally met with a 'what for?' and secondly, that the CO might not even visit our location. The first was comical, the latter not so.

With the Islands now having been retaken, the inevitable question as to our return was raised every time Bill and I toured the position. The truth was that we just didn't know, perhaps the Argentine's sudden collapse had caught out the planners? What was suggested was that we would be moving tomorrow but as yet, to an unspecified location. The general situation could be described as being in as state of flux. Whilst we had won the war, mixed messages were coming out from Argentina. Bill told of the fact that the Argentines had broken into our HF radio net, citing that we may have taken the Falklands for now, but they may take it later!

The news on the World Service told of the euphoria back home in the UK, with the Prime Minister Margret Thatcher standing at the dispatch box and telling of the Battle of the Falklands. Some news reporters were saying that the Argentines were dejected and just seemed relieved that it was all over. In response to Mrs Thatcher's speech, General Galtieri's Argentine Junta, back in Buenos Aries, were saying that it was just a battle and not a war. We weren't sure if this was just sabre rattling to appease the Argentine

A Sea King flies in past A Sub to the pick-up point for the waiting PoWs, 15 June 1982.

C Sub and the detachment now out of action. Left to right are Gunner Steve Thompson, Gunner Frank Muir, Sergeant Steve Sprotson, Gunner Richard 'Kaff' Tottle, Gunner Martin Straughan, and Gunner Geoff Wilkinson, 15 or 16 June (Courtesy of Steve Sprotson)

population, or that they were going to come back after re-grouping. What was being reported in the world news, was of the widespread rioting outside Galtieri's Presidential Palace, demanding his downfall.

It wasn't lost on either myself or my team that it was H1 that fired the first rounds of the war and it was H1 in the hot seat at its end. We had come a long way together, from that first tentative fire mission, to leading the race in most of the multi-battery missions.

Whilst we were no longer on an offensive footing, with the political situation being as it was, and with Argentina refusing to formally announce the end of hostilities, we still maintained our defences. As directed, Bill ordered that the Blowpipe Detachment and the LMG positions were still to be manned.

Later in the day, we received news that we were relocating as a regiment, with a tented camp at Fitzroy being identified as our new location, along with the rest of 5 Brigade. Two battalions were however, looking like they were relocating onto ships. Unfortunately, the fuel pumps supplying the helicopters with Avgas (aviation fuel) had broken, which was having a major impact on the flying program, in as much that flying had almost stopped. This was going to directly affect getting the fighting troops off the battle field and into their designated administration areas. The priority of any movement was going to go to 3 Commando Brigade. With the expected repatriation of the prisoners of war back to Argentina taking some six days, that we could expect to be here for the next forty-eight hours. With conditions being so harsh, Arctic tents arrived, with the hope of making life a little more durable.

As any movement for us had been put on hold, the emphasis changed to keeping busy and clearing up the position. In recent days, we had fired off over 2,000 rounds, with a corresponding amount of salvage, along with some 1,500 rounds of live ammunition that was prepared for the final push as a start. It was a mammoth task and was expected to last for many days. The weather continued with the same unforgiving intensity; however, the Arctic tents took the sting out of the conditions.

Wednesday, 16 June (Day 27)

The move was postponed. The weather is terrible, very cold and wet! With the lack of firing and with only an air threat then there is not a lot to do. About the best thing is 14 hrs of darkness.

Conditions were still atrocious and our move was postponed. Whilst I noted in my diary that there was little to do, that fact didn't detract from the task of cleaning up. With only ten hours of daylight to effectively work in, the terrible weather was compounding the problems of our clean up.

During a brief lull in the weather, we saw our first Argentine soldiers, who were escorted off the high ground to the north, to wait by the side of the road just in front of A Sub, the forward gun detachment. I along with a few others walked up the track to get a closer look and they were a very sorry sight. They were picked up by a Sea King shortly afterwards and flown on to Stanley.

Thursday, 17 June (Day 28)

During the dark hours we were told to move originally to a 'straight line' posn + tented area – like 'Amber Express', RSM's idea – Simon (GPO 97 Bty) said 'perhaps the enemy is within?'. Soon after 1st light the Battery started to move to Bluff Cove and settle down into the sheering shed and an outhouse. How long we don't know. All we have to do is tidy up after 2SG, re-turfing and collecting all ammo.

In the early hours, we were told that 4 Field Regiment was relocating back to Fitzroy. The RSM was pushing for a 'straight line' position, as we did on 'Amber Express'. Exercise *Amber Express* was a Regimental exercise recently held in Denmark, where the main base position was a tented scene, which might have been the norm in the Crimea and such like, but this was a world away from that.

The feeling amongst us in 29 Battery, was that as our Regimental Headquarters and 97 Battery were only effectively involved from the 7th June that the RSM was trying to flex his authority and get us back into a barrack mentality. Lieutenant Simon Frend's (GPO 97 Battery) comment on the RSM's plan over Regimental Net, summed up our collective thoughts perfectly – 'perhaps the enemy is within?'

Bill Moore resisted the move: 'Both Simon and I refused to move, owing to the still existing air threat. JR (John Russell) said that our refusal to move was a sure sign that the two GPOs had grown up.'The fact of the matter was that those making such plans had no experience of the air threat, not having

Flying back into our new holding position at Bluff Cove Settlement. The large building to the left is the sheep shearing shed, with the settlement to the right. The front building with the side view is the garage, which became the Battery command post, with accommodation upstairs. The gable ended building behind and left was the Kilmartins' farmhouse, with the Dobbins' to the rear right. The first of the guns can be seen on the 'green' at the settlement's edge, with peat sangars (predominately 2 SG) sited in the left foreground. This picture is taken from a position to the south-west of the Settlement, just to the north and below the ridge line, from where our intended location was planned to be. The exposed ridge line can be seen, with us moving further over the ridge to the south (800m) and relative security of the Fitz Cove. Our final position, whilst not visible, was situated just below the high ground on the far ridge to the east, beyond the waters of Bluff Cove in the middle distance. The faint outlines of the mountains to the east of Stanley can just be seen on the horizon, 17 June 1982.

A similar view today. The sheering shed remains as it was in 1982 and the few trees seen anywhere on the island have grown. The garage (front left) has been completely renovated, unlike the Kilmartins' original yellow roofed house, now used for storage which is steadily becoming overgrown. The red-roofed building was the Dobbins' (now deceased) farmhouse, which has been taken over and completely renovated by the Kilmartins today. Mount Challenger rises behind the settlement, to its right and just below the 'v' shape between the two mountains in the extreme distance, is a small diagonal mark on the low ridge line. That mark is the road and our final position at Wether Ground, 10 January 2017.

Looking back at Bluff Cove Settlement from the south-east, 17 June 1982.

Bluff Cove settlement today. The main buildings from the left. The red door of the refurbished garage, now craft workshop; the yellow roof of the original Kilmartin farmhouse and their red-roofed residence today, 10 January 2017.

seen the intensity of enemy air activity in 'Bomb Alley' as we had. The GPOs had given Regimental Headquarters a reality check and sanity won the day. By first light, the order was changed and that we, along with the FDC and the Blowpipe Detachment, were to relocate back to the settlement of Bluff Cove for the foreseeable future. Without knowing how long we would be there, utilising hard accommodation, albeit sheds and outhouses, was considered better than tents.

It was at this time that the David Gibbins returned to the Battery, having completed his detachment as a Forward Air Controller and immediately reverted back to being the BK; who, along with the residents, began allocating the living areas and organising the settlement to accommodate the Battery.

Most of the Battery were housed in the shearing shed; with the officers,

Inside Bluff Cove Settlement, with the Battery flag flying. In between and behind the two dispatch riders' bikes, used by Lieutenant Bill Moore and Bombardier Malcom Hagan for their trips up Sussex Mountains, is the original storehouse and shop. Seasonal workers could purchase supplies here. Behind and to the right is the garage, with the command post's 5m aerial mast visible. Behind the flagpole in the distance lies the exposed ridge line and the area of our planned first location at Bluff Cove, 17 June 1982.

That same view today, 10 January 2017.

warrant officers and the FDC, who maintained the radio link, taking residence in the 'outhouse'. The outhouse was in fact an empty two-storey garage near the centre of the settlement, with the officers and seniors being accommodated upstairs and the FDC, now set up as a Command Post below. The Battery's Cooks reactivated a peat-fired bread oven at the shearing shed, producing: bread, pizzas and pies, with the 'makings' supplied by the BQMS.

A further view inside the settlement, with the flagpole on the right. The building to the left is the generator and battery outhouse that provided the settlement's power supply. Fenced off is the large dark peat mound, 17 June 1982.

The emphasis at the 'O' Group was placed on our new surroundings and establishing a sense of normality, in the form of a camp routine, but it opened with the salutary warning that the war was not over. The routine was set, with reveille at 08:00 hours, that the accommodation was to be cleaned by 09:00 hours, before stressing that everybody was to be washed and shaved having had breakfast by 10:00 hours. All ranks were then to take part in 'Paper Chase', or simply litter picking, around the settlement until 12:00 hours, when we were to break for lunch. Picking up litter wasn't just something to do for sake of doing something, there was actually a lot of it lying around, which we had now inherited. We were to resume at 13:00 hours, until the end of the working day, with the Gun Detachments carrying out the daily servicing of their guns by half detachments, with the remainder of the Battery required to re-turf the area of the fence, immediately adjacent to the Kilmartins' house.

The next item was very well received, which detailed the first beer run. The BQMS was looking to acquired ten crates of beer, which he would sell, and it was suggested that crews pooled their cash.

The mood was brought back down to earth, by detailing the ablutions; more so, by the fact that we may actually be here until we leave the islands. The BQMS had also managed to get his hands on stocks of shaving kit and individuals were to see him if they were in need of replenishment. The BQMS had also managed to secure a supply of washing powder and a 50-gallon drum, heated by a Cook's Number 1 burner, effectively a weak blow torch used for cooking, to heat the water for hand-washing. We had been in the field for some time now and we were absolutely filthy and this was something to look forward to. Reference was made regarding the weather, in that these last two days had been the worst we had seen.

Looking back into the settlement at Bluff Cove from the north-west, with the Dobbins' house on the left and the Kilmartins' on the right. The right-hand of the two white buildings at the front was a pigsty. Peat sangars can also be seen, which at the time of our arrival were littered with live ammunition from the previous occupants, 17 June 1982.

The same view now, the pigs have long since gone, 10 January 2017.

Following on for the earlier Paper Chase, all rubbish was to be handed in at 13:30 hours and was to be separated into what could be burnt and what would be packed off out to Stanley. One contributor highlighted that faeces had been found in the main sheep shearing accommodation shed, left by the Scots Guards and emphasised that the ablutions were to be used at all times. A request was put out for people to look out for any 4 x 2-inch bits of wood, as it was intended to construct a shower. David stressed the importance of everybody needing to keep busy.

Even though we knew that hostilities had ended, there was concern that there may still be a small cadre of Argentines, such as stay behind parties, who wanted to keep fighting. As such, the trenches on the hill overlooking the settlement were to remain manned by LMGs and the Blowpipe Detachments. To maintain communications with them, the signallers were to set up a telephone system, between the trenches and the main shearing shed, with the password confirmed as 'II – MM' (India India – Mike Mike).

The final detail covered the not-so-insignificant matter of our live ammunition and it marked the end of our war footing. Whilst the sentries would be armed, individuals were to hand back all live ammunition, ranging from 9mm to grenades. Equally, any live ammunition found around the settlement from previous occupiers, was to be handed in as well. It was stressed that should we need live rounds again, that they would be re-issued.

Friday, 18 June (Day 29)

After a relaxed start it's just a case of tidying up. A lot of re-turfing and cleaning. The amount of ammo collected is amazing! White Phos, 84mm, 81mm, 0.5mm [incorrect size – should be inch], 7.64mm and 105mm. The CO visited us and told us we were going back with 2 PARA. Also, we don't know how long we have to stay here. Now that Galtieri has been deposed it's just a case of waiting. We have started to send the PWs back, but are keeping the Offrs and SNCOs back – who knows how long? The World news doesn't look too promising, but let's just wait and see. At the evening conf me + 14 are going to clean up the last posn. Beer on the posn.

Sergeant Joe Walker, B Sub's Detachment Commander, photographed inside the sheering shed at Bluff Cove, circa 17 June 1982.

The tidying-up of the settlement continues, with the emphasis placed on disassembling the peat sangars and re-turfing, as well as picking up the discarded ammunition. These settlements and farmsteads have relatively small grassed paddock areas in and around them, which meant that they required more work doing to them, than merely filling in holes in the ground. The thing that surprised not only myself, was the sheer quantity of discarded ammunition left just lying around. In contrast, we as a Unit could account for everything we were issued with. Apart from the limited expenditure of small arms fired at passing aircraft, every man still had their correct scaling; with the gun ammunition being specially looked after. To find so much just lying around we felt smacked of poor drills.

The CO visited and gave us the eagerly awaited news regarding our departure. We were going to return to the UK with 2 Para, but as yet, no date had been set. This was in keeping with the directive given, regarding the repatriation of fighting troops. The directive was that all troops who landed on 21 May would be going home first. The 'system' was keen to repatriate fighting troops with a garrison force and as such, 3 Commando Brigade, along with both 2 and 3 Para would be amongst the first to leave. This meant with 29 Battery being part of 2 Para's Battalion Group, that we would return with them. It was just the news that we were waiting for and morale soared. With Galtieri deposed, everyone appreciated that it was just a case of waiting, but knowing that we would be going home as part of the first wave, was good enough to be going on with.

The news from Stanley was that we were sending back the first of the PoWs, who were mainly conscripts, but were holding back the officers and senior non-commissioned officers. We didn't know for how long, but speculation was mainly based on the fact that without this level of expertise, that the Argentine forces would find it difficult regrouping. The signallers kept us abreast of the outside world, by ensuring that they tuned into the World Service on the hour. Being so far away and not having access to a wider news base, meant that this was our only source of information, but it didn't look too promising. Thankfully we're not politicians.

I was warned off that I would be taking a fifteen-man working party, in a Sea King, to the last position to continue with its clean up. Whilst we had achieved much before we left, there was still a small mountain of ammunition and salvage to deal with.

One thing that boosted morale almost as much as our impending return, was the news that beer had arrived on the position. A working party was required to unload the various stores being flown in, with the BQMS supervising the beer's wellbeing and 'bonded' storage.

David's 'O' Group that evening detailed a similar routine to yesterday, with a thirty-minute delayed start. Reveille was set at 08:30 hours and we were to be ready for work by 1030 hours. The emphasis until lunch at 12:30 hours was placed on Gun and vehicle maintenance, with the remainder of the Battery re-turfing the defensive positions. Re-turfing is essentially filling back in the defensive earthworks and returning the ground to its previous state. Work was to start again at 13:30 hours and continue on from the mornings efforts until 16:00 hours.

The shower in the shearing shed was constructed by Sergeants Irvine and Dobson and was almost completed, with the aid of a forty-gallon drum and a burner. It was hoped to have it up and running by the end of the day and patience was requested.

Once again, the subject of mines was covered, with the general caveat that you could expect them anywhere and, as such, David stressed the need to stick to the settlement's cleared area. A warning was also given out regarding the collection of souvenirs, especially live ammunition, with particular reference to 0.50 inch ('50 Calibre') rounds. Reference was made later, regarding potential booby-traps and drawing on our training and experiences from our recent tour in Northern Ireland, it was the suggestion that if it looks too good to be picked up, then it probably was.

Next on the list was the long-awaited news of the beer run and it was confirmed that there were ten crates as promised. The sale of beer was to start at 190:00 hours and the price was set at 35p per can, with a two can per man limit. The irony was that Staff Sergeant McQueenie could get beer, but could couldn't source torch batteries. Part of the reason for that, was the explanation that the rear echelon and the stores set up was in such a mess. There was conjecture that the NAAFI was going to set itself up in Stanley, which was of little use to us; however, the BQMS may be able to acquire some stocks for Bluff Cove. What was made clear was that there were no more cigarettes. The NAAFI is a civilian run tri-service institution and is effectively the military's local 'corner shop'/cafe, providing both a welcome diversion, along with stocking basic essentials. It appeared that an old washing machine had been found and had been pressed back into service. Being electric, it was only worked when the generators were working, with Sergeant Maxwell detailed to oversee it. To prevent our presence from dominating the Islanders lives, nobody was permitted to see them, without prior clearance from either the BK or the GPO.

Individuals were reminded to get their mail in, in preparation for the next mail run. Reports were that incoming mail sacks had been offloaded from HMS *Fearless* and were being sorted, possibly by 2 Para, before sending out. Whilst we were getting mail, the salutary fact was that there was no ship of goodies. There was also no decent water to be had and that Stanley was itself in rather a bad way.

David concluded with the news that a new Air Defence Battery was to be deployed to Stanley and that 97 Battery were warned off to stay and garrison the Islands. The best news was saved until last, which was that we were to return with 2 Para.

Saturday, 19 June (Day 30)

Soon after the working day started it became apparent that I was not going off. The shower was starting to work after a trial run last night and that drained the workforce. That inevitably started friction between the hierarchy and that shortened tempers. Eventually after a big conf it sorted itself out and it's arranged to go off tomorrow as planned. Mail is in but it's being sorted out at 0C's loc. Yesterday we had an issue of long johns + socks boots and combats!! The second can of beer went down well. Had a bath in the house (Kevin & Diane's). That went down very well along with their stew, tea – coffee, gin & tonic. Told that we were moving to a ship.

The day didn't start off a planned and it quickly became apparent that nobody was leaving the position. The reason was that Sergeants Irvine's and Dobson's shower was proving to be a great success, with individuals queuing to use it, which in turn was draining the workforce. We had been without proper washing facilities for the best part of a month and were absolutely filthy, and understandably individuals were keen to use it. It now boiled down to where the Battery's hierarchy placed the priority for the position's clean up, or the cleanliness of our soldiers and that led to friction and shortened tempers. We knew that the work had to be done, but it was questioned as to whether it had to be done at the expense of the Battery's morale.

A conference was called and it was decided that the position wasn't going anywhere and that we were to continue with the showers. This fitted in perfectly with yesterday's clothing issue of underwear, socks and combats. There were also boots for those who needed them. The simple decision to continue with the showers, coupled with the ability to change into clean clothing had such an immediate positive effect, that it was evident that the correct decision had been made.

Kevin and Diane Kilmartin were a young couple, who along with Tim and Jean Dobbin, were the only residents at Bluff Cove and owned the smaller farmstead. They had kindly invited the officers to dinner and offered the use of their bath beforehand. Being the most junior I was the last to go, but it was certainly worth the wait. It was when I piled my old clothes next to my new issue that I realised just how filthy I was. I don't know if people remember any of their various bathing experiences throughout their lifetime, but I can say beyond doubt that this bath is firmly etched in my memory.

After quickly returning my things to the garage, I and the others went in to join Kevin and Diane. The plentiful supply of mutton stew with all the trimmings was fantastic, with tea and coffee to follow. The evening was topped off with that quintessential English tipple, a gin and tonic. Over dinner it transpired that Diane and James went to the same university (Sheffield) and at the same time. We all agreed that it had been a great evening.

Later that evening news came through that we were moving to a ship, which was unspecified at this time. It was yet another indicator that things were moving in the right direction regarding our return, and morale was generally on the rise.

Sunday, 20 June (Day 31)

At 1st light we were told that we weren't going. At lunch approx 30 took off for showering on the Sir Geraint. *The 1st helo took off without me to* Fearless *in Stanley, we got ½ way there till the helos received their orders. The* Sir Tristram *is along-side – a burnt hulk. We're here for washing (showering) but with the troops it's very inadequate. Hitched a lift in the back of a Huey [UH-1] Iroquois!*

The day got off to a bad start, when we received news that we were not returning with 2 Para and that we were to remain, for an unspecified time. Understandably, morale dipped somewhat. As there were no details to support this, the feeling was that whilst this was a setback, that it wasn't the end of the world, as individuals clung onto the directive that all first wave troops would return as a priority. Whilst requests for further information went in, nothing forthcoming came back in return and the longer it went on, the more concerned we were.

Whilst our shower in the sheep shearing shed was working, the throughput was very slow. As a result, a request was put in for 'shower runs', which were granted. At lunchtime, I left the position with a party of some thirty to fly onto the LSL *Sir Geraint*, which was at anchor off Fitzroy, with the system delivering as requested. The shower run was always intended to take place on the *Geraint*, which was anchored close

The burnt-out superstructure of the LSL *Sir Tristram*, taken from *Sir Geraint's* cargo deck, which was moored alongside. The *Geraint* visit was for a small party of the Battery's Gunners to have a shower on board. Some areas of *Tristram* were available, but not used, 20 June 1982.

A close-up of *Tristram's* extensive damage caused as a result of the Argentine air attack at Bluff Cove on 8 June, with the loss of two lives. The photograph was another taken from the deck of her sister ship, *Geraint* during the shower run, 20 June 1982.

A further view of the damage on the port side, 20 June 1982.

to the point of the attack on *Sir Galahad;* however, there was a suggestion that *Sir Tristram* could also be pressed into service. The *Geraint* was tied up along-side *Tristram*, with *Galahad* at anchor which was still smouldering some 500m astern. Looking at *Tristram's* bomb damage, I couldn't see how there was anything still left working. I accompanied the shower party, not to shower, but to oversee events and ensure that everyone made it back to the Battery location. Considering their 'palatial' surroundings and the timeline, I was disappointed to see both the state of the troops on board, namely the Welsh Guards and the cleanliness of the ship. Their morale was low and, in particular, that of the attitude of the junior officers, which was standoffish to say the least. I couldn't wait to leave. Whilst the troops showered, I went topside to take a closer look at *Tristram*. The scale of the damage was staggering and could only guess as to what I could not see below and within her decks. The intense heat of the fire had twisted the bridge superstructure in on itself, with extensive fire damage visible continuing aft. I when I looked over to *Galahad* and saw her in a similar state, and knowing of the loss of life met there, I couldn't believe that so many on *Tristram* survived the attack. The high point was riding in the back of the Huey for our return, which had more of a feeling of a pleasure flight,

Taken from *Geraint*'s rear flight deck, *Galahad* can still be seen smoldering from the air attack at Bluff Cove some twelve days earlier. In the photograph, the ships are actually at anchor just outside Fitzroy Harbour. Of the forty-eight who lost their lives, thirty-two were from the Welsh Guards. On 25 June, she was towed out to sea off the Falklands and sunk as a War Grave, 20 June 1982.

coupled with the added buzz that it had been procured.

This Argentine aircraft was pressed into service as it was still in a flying state, being utilised as a 'run-around' to ease the helicopter shortages. Under/behind the pilot's seat was a case of whisky, which was used for bartering and we were warned to keep our hands off it. As an after note, this Huey eventually made its way back to the UK and even featured in the opening sequences of a James Bond movie; and I was to meet the pilot, Rob Tierney, again in 1989, whilst training to become a qualified helicopter instructor at RAF Shawbury, where Rob was the base's head of ground school. In 1982, Rob was the RAF Liaison Officer to 5 Brigade, which was essentially a desk job; however, Rob was an ex-helicopter test pilot and was more than suitably skilled to utilise his aviation skills and press G-HUEY into service.

The evening's 'O' Group was relatively straightforward, in as much that we were to pick up from where we were previously detailed. With most of the settlement now clear, work continued at the Fitz Cove position, just over the hill.

With still no update at the end of play, morale remained generally down.

Monday, 21 June (Day 32)
Took a party of 15 off all day to the last gun posn, to clear ammo + salvage – A huge task. It was heavy drizzle all day. The weather has not been too bad these last few days. Bill & JR [Capt John Russell] went off to the CO's 'O' Gp. They said that we will go back hopefully before August. Heard that the 1st troops will be going home

soon! 2 letters from Jill, seemed a little out of sequence – let's hope it sorts itself out soon. Morale is a little undecided, with all the indecision that is going on, as to our move from here to ships and ultimately home.

Shortly after first light, I took off with fourteen others to continue with the last position's clean up. Whilst we broke the back of the work before we flew out, there was still a mountain of ammunition and salvage to deal with, which brought home the realisation as to the intensity of the Gunner effort in those last few days of the war. Again, conditions were poor, which made for a miserable time, made all the worse by contrasting the weather against the relatively better weather seen over the last forty-eight hours. As we were out all day and as there was no shelter, lunch was nothing more than a bar of chocolate and other such snacks, but a hot cup of tea always raises the mood. The priority was to repackage the live ammunition and it's only when we centralised the ammunition from each of the six guns, that the true scale of our support was evident.

While we were away, Bill and John Russell were summoned to attend the CO's 'O' Group. They were to learn that the first troops would be returning soon, as originally planned; however, that that was not to be our fate. The military planners had conducted a threat assessment and concluded that without credible Artillery support, the remaining garrison troops would be vulnerable to any counter-invasion. To lose four out of five gun batteries was too much of a risk and because 29 Battery were part of 4th Field Regiment, who were remaining, we would naturally fit back into the Regiment, along with 97 Battery. The reality was that 29 Commando Regiment and 4th Field Regiment were the only Light Gunners and training replacements would take a number of weeks. As such we were required to remain in place, until possibly August.

Morale was for the majority rather low on hearing the news. Some were pragmatic, understanding the reality of the situation, but at the end of the day we were still soldiers and we would do as we were told. The one thing that did brighten things was a mail run and I was to receive two letters from Jill, albeit out of sequence.

Tuesday, 22 June (Day 33)

A nice day in camp, weather OK. Did my washing in the house in the AM. In the afternoon we were told that 2 & 3 PARA were going home at the end of the week and that we were ready to go in about 48 hrs. Went down to the house in the evening. Bill took a message from the CO to be prepared to stay till the 20th July! 4 weeks!!! A kick in the teeth. Letters from home which was good news and Jill also enclosed some photos. It was nice to catch up on the news. The whole Regt looks to go back together.

After what had seemed like an eternity, the weather broke to become a fair day. The day was more of a stand down from the working parties, giving individuals time to sort out their own personal administration. I secured some of the washing powder and used the Kilmartins' washing machine to make a start on my combats. One wash was never going to be enough, but it was a start.

After lunch, news came through of both 2 and 3 Para's return home, which was scheduled for the end of the week. News also came through that we were to be ready to go in forty-eight hours, but there was nothing further to support that, in terms of detail. When this filtered through the settlement morale took a massive upswing. A further mail run helped lighten the mood and Jill enclosed some photographs in her letters.

Early evening saw the officers invited back to Kevin's and Diane's, which was rounding off a rather good day. Just as things were coming together, Bill was summoned to the radio to take a message from our Regimental Headquarters. The news from the CO was just as bad as could be, as the message told that we were to be prepared to stay for another four weeks, until 20 July and then return home as a Regiment. Having already been told that we were going home on two previous occasions, to be told that we were not for the third time felt like a kick in the teeth.

Wednesday, 23 June (Day 34)
In the morning the BC and John Patrick [BC 41 'OP' Bty – 3 PARA, 29 Bty's previous BC] arrived to tell us the bad news. They stated that it was the worst case; however, it still made everyone a little miserable (understatement). But by the end of the day – people were getting over it. It was a miserable day with drizzle not helping! I was evicted with JR to the caravan (Romany type). JR moved to the house (Tim's) and the SMIS (signals Sergeant Major) moved down to fill in. James & Bob + rest of the Ops will join us on Friday. All the Bty kit i.e. suitcases + kitbags + Bty property was unloaded in Stanley by the Ops today. People are now just ready for home.

Yesterday's blip of fair weather once again gave way to a miserable drizzly day. The helicopters were still flying and one was to bring in Tony Rice along with John Patrick, our previous BC and now back in his 'normal' role of Regimental Second in Command. They came to personally confirm the bad news, but were at pains to point out that this was hopefully the worst-case scenario. Even having heard it the previous evening, individuals found the news difficult to take. As I mentioned previously, by the end of the day, we were more pragmatic over events and accepting of our lot; but the general feeling was that we were just marking time and were ready to go home.

Knowing that were now going to be here for some time, emphasis was placed on making the accommodation as comfortable as possible. To that end, both John Russell and I were 'evicted' to a caravan on the rear edge of the settlement and after a quick airing, we settled in to our new surroundings and mused that it did have some plus points. The caravan was primarily used by visiting shearers and had been unoccupied for some time, hence the need for freshening up. Being on the edge it was remote and therefore quiet, so we didn't have the continual background noise of the Command Post underneath us and importantly the beds were proper bunk beds. Whilst I commentated that it was a Romany type at the time, it was more of a mini mobile home/bunkhouse type, but thankfully it was structurally sound. Having said that, John was later offered a bed in the

Dobbin's house and didn't need much persuasion in saying yes. Due to his quick change, the FDC's Signals Sergeant Major moved in to take his place.

To our general amazement, we heard that our previously thought long lost suitcases and kitbags had actually turned up and had been off loaded by the Forward Observation Parties in Stanley. We were also informed that these Observation Parties were returning to join us here at Bluff Cove. The caravan had two spare bunks and they were allocated to James Watson and Bob Ash.

Thursday, 24 June (Day 35)
Having spent all day away with SSgt Mutter & 12 we cleared the position up by the track. It all went extremely well, the Wessex 'Pinger' pilot did exactly what we asked and the lads did well. At the brief, David said from the CO that 137 Bty (40 Fd) was due to take over here on the 20th July. David came in at 1810 and said we were going home via a ferry in 5 DAYS TIME. Apparently we sail in 5 days ... guarding Argie PWs. With my 2 cans of beer I celebrated and then went for a bath.

Having secured a helicopter, I, along with Staff Sergeant Mutter and twelve others, went back to the last position to continue with the clean-up of the ammunition and salvage. By the end of the day we had cleared the position of the live ammunition and salvage, with the Wessex's pilot playing a significant part in its success. He was a 'Pinger', or anti-submarine pilot by trade, but was now carrying numerous underslung loads, under the control of a group of Gunners. He did exactly what was asked of him, which considerably eased the workload.

At David's evening brief, he detailed the way ahead, as well as the plan for our continued stay at the settlement. With regards to the Islands, a new Headquarters, run by a '2 Star' (Major General) was going to be set up; however, that there was an issue with the available real estate, in as much that this new set up, along with all the personnel and equipment, was probably too big to fit within Stanley. I recall a certain degree of amusement from this, as it was Stanley or nothing. The general suggestion was that the decision-makers high up in the MoD were making plans, without actually understanding the reality of life down here.

David announced that we should expect to receive our suitcases and kit bags tomorrow. Individuals were to record what was missing, with a limit set at £250 per person for general clothing and personal items; however, high value items, such as cameras, were to be reclaimed on one's individual kit insurance. It was stressed that claims were to be passed at the CO's discretion and that David was to compile a list, stating the approximate cost of the losses.

The brief went on to more local matters. Firstly, that we were to lose both the FDC and the Blowpipe Detachment, which were going to redeploy back to Fitzroy, but as yet, no time scale had been set. With regards to our particular set-up, we could expect to receive extra tents on 2 July, with the more substantial and semi-permanent huts by the middle of the month. Whilst hostilities had ended, casualties were still being taken, at a loss of '2 feet per day', due to mines and we were briefed to resist the temptation to wander unnecessarily, particularly as the bridge between Fitzroy and Bluff Cove was out.

We were to expect to be relieved in place by 137 Battery, from 40 Field Regiment RA on 20 July; with 97 Battery, the Blowpipe Detachment and our own Regimental Headquarters to be relieved by the balance of 40 Field Regiment by the end of that month. David did emphasise that the CO is fighting our cause and is 100 per cent behind the Battery. David cited that the CO had sent a blunt three-page signal, which considering that brevity is the key to signal writing, spoke volumes. David then went onto say that he would be carrying out a stores' inventory, in preparation for 137 Battery, to make up for any known deficiencies. Regarding advice as to them as to what to bring; 'everything' was the cry.

On a happy note, we were told that fresh fruit had arrived in Stanley, with apples soon to be dispensed. David briefed that the 88 Battery's Observation Parties, that went to make up 41 Observation Battery, had left the islands, having managed to find space on a C130 Hercules transport plane that was repatriating compassionate/welfare cases back to the UK. There was a general affinity to 41 Observation Battery, due to John Patrick's association with Corunna and we didn't begrudge them their early departure.

With regards to our vehicles, the brief directed that two rigging teams were to be sent to Stanley, to prepare our 'redundant' gun limbers (1-Ton Land Rovers) for flying back to Bluff Cove. Also, that our suitcases were to be reclaimed. These tasks were to fall to Sergeant Dobson, plus three for the former and for Sergeant Jones plus three, to reclaim our baggage.

Whilst we had been concentrating on clearing our last position, there was still the requirement to go back to Head of the Bay House. As such, a Sea King was to take a party of fifteen, made up from eight from Gun Troop and seven from Command Troop to complete that task. By this stage, the Battery's personnel had reverted to their peacetime sub-unit groupings (Troops), from their operational detachments. There was a request from the settlement for a party of ten, to round up their sheep and to be prepared for a five-mile hike, starting at 0:930 hours and to expect for it to last until approximately 13:00 hours. Command Troop were to detail five men as part of that request. There was also concern expressed by the settlement about the amount of equipment we had generally lying around. To suggest that equipment had been abandoned would be unfounded, we just had a lot of it. As a public relations exercise, we were to make every effort to move the stores and equipment into storage; however, if there was no space available, to move stores from one shed to another, so at least as to make it look as if we were doing it!

The fact that we were expected to remain here for some time was lost on nobody. As such, ideas of how we could keep ourselves busy and amused were to be passed. For example, there were boat repairs to be done, with others such as fishing to be rotated, but all projects will be adhered to. Finally, David required twelve empty ammunition boxes for the 'Battery Goodies' (souvenirs).

Shortly after ending the brief, at 18:10 hours, David was summoned to the radio and told that the Battery was returning home in five days' time. It was to be a rather an unconventional return by standards, as we were detailed to act as the guard force, to the ferry returning Argentine PoWs, but that didn't matter one bit. It would be a huge understatement to say, but it was extremely well received. Having said that, there was a collective element of being guarded, having ridden an emotional rollercoaster in recent days. I along with others, celebrated the news with our two cans of beer, after which I went to the Kilmartins' for a bath.

It transpires that the BC, who had remained in Stanley was fighting our cause, at the highest level, in trying to get us an early return to the UK. One of the first decisions made after the surrender was that all initial fighting troops, namely those who had taken part on D-Day, would sail home as soon as possible. That decision was now taking shape, with 3 Commando Brigade earmarked to return on *Canberra* and both 2 Para and 3 Para returning on *Norland*. It was his argument that as first wave troops, we should also be included amongst *Canberra*/*Norland*'s numbers. Eventually, the argument held sway and we were cleared for an early return, with the Battery being used as a guard for the returning PoWs on *St Edmund*.

Friday, 25 June (Day 36)
Today we met up with our kit i.e. suitcases and kitbags. Some were missing but mine was untouched. The Ops came to Bluff Cove to stay and Bob & James moved down to the caravan. It was good to hear of the humorous side to the war, of people's little snippets. RAIN!!! WIND!!! COLD!!!

Today saw a subtle change of mentality, as we finally caught up with our long-lost non-operational personal baggage. Up until this point, all we had was our operational equipment and to be reunited with our suitcases and kitbags made for a more 'in barracks' feeling. One or two individuals had kit missing, but mine came through unscathed. As planned, the Observation Parties finally made it here and James and Bob took residence in the caravan. It was the first real time we had to sit and swap stories and to hear of some of the more humorous side to the war, not only from their side, but from on the position as well.

At the evening 'O' Group, David went into full BK mode and set out the plan to recall all of our specialist Forward Observation Parties stores and main equipment. The reality was that individual parties didn't require these stores and having them centrally-controlled eased accountability. Our holdings of laser binoculars however, were identified as having to go back with us. Our replacements were to draw up a list of what stores they possessed, highlighting any important deficiencies, with Warrant Officer 2 Bullock (callsign '13'), as one of the Forward Observation Officers, taking the lead. All radio equipment was to be handed into and coordinated by Sergeant Maxwell. David nominated himself to take the lead with our vehicles, with checks to be made on the vehicle's tools, as well as their canopies and such like. All our general stores, known as 'G1098' were to go to the BQMS by 14:00 hours; however, individual issues of binoculars, compasses and watches were to remain as originally issued. David set a deadline of 12:00 hours, as the time that the final list for any missing/lost belongings was to handed in by, with any financial claim to be given to James as soon as possible. David concluded the brief with instruction that both Troops were to parade, with working parties required to sort out the G1098 stores.

Saturday, 26 June (Day 37)

Again it's a dismal day. Rumour control confirmed that we board the St Edmund on Monday. Bob & I flew to Stanley. Bob to meet up with the hooking up teams who were left to do the 1 x Tonners + L/R + Pack How. I went for a 'cabby'. We drove around town, many soldiers [including prisoners], various burnt out helos and en posn. We tried to go to the west store, but it was shut. We then went to the airfield. Photos of the 155mm and a Pack How Gun Posn. It was shelled, the kit was all over the place. AA guns were dotted around and a trailer with 2 x Exocet missile pods. It was a good sight to see the shell holes! We then flew back early afternoon with goodies from the house that Bob stayed in.

Despite being yet another dismal day, a helicopter came in as planned and took a small party, led by Bob to Stanley, with the aim of meeting the hook-up teams and sorting out the gun limbers. Being at a loose end, I went along for the ride, with Bombardier Armstrong 'K' joining us at the last minute. Bombardier Armstrong took the opportunity to come in his capacity as the Battery photographer and we were both eager to see Stanley at first hand. The hook-up team was split in two, with Sergeant Jones plus three, making sure that the vehicles were serviceable and Sergeant Dobson plus three, leading with the underslung hook-up preparations.

At a chance meeting with John Osmond (pictured facing) in 2015, he recognised the aircraft in the top photograph on the next page and offered up his own picture of the same. John was a Lieutenant RN Aircraft Engineer Officer with 824 Naval Air Squadron during the war, and it was coincidence that these two photographs were taken almost at the same time, albeit some ninety degrees apart, 26 June 1982. (Courtesy of John Osmond)

Our transport, a Mark 2a Sea King, parked on Stanley Racecourse having dropped us off as part of Captain Bob Ash's working party check-up, 26 June 1982.

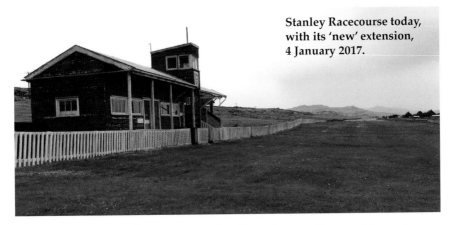

Stanley Racecourse today, with its 'new' extension, 4 January 2017.

Waiting for us at the racecourse landing site was Sergeant Jones in one of our gun limbers, close by to the robbed-out shell of an Argentine Puma helicopter. The trip into Stanley took us past Government House, where on the road nearby were at least four or five containers, some of which were opened with food on show. Argentine forces were clearly not short of rations and this proved that it was their administration that was at fault.

Whilst we had transport, Bob took me to see what was left of an Argentine 105mm Pack Howitzer gun position on Stanley's outskirts and just to the south of the racecourse; which had all the scars of successful counter battery fire, some of it ours. It was here that one of the ironies of the war unfolded, which centred on the Argentine Pack Howitzers, which had been purchased from the British MoD when they were superseded by the new Light Gun. This came to light when it was spotted that the Guns on the position that Bob and I were visiting, were still marked up in 7 Parachute Regiment's colours, as well as displaying the Royal Cypher and looked as if

The lower slope of the racecourse below the main building, with two Argentine Huey helicopters parked on the edge. The buildings here mark the south-western edge of Stanley's built up area. Today, the area forms part of a residential suburb, 26 June 1982.

A view back to the racecourse, the main building to the left, with the small covered grandstand behind the low white fence opposite. The grandstand sits on the edge of the residential development, 26 June 1982.

Immediately behind the position from where the previous photograph was taken is an Argentine A109 helicopter, 26 June 1982.

they had just come off 7 Parachute Regiment's gun park. The irony wasn't lost on us that 7 Parachute Regiment's old guns had shelled our troops and that we took them out under counter battery fire with their replacements! I noted in my diary of how good it was to see the shell holes; I wasn't looking at the damage caused in human terms to their gun crews, but from a detached unemotional one of wining the fight. What was clear was just how lucky we were at Wether Ground, having come out of the 155-mm's harassing fire unscathed. To see at first-hand the results of effective directed artillery fire, brought home as to what could have happened to us, should they have been able to observe and correct their aim.

Considering the amount of time the Argentines had to prepare the position's defences, we thought it was woefully inadequate. The Guns were positioned out in the open, with only a small, low, turfed bank directly in front of them for protection. The concept of protection, not only for the gun itself, but for the crews as well, was something they seemed to completely lack. Equally we were surprised at just how sloppy the areas around each platform were. Littler was everywhere and their seemed to be no form of ammunition control in place. The standards we saw were thankfully poles apart from our own.

Our Northern Ireland training had taught us to be wary of attractive 'items' being potentially booby-trapped, with general warnings to that effect

A cannibalised Argentine Puma sits by the side of Ross Road West, near the First World War Memorial, on the shore side route into Stanley, 26 June 1982.

The area where the Puma was parked is now the site of Stanley's Battle Memorial Wall. Tony Rice is standing on the kerb, with Bob Ash viewing the wall tablets, 4 January 2017.

in place, particularly in and around Stanley and we were mindful to leave things as they were; however, before I left the position, I went over to the closest gun and picked up an empty shell case as a souvenir of my visit. Positioned close by the limbers, was one of the remaining Argentine 155mm Field Guns, which Bob and I both looked over, with a professional eye.

Whilst driving around Stanley, I was surprised when we passed a lorry-

Further down Ross Road West lies the wreck of the *Jhelum*. This photograph was taken from the front garden of the house Captain Bob Ash and his observation party temporarily occupied when 2 Para swept into Stanley immediately after the ceasefire. We went there to try and source any Argentine rations, in order to supplement our own supplies, 26 June 1982

The wreck of the *Jhelum* today. The house is now the residence of the islands' Chief Executive, 4 January 2017.

mounted twin Exocet missile launch system abandoned on the side of the road. It just looked to be so out of place in the road. As we drove slowly through the streets we passed numerous groups of PoWs, who appeared to be conscripts and looked a sorry sight indeed. There was no feeling of animosity towards them, the forlorn expressions on their faces told of the wretched time they had endured and it was hard not to feel pity. The area around the waterfront was littered with rubbish and as we drove past, we witnessed small groups of prisoners being put to work in clearing up their mess.

Bob's intention was that we would try and see if we could get anything from the West Store, but unfortunately it was shut. As a fall back, we went to 'Bob's' house, intending to go in search of Argentine rations that were left by them, after vacating it post the surrender. The house was on the shore road towards Government House and Bob and his Observation Party came across it when 2 Para entered Stanley. The Argentine Forces has previously evicted the owners and taken the house for themselves and appeared to have been in residence for some time. What little was on offer was gratefully taken to provide a much-needed change to our rations. The monotony and scarcity of the rationing is endorsed by Gunner Kirvell's previous recollections of our fare and was felt by many.

Whilst we were away, rumour control confirmed that 29 Battery would be embarking on *St Edmund* on Monday, as previously planned.

The evening 'O' Group was dominated by our impending return home on *St Edmund*; however, it started with the news that the Gunners were to establish a permanent camp at Fitzroy, with our rear party relocating to that location. David briefed us that we were to leave at 09:00 hours

Located on Ross Road West, Government House sits on the western edge of Stanley, with the racecourse (out of view) just behind. Argentine stores, almost certainly having been dropped off by helicopter, can be seen in the middle of the paddock. On the right-hand side, containers with a considerable amount of food stores inside can be seen, 26 June 1982.

The same view of Government house today. The site of the Battle Memorial Wall, and the location of the damaged Puma, is on the elbow of the bend near the water's edge, 4 January 2017.

A close-up of the food containers and Government house from Ross Road West, 26 June 1982.

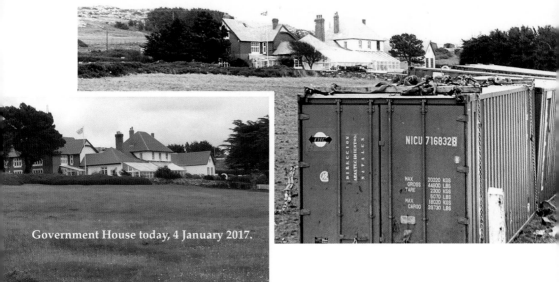

Government House today, 4 January 2017.

Taken from a spot by the First World War Memorial, this composite photograph shows the view along Ross Road West towards Stanley. The roofs of Government House can be seen just behind the gorse bank on the near right. The area of the Puma is just out of sight around the bend, 26 June.

The same view along Ross Road West today. Government House is obscured by the gorse bank, with the white fence being the only clue to its location. The triple gabled building on the right is the Secondary School, Library and Leisure Complex. The blue roofs are those of the islands' hospital, 4 January 2017.

by Chinook, along with our personal kit, to *St Edmund*. Once we were all embarked, we would sail to Ajax Bay, where we would pick up sixty members from the Blowpipe Troop, along with the Scots Guards. In three days' time (Tuesday), the Scots Guards would disembark, with us then sailing back around to Stanley, to pick up our PoWs. On our arrival at Stanley, we were to disembark the Blowpipe Troop, but were to pick up our Regimental Headquarters, along with two Troops from T Battery RA, the Rapier Air Defence Battery. When everything was in place, we were

This is the junction at the bottom of Philomel Street and Ross Road, in the centre of Stanley, where a number of Argentine Panhard AML 90 were parked up. Due to the nature of the ground in the surrounding area, they didn't venture out of Stanley. An Argentinian PoW walks by, with another group of prisoners clearing up the mess that they caused, 26 June 1982.

The same junction today. The house on the corner is now the location for Falklands Conservation, 11 January 2017.

to sail in the company of HMS *Antelope* to Ascension, with the expected passage taking ten days. The reference to HMS *Antelope* in the brief was clearly an error, as Bill and I watched *Antelope*'s unexploded Argentine bombs detonate on the night of 23 May. What was important though, was that we were to be allocated a naval escort. Once embarked, emphasis was placed on relaxation, with films, selection of the best recreational areas and food being the order of the day. We were reminded that things were going

Saint Mary's Catholic Church, 26 June 1982.

Christ Church Cathedral, with its iconic whalebone arch, 26 June 1982.

to be cramped whilst the Scots Guards were with us, but we would readjust once they had disembarked. As such, the message was don't unpack. The briefing concluding that we would be securing the best accommodation that *St Edmund* had to offer.

An abandoned pair of Argentine vehicle-mounted Exocet missiles in Stanley's 'suburbs', 26 June 1982. It was either this unit, or a similar one, that sank HMS *Glamorgan* on 12 June 1982.

A Royal Marine BV snow vehicle parked in a Stanley backstreet, 26 June 1982.

A Stanley residence showing damage caused during the war, where three Falkland Islanders were killed, 26 June 1982.

Gunner Freddie Martin (left) and Bombardier Malcom Hagan (right) stand by a large pile of surrendered weapons, 26 June 1982. What was not known at the time was that many of the weapons were still loaded, having 'one up the spout'.

Argentine Pucaras at Stanley Airport, 26 June 1982.

Gunner Freddie Martin is pictured standing next to a Pucara at Stanley's airfield, with Bombardier Malcom Hagan at the right rear, 26 June 1982. The aircraft were taped off as they had been booby-trapped by the Argentines prior to the ceasefire. As with the others, the crew's seats had been fired off, disabling the aircraft. This aircraft was taken back to the UK and stood as part of the exterior display at the Army Air Corps' Museum of Army Flying for many years.

The author sat on an Argentine 105mm Pack Howitzer, 26 June 1982. The gun position was located just to the south-west of Stanley's Racecourse.

The view over the Argentine gun position to the north-east and the western edge of Stanley Harbour. The lack of any form of self-defence or protection for the gun crews was starkly evident, 26 June 1982.

Another view of the position and an Argentine 105mm Pack Howitzer, 26 June 1982. The Pack Howitzer still carried the markings of 7 Regiment Royal Horse Artillery. It was subsequently sold as surplus to requirement. An up-turned gun can be seen on the background. Also evident is the lack of discipline on the position, with litter strewn everywhere.

An Argentine 155mm Field Howitzer pictured abandoned on Stanley's outskirts, 26 June 1982. 29 Battery's 1 Tonne Land Rover gun limbers can be seen lined up at the rear. Captain Bob Ash is standing left, with Second Lieutenant Tom Martin (author) at the front right. Sergeant Jones (REME), our driver, is standing next to one of our limbers which was used to ferry us around Stanley.

A grainy picture of the author standing by the Argentine 155mm Field Howitzer, 26 June 1982.

Stanley Harbour looking west to the mountains and the Argentine defensive ring on its eastern approaches, with Stanley on the left, 26 June 1982.

Sunday, 27 June (Day 38)

We were ready in our administrative set up to go. We packed our kit and were waiting for the BC's return for the news of the St Edmund. *In the end we were told that we were delayed for 4 days!! Alarm and despondency!! But when the BC came back we were definitely going tomorrow morning. Thank God. The Chinook was coming at 0900. We sail to Ajax Bay with Blowpipe + 2 Coys of 2SG. 2SG get off and we pick up 530 Argie PWs. Menendez is amongst them!!! Back to Stanley & pick up T Bty RA. It's then a 10 day sail to Ascension and a flight home!! (The feeling is … we'll see it when it happens.) After a curry in the cabin and a few beers it's time for bed. Just before we went to bed, I was called to the garage & told that I +29 (30) were going back on the* Sir Geraint.

The day began with the expectation that we were to embark on *St Edmund*, and as such we were all eager, packed and ready to go. It was hard to disguise our feelings when faced with yet another delay, albeit only for four days, especially after the initial bomb-shell that we were to remain and garrison the islands. Thankfully the BC flew in and confirmed that we were definitely going tomorrow morning and that we were to expect a Chinook at 09:00 hours.

The initial plan had been somewhat modified, in as much that we were to sail to Ajax Bay along with the Blowpipe Troop and two Companies of Scots Guards. We were to then disembark the Guards, pick up 530 Argentinian PoWs, with the Argentinian Commander General Menendez amongst their midst. These PoWs were not general conscripts, but their regular forces, with the majority being marines. After picking up the prisoners, we were to sail back to Stanley, where T Battery would be waiting to join us for our passage to Ascension and a flight home. There was just one small point that had appeared to have been overlooked, which related to the PoWs in that, when we get off, what happens to them? This was cleared up when it was decided to sail to the neutral port of Montevideo in Uruguay, disembark the PoWs and then sail on to Ascension. Whilst this would lengthen the sea passage, it was a price worth paying to get off the islands. Notwithstanding

A group of Argentine PoWs on the decks of the *St Edmund* 'prison ship', 29 June 1982.

Argentine PoWs in the mess deck, 29 June 1982.

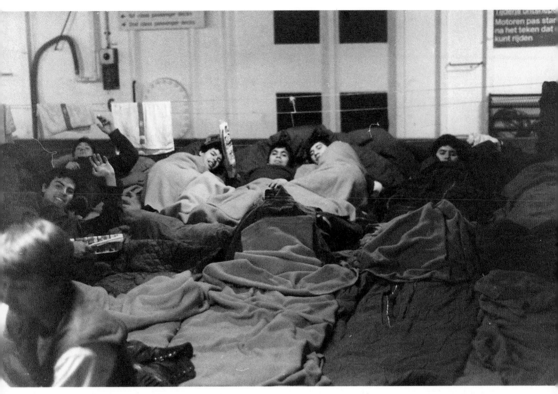

Argentinian PoWs on the ship's vehicle deck, which was used for accommodation, 29 June 1982.

Another view of Argentine PoWs taped off into accommodation pens on the vehicle deck, 29 June 1982.

This is a copy of a cartoon taken from one of the Argentine prisoners on 29 June. Entitled 'The San Carlos 6', the '6' in question are, left to right: C.P.I.M. Joan Tomas Carrasco, SARG Miguel Alfredo Moreno, SARG Neildo Riveros, SARG 1RO Guillermo S. Potocsnyak, SARG 1RO Jose B. Rivas, and SARG 1RO Vincente Alfredo Flores.

that, when we were due to arrive in Ascension, flights would be put on for our immediate return. To say that we were becoming quite cynical by this time would have been a huge understatement and it general feeling was 'we'll see it when it happens'.

At the 'O' Group that night, David set out the routine for our move:

Reveille was set to be at 05:30 hours, with the generators to be switched on at that time, with individuals having breakfast under their own arrangements. By 07:00 hours, that the area was to be clear, with the de-kitting of our Arctic clothing also commencing at that time, with Battery Headquarters, Command Troop and Gun Troop following in that order. The dress for the trip was to be our old temperate clothing of combat jacket and lightweight trousers, with berets. As soon as we were on board, we were to wear training shoes, or even normal shoes. The exact order of embarkation would be finalised into three chalks of thirty-three; however, there were to be no underslung cargo nets, so individuals were to carry their own kit.

When onboard, the BC would head-up a PoW's committee, with the assistance of a Major from the Army Legal Corps. It was confirmed that Menendez plus five of his staff and that Goff, another senior Argentine and seven of his staff, would be amongst the numbers, but that they were to be kept separate. Of the rest, there were in fact 113 conscripts, with the balance being 270 officers, 107 non-commissioned officers and four civilians. Once embarked, the priority was to get everybody's dhobi (washing) done as soon as possible, with the lowest rank going first. As we were now leaving, the shearing shed was to be cleaned, and handed back to the settlement. To provide an independent internal communications set-up on *St Edmund*, Command Troop were to ensure that all of the field telephones went, along with a 1km pack of Don 10 telephone wire. To augment this, the seven 349s handheld radios were also to be taken. Finally, there was the issue of NAAFI stocks to consider and the advice was to take plenty, especially cigarettes.

Once again it transpired, that the BC had not let up on getting his Battery home at the earliest opportunity and some thirty berths were found on the LSL *Sir Geraint*. After the evening brief, I retired back to the caravan, for a curry, eking out the last of my curry powder, a few beers and decided to get an early night, only to be summoned back to the garage and to be told my fate by David. Being a very unwilling sailor, everyone took much joy at the thought of me having to sail in a flat-bottomed boat back home. Some thirty years later I was to ask Bill if he recalled how I was chosen, to sail 8,000 miles through some of the roughest seas in the world in a flat-bottomed boat? His rueful reply summed it up: 'You would probably sue me if I told you.'

Monday, 28 June (Day 39)
After reveille at 0530 & packed up (handed in all arctic kit) we hung around all day waiting for the helo. We were told that the ship would not sail without us, however nothing happened and due to the weather the helos couldn't fly to Stanley. At 2000 we went to Kevin's to see a slide show of his Antarctic experiences – very enjoyable.

It was an early start to the day, with reveille at 05:30 hours. The reason being was that we had to be prepared to leave at first light, or at least shortly after it, and we were not privy to the flying schedule; however, we were assured that *Sir Geraint* would not sail without us, which helped to ease any growing angst. After breakfast and packing up, the *Geraint* party handed in all their Arctic clothing, of which I was sorry to see go. It was by far the best and most comfortable clothing I'd ever been issued and to go back into our original temperate combat clothing left me feeling vulnerable to the conditions. In true military fashion, it was a 'rush to wait' job and time seemed to painfully drag on. The weather wasn't ideal and some questioned whether it was good enough to fly out, but there were helicopters passing by, which had us scrambling down to the landing site, only to see us turn back as they flew on. Eventually two helicopters did arrive and we quickly made our farewells, before making our way to the landing site. Expecting to do a 'rotors running' embarkation, I was surprised to see them both shut down and the crews get out. On asking what the problem was I was informed that they hadn't come for us, but for a 'tea stop' before going on to San Carlos, recounting that we had a reputation as one of the best around! I asked if they could drop us off in Stanley, but was told that the weather between here and there was unsuitable. Consequently, we made our way back to the accommodation somewhat despondently.

Later that evening, the officers were invited by Kevin to go around and see a slide show of his experiences in the Antarctic. It was both enjoyable and informative, but equally important, it was a welcome distraction from the earlier disappointment.

This photograph marks the beginning of a roll of film taken from an Argentine prisoner aboard *St Edmund* and developed once the Battery returned to Aldershot. It records the prisoners' build up and subsequent deployment to the Falklands, following the initial Argentine invasion of 2 April. As such they are dateless. The camera roll begins on mainland Argentina, with what looks like a row of twin-barrelled anti-aircraft guns under covers, prepared for sailing.

Mainland Argentina, with an airbase in the background.

Two Argentine officers at what is probably the docks on the mainland.

Leaving port.

An Argentine support/supply
vessel en-route to the Falklands.

An Argentine C130 on
Stanley airfield.

Argentine troops setting up camp on Stanley's outskirts

An Argentine field kitchen.

This looks like a shallow protection shelter with a peat-covered domed roof. The buildings in the background suggest it is on Stanley's outskirts.

Argentine person outside a comple sangar.

Enemy troops posing during the mid-phase of their bunker construction. The angle irons will be covered in corrugated tin and covered in peat/soil, which will act as overhead protection against artillery and mortar fire.

Posing outside a completed bunker.

The terminal building at Stanley Airport.

The airport building as it appeared on 4 January 2017.

An Argentine officer beside a power supply trailer for one of the twin-barrelled anti-aircraft guns seen earlier on the dockside.

Stanley airfield from the access road.

The view across the southwestern edge of Stanley, looking diagonally over to the inner harbour entrance. The two large grey tanks in the foreground supplied fuel oil to the main power station, which is out of sight in the gully, this side of the houses. These tanks were deemed to be hazardous by the Argentine forces and were destroyed soon after our landings at San Carlos.

A similar view today, the roofs of the power station are just visible in the gully.

Enemy personnel outside what looks like a protected tent.

An Argentine officer posing in downtown Stanley.

In this comparison taken on 11 January 2017, the author is pictured outside Bennett House B&B; the red post office box was moved some time ago. We stayed here for our last two nights on the islands.

Two more Argentine officers posing in the streets.

The same street view on 11 January 2017.

Argentine team photograph.

The view from Stanley's south-western outskirts, looking over the inner harbour, as an Argentine Chinook transports an underslung load from west to east. Two large fuel oil tanks can be seen on the far shoreline.

Another Argentine image taken looking towards the inner harbour entrance.

The same view today; the main difference is that the original was taken on the outer edge of the built-up area, this picture was taken well within a suburb.

An Argentine fire trench, sporting a .50 calibre machine-gun. The protected tent/shelter seen earlier is further up the slope.

Posing this time with weapons.

A seemingly relaxed and happy bunch of Argentine prisoners of war pictured with their Royal Military Police guard.

Chapter 11
The Return Home

Tuesday, 29 June (Day 40)

The weather looks worse than yesterday but a Chinook arrived to take them on to St Edmund at San Carlos. Straight after that a Sea King + Wessex took me and 27 to Geraint. Its been cleaned up and it looks a different ship. Back to civilisation … a shower + sheets. An excellent day. Told it's 12 days to Ascension (July 12, one to two days there and fly back to UK ETA 15 July). Sent a signal to Tony Rice to that effect.

My impending departure and the underlying excitement of finally going home, meant that I didn't sleep well, fuelled by also waiting to see what the weather had in store. Dawn broke to a dull and rather misty vista and I gauged the weather to be worse than yesterday. Needless to say, that morale took a hit and whilst we had an assurance that *Sir Geraint* wouldn't sail without us, I couldn't see that the system would be true to its word. As the day went on the chance of leaving faded and by mid-afternoon I'd resigned myself to staying put. With just under an hour of daylight remaining, 'BN' the sole surviving Chinook flew in and took the first designated party to *St Edmund* at Ajax Bay, where preparations were made to take the PoWs to either Argentina, or Ascension before onward passage to the UK.

Just before last light and when all hope of flying out ceased, two helicopters came in and my party was quickly rounded up and told to go. Hurried farewells were made and we made our way once again to the landing site. True to their word, the ship clearly hadn't sailed, but this may also be due to the Force 10 blowing out in the open sea. One very pleasing sight on arrival was that considerable effort had been put into getting the ship cleaned up, which off-set the thought of the impending voyage home based on my earlier visit. I was given very clear instructions prior to leaving. My brief was to get the party back to the UK, where on arrival back at camp, secure the weapons in the armoury and then take a week's leave. On return, I/ we were to continue with normal barrack

A copy of *The Penguin News*, dated 14 June, which I found on the *Geraint* when I embarked for the long journey home, 29 June 1982.

routine, until the rest of the Battery caught up.

We were the last to embark and were shown our messing arrangements. I was introduced to Major Roger Dillon RM who, as the senior officer of the embarked troops, informed me that we were delayed in sailing. He said that we were just to settle into our new surroundings and that there would be a full briefing in the morning, as there were still matters to be clarified. Notwithstanding that, we did receive a short brief for the return voyage. We had expected to sail all the way back Portsmouth, which would take approximately some four weeks, via a short resupply stop at Ascension; however, the news now was that we would in fact be flying back from Ascension, which was, to say the least, very well received. After ensuring that my detachment was settled, I went to the communications room and sent a signal to the BC, informing him of our good fortune. I also included in it a request from *Sir Geraint*, that another helicopter lift would be required; essentially the ship was short of ten personnel from callsign '49' – one of the Observation Batteries – who were still expected and were believed to have been redirected to Fitzroy.

After sending the signal, I set off for the small ship's wardroom and made my acquaintance with the other officers. We were very much a mixed bunch, with ten coming from the Royal Marines, including the Commando Forces Chaplain, seven Gunners including myself, two from 5 Brigade's Signal Squadron and a Royal Engineer. What wasn't lost on me was that I was the youngest by some margin.

Sir Geraint was one of six Royal Fleet Auxiliary's Landing Ship Logistics and was commanded by Captain D. Lawrence. She was commissioned in the summer of 1967 and even by 1982 standards, felt a little old. *Sir Geraint* was 366 feet long, with a beam of sixty feet and came in on a full load at 5,670 tons; this meant that it didn't take long to get orientated. As far as I was concerned, it wasn't that *Sir Geraint* was not very big, but the fact that she had a flat bottom, specifically designed for beach, or shallow water landings. Having felt like being the worst sailor in the world on the voyage down, the prospect of sailing even to Ascension, in a ship not even half the size of *Norland* and with a flat bottom, filled me with dread. Having said that, and on balance, the option of taking a berth home, far out-weighed the prospect of a stormy homeward sea passage.

Wednesday, 30 June (Day 41)

Still haven't sailed. Weather is bad, 70 knot winds at sea. Tristram has dragged its anchor and run aground. We'll have to wait and see. At 1400 we set sail. The seas were mountainous and conditions were the worst I've been in. Many sea sickness tablets so far, not too bad. Force 10.

Reflecting on my first night aboard couldn't have contrasted more from conditions back at Bluff Cove. It's only when one is deprived of something that's taken for granted, that you appreciate its true worth when reacquainted with it. It felt like total luxury to have a bunk with clean sheets, 'heads' – naval slang for toilets – and showers next to the cabin and 'proper' food. After a leisurely breakfast, I met up with Sergeant

Taylor and we went down to the main troop accommodation to check up on the others.

Just before 10:30 hours, a pipe went out calling for all the heads of each sub-unit, to attend a briefing in the officers' dining room. The embarked troops were from nineteen sub-units and totaled 295 all ranks. Here Roger Dillon set out the routine and laid down the ground rules. He opened by saying that every day at 08:00 hours he would attend the Captain's morning briefing, which would be followed at 10:30 hours, by his briefing, when information would be cascaded down. The limitations of communications were highlighted and as to what we could expect. Emphasis was placed on the fact that individuals had to be mindful of tempers flaring, considering what we had all been through. In fact, anything that can help to keep people amused would be considered, with mention made to the fact that the ship's crew would aim to build a small swimming pool on the upper cargo deck. Mention was also made that there may be a chance of getting some of the troops 'on the ship's wheel'.

Roger Dillon went on to say that we could expect the current weather to continue for another three days and that it was causing problems inside the anchorage; however, it wasn't all bad news, with the announcement that we had plenty of food, with rules covering drinking and smoking to be published soonest. As was now standard practice, a lifeboat sentry would be required throughout the day and the night, that everything was to be secured for sea and that sea sickness tablets were available. We were brought back to reality by the announcement that we were still to observe 'darken ship' routine. Whilst the war may be over, the threat of disenfranchised air force, or 'rogue' Super Etendards had to be considered, at least until we're out of range to the north.

The briefing concluded by reminding everyone to close all doors, to enable the air conditioning to function properly. Morale was high and the general tone set was for an enjoyable and relaxing passage back. The only hard rule was that everybody had to get up in the morning and wash & shave before breakfast. After that, individuals were left to either of their sub-unit's, or individual disposal.

True to the brief, conditions outside were still truly awful, with hurricane-force winds continuing to batter Stanley's harbour and the ships in the anchorage. One such casualty was *Sir Geraint's* sister ship *Sir Tristram*, which had been towed back to Stanley from Fitzroy. *Sir Tristram* had dragged her anchor and had run aground close by, causing alarm within *Sir Geraint's* crew, which wasn't lost on the embarked troops. Captain Lawrence was faced with the dilemma of suffering a similar fate as *Sir Tristram's*, or to put to sea and ride the storm. After finally deciding that enough was enough, especially after being delayed by twenty-four hours before we arrived and now some forty-eight hours in total, that *Sir Geraint* had to press on and we would have to accept the fact that conditions would be rather unpleasant. A pipe went out stating Captain Lawrence's intentions and warned everybody to secure all loose items. Expecting the worst, I sought to take the maximum dosage of sea sickness tablets in preparation of setting sail and was dreading getting under way.

Shortly afterwards, we set sail at 14:00 hours out of Stanley Harbour on our 3,800-mile passage to Ascension. The waters in the anchorage were relatively calm, with just the strong winds lashing up the comparatively small waves; however, things were about to change as we passed out of the sanctuary of the Islands and into the teeth of the Force 10 storm and the South Atlantic.

Conditions certainly met with expectations and I didn't think that things could get any worse. As I looked out at the mountainous seas my heart sank. These were by far the worst conditions that I'd been in and I was just waiting in anticipation for the sickness to kick in. Whilst it was just as rough during the later stages of the voyage south, when looking out from *Norland* you appeared to be above the waves, due to the height of the promenade decks above the water; however, the considerably lower sides of these landing ships, felt that we were very much amongst it. I don't know if it was fear, or the tablets kicking in, or a combination of both, but I wasn't feeling too bad at this stage and I even felt comfortable with the prospect of eating later. The fact of the matter was that I'd found my sea legs and I was soon to wean myself off the sea sickness tablets.

As briefed, the ship would be unable to establish contact with the outside world after a day from land and would not be able regain contact until within a day of land, at journey's end. To that end, a last flurry of signals was sent confirming numbers on board. In-coming communications would be difficult, but expected to be in operation.

At some stage during the day and prior to sailing, *Sir Geraint* received a mail drop, which contained within it, and hot off the press, an edition of 'The Penguin News' – the Falkland Island news magazine, which succinctly gave the news of 14/15 June.

Thursday, 1 July (Day 42)

After no sleep at all during the night I was feeling remarkably fresh. A small b'fast went down a treat. The weather has abated and it's now only 4-5, but in the LSL it's horrendous. At noon we were about 300 miles NE of Stanley. The 'Poseidon Adventure' was the matinee. At 1525 we had abandon ship drills.

The overnight weather was so bad, that sleep was impossible and it was as much as I could do to wedge myself in my bunk. Notwithstanding that, I was feeling quite fresh, considering the roller coaster ride. Despite the conditions, I wasn't feeling queasy and was to my surprise looking forward to breakfast, which 'went down a treat'. The weather abated as we sailed further north and by late noon we were some 300 miles northeast of Stanley; however, the conditions were by my assessment still horrendous. After lunch, as became the norm, a film was played on the dining room's video system. Today's matinee was 'The Poseidon Adventure', the irony of which wasn't lost on those watching. As soon as the film ended, we had the standard 'abandon ship' drills. Looking back to from where we were when we first left Portsmouth, this drill went very well. The other thing that became routine, was the naval tradition of 'sundowners', or pre-dinner drinks, which were normally taken outside, albeit briefly, in the leeward part of the aft lower deck, when the weather was bad.

Friday, 2 July (Day 43)
At noon we were 900 miles off Buenos Aries and 2700 miles to go!! Weather Force 6 heavy swell. No feeling of sea sickness yet. This afternoon's matinee was 'Sea Wolves', anything to pass the time away. Even Spike Milligan books the second and third time round are funny. Clocks back 1 hr.

We were making steady progress northwards and the general weather situation was one of gradual improvement. Having said that, it was still blowing a strong breezy Force 6, which felt like a gale, with the sea running with a heavy swell. Whilst *Sir Geraint's* flat bottom compounded the situation, I was still feeling relatively good.

Time started to drag, not helped by the weather causing limitations of movement out and about, as well as with there being nowhere to go. There was little to pass the time away apart from reading on one's bunk. The small wardroom library was well used, with the more popular books even having a reservation list. The one thing that did mark progress were the clocks changing.

Vaughan Lewis was *Sir Geraint's* Navigator and he produced a daily update on the notice board, as to our progress north to Ascension. The following is a typical example of Lewis's daily updates: Buenos Airies [Aries] 900 miles on the PORT (left) side. Weather moderate.

Saturday, 3 July (Day 44)
At 1200 we were 800 miles off Uruguay and 2300 miles to Ascension! The films were not too hot. Its been blowing Force 9 since last night and all today. Clocks back 1 hr.

We were by this stage well into the general routine of things, but conditions were a significant factor in trying to do anything. The weather had worsened overnight and had picked up to Force 9, which is categorised as a strong gale, which was almost as brutal as when we first left Stanley. In conditions like these time just seemed to stand still and not even trying to watch a film could stop you from clock watching. The only light at the end of the tunnel was that the clocks went back again.

Lewis: 2400 miles to go. Weather predicted 20 kts SW wind.

Sunday, 4 July (Day 45)
Still no change in the weather. At 1200 we were off Rio de Janeiro and just over 2000 miles to do. The afternoon film was a washout. By dinner the weather shows no sign of letting up. It's not that it's making me sea sick, but it is wearing everybody down. Morale is good. All one can do is go from meal to meal, read and watch TV. After 'Zulu' in the evening the sea outside seemed a little calmer.

We were almost at the half-way point, but the weather was showing no signs of changing. *Sir Geraint's* flat bottom was compounding the general misery that was running through us all. The pitching and rolling was taking its toll on everybody and whilst I wasn't feeling sea sick, having to constantly wedge yourself into either your chair or bunk was fatiguing. Time was marked by the passing of meals, interspersed with films and reading. Having said that, morale was generally good, as everybody appreciated that with every mile sailed, that we were a mile closer to getting off and that can't be underestimated. I noted things were noticeably better after watching the classic war film 'Zulu'.

Lewis: All America goes potty – Temp 60 deg.

Monday, 5 July (Day 46)

Sometime during the night the storm abated. The wind is still fairly strong. There is still a swell on the sea, but it's not too bad. At 1200 we were 800 miles off Rio de Janeiro and 1700 miles to go. The sun is out and it's quite nice outside. Another book and film gone! Had a party till 0230 with the Marines. (at 2000 it was 1600 miles 'to do')

At some stage during the night the weather abated, but whilst there was still a strong wind, the sea was noticeably calmer. The pleasant conditions saw most individuals take time on the upper decks to just chill out in the sun. Later at sundowners, those of us at the ships' rail were treated to a surreal experience. We were stood about idly chatting and/or looking out to sea, when we heard the sound of bagpipes! On closer investigation, we found Captain Willie Nicholl slowly walking around on the upper deck playing a lament. The mystery of his odd shaped box had now been solved. This box had been part of his pre-landing personal baggage and we couldn't work out why he was entitled to 'excess baggage'. It had for most of the time until now, been left by his bunk in our cabin and was generally considered to be a trip hazard. After some fine tuning in a sound-proof space, Willie had made his way topside and proceeded to play a number of traditional Gaelic laments. What was beyond doubt, was that he could play the pipes and continued to do so, particularly at sundowners.

As I noted in my diary, 'another book and film gone!'

Lewis: Rio de Janeiro 800 Port side, weather N/E Trades 15 kts.

Tuesday, 6 July (Day 47)

What a beautiful day. The sea is dead calm and the sky is clear, but some cloud. 1330 miles to go. 30 °N 30 °S [should read W and not N?] Temp outside is 20 °C. Test fired all Argie weapons. I fire an FN (Marine type), shooting at 50 (barrels/ gallon) drums. The Gunners have preference on firing the Bofors [40mm AA Gun]. A very pleasant afternoon was spent sunbathing and exercising.

The ship still had a considerable amount of ammunition on board, which Captain Lawrence was keen to get rid of. Essentially as any returning ammunition would cause a logistical headache on return to UK waters; where the ship would be required to go into quarantine, until certified clear of munitions. Equally, there were fifty 50-gallon drums of aviation fuel on the flight deck that required 'disposal'. It was a beautiful day and the sea was very calm and the snap solution was to hold a 'range day'. The plan was as simple as it was practical, individuals were invited to put on show and fire any trophy weapons, thereby ensuring ammunition could be expended. Ammunition brought out onto the flight deck was both plentiful and varied. There were: two crates of L2 grenades, a number of 66mm anti-tank launchers, a few 84mm Carl Gustav rounds and over 10,000 rounds of 7.62mm rifle ammunition.

The detail was simple, personnel were numbered off, a drum of aviation fuel was dropped over the side, weapons were loaded and when the drum was deemed a safe distance astern, the order to fire was given. Individuals would fire until their allocation of ammunition was expended. I asked one 'owner' if I could fire his Argentine 7.62mm, a marine-type of folding-butt FN rifle with which he had acquired a few magazines. I'd fired thousands of 7.62mm from our almost identical SLRs, but this felt very different, considering where it had come from. What was surprising, was the firing of the 66mm. Peace time training only allowed for its firing by way of a 'sub .22 calibre' adaptor. The blast from the full charge 66mm was a massive step up in both noise and effect.

The 'interesting' element of the day's expenditure was that of the L2 Grenade. This grenade has a seven-second fuse once the pin is pulled and the handle released. Rather than just pull and throw, the 'sport' was to attempt a form of depth charge. Throw too soon and the grenade sinks well below the surface, causing a blackish slick on the surface. Too late and one gets an 'air burst' with the consequence of getting shrapnel coming back at you. The perfect throw allowed the grenade to explode just below the surface, with the visual effect akin to that of a depth charge. Sport indeed!

The Bofors ammunition was going to require another session and as these guns were of a larger calibre than most were used to, the decision was that the Gunners were to take preference on firing it off.

After clearing up the empty brass case on the flight deck, we made the best of the sunnier and milder weather to sunbath. I was acutely aware of my earlier sunbathing experience on the voyage south and was mindful not to over-do it, but like others, did manage to do some exercise on the flight deck.

Lewis: 70 deg getting warmer.

Wednesday 7 July (Day 48)

Duty Officer!! Not a bad day to start with. At mid-morning I fired the 1st rds of the Bofors. Very good at Schermulys, 3 air – 1 sea burst!! Again the Chinese in the morning go 'Blekfust!'. After all the official duties there was the bronzing on the rear flight deck, but by mid-afternoon the weather clouded, but all in all –a good day. (Have Chinese meal). At 0400 approx we crossed into the tropics. At noon we had 965 miles to do. Flight is confirmed to UK as ETD Ascension 2000 on the 10th. Some physical ex was taken in the late afternoon.

At 04:00 hours we had crossed into the Tropics and the weather continued to remain fair, with temperatures now noticeably warmer. The Chinese stewards in the mess announced that meals were ready and the first call of the day – 'Blekfust!' – was generally mimicked in a similar light-hearted fashion. I was the duty officer for the day and after a quick breakfast went about the small number of things I had to attend to. The biggest one being 'Rounds', where a general inspection of the ship is made in the company of the duty Sergeant. Having done 'extras' on *Norland*, these were by comparison rather relaxed.

Midday saw the promised range detail for the Bofors come to fruition and at noon we assembled as briefed. The ship had some 400 rounds of 40mm, which were set in clips of four. On the leeward side on the forecastle, a plentiful supply of Schermuly parachute flares were assembled to act as targets. The landing ships were fitted with two bow-mounted 40mm Bofors guns, and the gun crews were positioned and briefed on the leeward gun prior to 'range clear'. Checking to see that it was all clear was simply a matter of looking out to the horizon and if nothing was sighted, then the all clear could be given. Once settled in, the gunner would shout 'PULL', where upon the flare party would fire the 2-inch parachute flare up wind and well out to sea. After the flare had deployed and floated into safe firing arcs, the clearance to fire was given, for which there were four rounds allocated per man. As a field gunner and the only gun-end officer, I was given the first go, just to 'to show how it's done'. This wasn't out of 'politeness' and I knew I was being set up in a lighthearted way, with the anticipation of failing eagerly felt by all those there, but against the odds hit the target.

After completing my duties, fired the Bofors and had lunch, the only thing left to do was to sunbathe on the rear flight deck. By mid-afternoon it had clouded over, ending the sun session, with PT taking over a little later on. The evening fare was a Chinese, which was greatly appreciated. The day ended with the news that a signal had been received, detailing our return flights, the news of which spread like wildfire and morale soared. Our flight was confirmed as departing Ascension at 20:00 hours on the 10 May. As I noted, it had been 'a good day'

Lewis: Isla de Trinidad 300 miles port side, 1000 miles to go.

Thursday, 8 July (Day 49)

Stiff on waking! A reasonable night's sleep after the last few nights. 2 hrs sunbathing in the morning were most appreciated. At noon we were 585 miles to go at a temp of 25 °C. Horse racing in the afternoon proved to be a high point. We didn't place in the first 5 races, but in the last we came 2nd as a syndicate. 1st was 9 Sqn RE who won £295 and second was us with £145. That meant we had our original £5 + £6 [winnings]. At night we had a diner night. What a night, with a games evening. The Gunners won overall. I even won the matchbox game. I spent an hour around 2359 polishing & having a tour of the engine room and after watching a porn film retired. What an evening.

When I woke, I was noticeably stiff from the PT, but a couple of hours sunbathing helped to ease things somewhat. What was rather difficult, was finding a space to lay my towel down on, as everybody sought to enjoy the conditions. The weather continued to be fair and temperatures were up into the mid-twenties. The consensus was that we should enjoy and celebrate the balmy conditions. To that end, in the wardroom, proceedings started off in the afternoon with horse racing.

We were invited to form syndicates, one for each of the six horses, for the planned six races. Whilst our syndicate didn't win outright, our placing in the last race meant that we went away in profit. For my original £5 stake, which I took back, I received £6 in winnings and I felt very pleased with life. The evening meal was transformed into more of a traditional dinner night, with a games evening following on afterwards. These games were all physical in their make-up and, considering the proceedings, were less than easy. Games ranged from 'sitting' up against a bulkhead (wall) without a chair until your legs give way, to 'bottles'.

The game 'bottles' is where from a standing position and a bottle in each hand, you bend forward and 'walk' the bottles forward whilst keeping your feet in the same place. You 'walk' as far as you can go, then reach forward and place one of the bottles upright, before trying to stand up again by reversing the process. Individuals lose if either they or the bottle fall over, with the winner covering the greatest distance. Jumping in and out of portholes was harder than it sounds and more than one person landed in a heap. One other game that I did rather well at was the 'plank'. Here two lines of three bar stools are placed, so as one stool sits under one's feet and one under one's head, with the other during the setting up, under the small of one's back. When both players are set, the middle stool is removed, with the player maintaining their 'plank' profile and the middle stool is passed around one's body as many times as possible, before collapsing to the floor.

I was to win the matchbox game, much to the annoyance of the younger marines. Here you sit on a chair/stool and matchbox is placed on the ground behind you. The aim of the game is to pick up the matchbox without the use of your hands, whilst not touching the floor. The general consensus was that I had youth on my side.

The evening's entertainment required a considerable amount of cleaning up, but that was a small price to pay for such a great night's entertainment. By this stage of the passage, the ship's officers and crew were giving 'tours' of their particular roles/workspaces, which was a very welcome distraction and certainly helped to pass the time. After the clear up I was to take up such an offer and take a tour of the engine room. Whilst it was very interesting, the overriding thought going through my mind, was what it must be like to work in when conditions were rough. When I went back up to the wardroom, an adult film, belonging to one of the ship's officers/crew was playing to a packed house. After watching the remainder of it I turned in and, as I wrote, 'what an evening'.

After the games night, the ship had run dry of beer, and spirit options were limited. By the time that we arrived at Ascension, the only alcohol left in the bar was a bottle of Kahlua (coffee liqueur) and a bottle of Cinzano.

Lewis: 75 deg East winds Force 4 20 kts.

Friday, 9 July (Day 50)

Hours to do. The weather is overcast but still very warm. Coffee in bed at 1000 by Mike Fallon (BC Spt Regt) and then the brief for getting home. Finally packed! After 2 hrs in the afternoon sunbathing it was just a case of retiring to the shower. The duty free arrived and also the bar bill. At noon we had 216 miles to do and it was 26 °C. Timings have slipped back 2 hrs already. All is in order for getting off.

The day started off at a very leisurely pace, with most suffering to some degree from last night's entertainment. Major Mike Fallon, 132 Observation Battery's BC, from the School of Artillery's Support Regiment was served coffee in bed at 10:00 hours! Much the same as John Patrick's 41 Observation Battery supporting 3 Para, 132 Observation Battery, provided observation parties to the Gurkhas. This was followed by a briefing, detailing the plans for our return flights home. After cascading the news, it was time to finally pack, not that there was much to do. It was 26 degrees and sunbathing was again the order of the day, albeit with caution. The incredible thing was that we could order Duty Free, which arrived in the afternoon, along with our bar bills. As we closed on Ascension, so the signal traffic increased, along with snippets of news. The general feeling was that we were 'hours to do', effectively having rounded the last bend, before the final straight finish to the line.

Lewis: Almost there

The 'O' Group confirmed the details that we had been eagerly anticipating, from when the news first broke. In summary: back in the UK, that the Commando Forces Headquarters had been told of our numbers and on which packets (persons per aircraft) that we were to be on. This in turn was going to be passed on to our parent units, as an 'Immediate Signal' at noon today and that information should reach them by tea time. My small sub-unit was detailed for the second aircraft, 'Packet B'. It was confirmed as an RAF VC10 transport aircraft, Flight Number 2611.

To prevent confusion around timings for our departure, all timings were to be 'Zulu' i.e. GMT; noting that Ascension is one hour behind and the UK one hour ahead of GMT. Our planned arrival time back in the UK was expected to be 08:10 hours local time. We were detailed to disembark from the rear flight deck during the afternoon, ahead of our baggage, which would be netted and flown to Wideawake Airfield. As such, lunch for our packet was to be our last meal onboard. Finally, we were to fill out and hand in our Next of Kin (NOK) cards, with rehearsals for the fly off starting at 14:00 hours, and we were then all set for getting off.

Saturday, 10 July (Day 51)

At 0600 I woke to see Ascension Island on the horizon. We reached it and RAS'ed [Replenishment At Sea] at 0800. Outside temp is 26 °C. Final prep before disembarkation. To relax there was sunbathing in the morning and fishing, Trigger fish, small type of fish and Razor fish. In the afternoon there was a film and the Chinese caught 4 fish of about 56 lbs. We left the ship and arrived on the island at about 1730Z and at 2000Z we left for the UK. We will stop in 5 hrs time

ROUTE BACK TO THE ASCENSION ISLES

2nd JULY - BUENOS AIRES 900 MILES ON THE PORT(LEFT) SIDE. WEATHER MODERATE

3rd JULY - 2400MILES TO GO. WEATHER PREDICTED 20KTS SW WIND

4th JULY - ALL AMERICA GOES POTTY - TEMP 60°

5th JULY - RIO DE JANEIRO 8 OOM PORT SIDE WEATHER N/E TRADES 15 KTS
6th JULY - 70° GETTING WARMER

7th JULY - ISLA DE TRINDADE 300M PORT SIDE 1000 MILES TO GO

8th JULY - 75° EAST WINDS FORCE 4 2 OKTS

9th JULY - ALMOST THERE

10th JULY - THERE(SUNTANS CANNOT BE GARUNTEED AS CAN ANYTHING ELSE ON HERE)

VAUGHAN LEWIS
NAVIGATOR

This is *Geraint*'s final day's progress report for our journey north. The ship's navigator, Vaughan Lewis, put this on the general notice board, adding a day each day, until we reached Ascension. As far as we were concerned, every day was the same, but this gave us some idea as to how our passage was progressing, 2 to 10 July 1982.

in DAKAR and change crews, arriving in the UK at 0800 UK local.

Lewis: There (suntans cannot be guaranteed as can anything else on here).

The day couldn't have started off any better. I woke at 06:00 hours to a glorious day and the sight of Ascension on the horizon. After quickly getting ready, I went back out onto the rail to watch our steady progress in. Conditions couldn't have been better and *Sir Geraint* RAS'ed at 08:00 hours and once again I was impressed by the evolution. After breakfast, final preparations were made and now it was just a case of killing time before we disembarked. Predictably, sunbathing was on the agenda. Whilst catching the sun, we spotted the Chinese crew on a sister landing ship also at anchor nearby, who were fishing off its stern, which soon saw us following suit. We broke out our survival kits and tried our hand at fishing over the side rail. Initial success saw us land a few Trigger fish, which we thought of using as bait for something larger. Unfortunately, trying to turn the Trigger fish into bait proved almost impossible, due to its extremely tough make up. Pocket knives failed and we resorted to using a bayonet, which also proved to be completely ineffectual. I spotted a fire axe stowed on the side and attempted to dispatch the fish with it. The first blow glanced off and hardly left a mark. The second and last blow hit the fish square on, but only to see it shoot off, as if it were a 'tiddly wink'! At this point we gave up and tidied up our mess to watch the Chinese show us how it's done.

We could clearly see their fishing tackle, which used a rope for line, a long steel wire cable for the leader and a hook which looked like it was at least six inches in length, which was baited with an entire fish. In contrast, we were using small hooks, with silver foil as a lure and 'standard' course style nylon fishing line. They landed four large tuna with great excitement, which they held up against each other for photographs, which were almost as tall as them. Mindful of the sun, the afternoon was spent relaxing by watching yet another film, but like me, most were watching the time.

The transition though Ascension was uneventful and after completing the usual paperwork, we boarded the VC10 as planned. The flight crew looked after us very well and I paid a long visit to the flight deck, during this leg of the journey. When it came to landing at Dakar, I was invited to remain on the flight deck to watch proceedings which was, to a lay person, very impressive. We were allowed off the aircraft, but had to remain in close proximity, whilst it was refuelled and turned around. Whilst it was good to stretch one's legs, the smell and heat, even at midnight, was oppressive.

Sunday, 11 July (Day 52)

We arrived at RAF Brize Norton, in Oxfordshire at 08:10 as planned, with no idea what sort of reception to expect. We had been out of communication for so long, with the only correspondence being that to confirm the various flight details for those returning. It did transpire that there was an update for us, but we had left Ascension before it arrived.

As we taxied into the arrivals dispersal, we saw a few banners, the sort of ones made from bed sheets, and a small crowd pressed against the fence. The formal reception was waiting at the bottom of the steps, as we disembarked the aircraft, which was a group of senior officers, who saluted and shook hands with every one of us as we filed off. As we reclaimed our baggage, we could hear an enthusiastic crowd waiting outside the building. I was standing near the exit, ensuring that my party had collected their baggage and weapons, only to be confronted by Lance Bombardier Owen, who came rushing back into the main part of the building looking visibly shaken. When I asked him what the problem was he said 'it's like a zoo out there!' I went over to look out through the exit doors to see very excitable families and friends at the threshold. I basically suggested that he might like to go out and put them out of their misery. As he approached the doorway, two pairs of hands grabbed him by his webbing and launched him into a melee!

Eventually my party had passed through Arrivals and I left the building to be met by Captain John Gray, our Regimental Quartermaster, who was in charge of the Rear Party when the Regimental Headquarters sailed. He informed me of the transport arrangements back to Aldershot and the fact

This was the scene that greeted us outside of the arrivals terminal at RAF Brize Norton, 11 July 1982.

that I had welcome party waiting for me. On looking around I eventually spotted my parents and Jill. After a quick hello, it was time to depart for barracks; with the party on a coach, and me journeying back with Jill. We arrived at Lille Barracks and stopped at the Guard Room, where weapons were immediately put into the armoury which was located behind it. I assembled the party back outside the Guard Room, with the intention of giving them their orders, but instead found that we were all to be presented with a pint of beer!

Very soon after this most pleasant surprise, I found myself doubly surprised to see Tony Rice walk up and greet me. Considering I had left approximately a week before their planned departure and flew back from Ascension, with the expectation of seeing them in a few weeks' time, I was rather lost for words. He explained that he'd continued to champion the Battery's cause and eventually the power- that-be acceded to his demands. In fact, the main body of the Battery flew out on a Hercules C130, shortly after I departed for *Sir Geraint*, all the way back to the UK and had been back in camp for almost two weeks. He confirmed the leave arrangements and I finally dismissed the party to a well-earned week of leave.

The rear party finally made it home around the 9th August, where time felt like it was passing at a glacial pace for David and his team. After handing over our stores and guns to the incoming Battery, the rear party were then in the mix for a long-overdue ride home. Their chance came because of a most unfortunate accident on Stanley's airfield, where a Sidewinder Anti-Aircraft missile exploded within the airfield's dispersal area, presumably from a Harrier, seriously injuring an ammunition working party. A Hercules was immediately pressed into service, to medically evacuate the casualties back to the UK. What should have been a joyous feeling was very much overshadowed by events and the general feeling was very subdued. Once at Ascension, they changed aircraft and returned in the relative comfort of a VC 10, arriving back at Brize Norton, before finally ending their journey in Aldershot, some twenty four hours after leaving the Falklands.

Chapter 12
Epilogue

ALMOST IMMEDIATELY AFTER our return, the members of the Battery dispersed on leave to their families; however, my family lived in Shropshire and whilst I was keen to go and visit, I elected to remain both in the officers' mess and locally with Jill, now my fiancé, and at the weekend, with her parents in Pirbright some five miles away, pending my trip north.

The Royal Tournament
It was about three to four days after we returned, that I was busying myself one morning in the mess' laundry room, trying to get the dirt and grime out of my 'combats', which was, understandably, taking more than one cycle. It was during this time that Captain John Gray, our OC Rear Party, called in to the mess, with an air of desperation about him, 'Ah Tom, glad to have caught you', he said with a breaking smile. He told me that he'd been hunting high and low for 'one of us' and was rather relieved to have found me. I sensed something was amiss, when he opened with: 'Have you ever thought of being on the small screen … I can see you right there on the telly and you're just the chap I need!' I asked quizzically what was going on, honing in on his last statement of 'you're just the chap I need'. John went on to explain that the MoD press office had been in contact with the Regiment, with the express aim of securing the services of a 'veteran', to represent the Army in an interview by Raymond Baxter, a stalwart of the BBC, to be conducted at Earls Court, for the upcoming Royal Tournament.

Thinking 'why me', I started to say that I was going to be away, but before I could get too far, he cut me off and stated that it was a done deal. The simple fact was that I was the only person that he could find and that he needed a name by lunchtime. The reality of the situation was that it was the sort of conversation that a Captain has to a Second Lieutenant and that there is only ever one outcome.

I was told to be outside the mess at 09:30 hours on Tuesday, where I'd be picked up and taken to London. I asked what was the dress code was. 'Oh yes … Service Dress, cross belt, medals, (I had the Northern Ireland General Service Medal) and get a Falklands ribbon' This latter edict was bordering on the impossible, as the South Atlantic Medal hadn't been formalised. Thankfully over the next few days the ribbon had been approved and I went off to visit my tailor. I was relieved to find that they had just taken receipt of one of the first rolls of ribbon and that he could help.

At the appointed hour, I was waiting in the entrance to the mess, when a very large chauffeur-driven car pulled up. The grey-suited driver, complete with hat, got out and opened the rear door for me to get in. He explained that he was from the BBC and that he was assigned to me for the day. Eventually we arrived at Earls Court, where I was met by one of the production team.

It was explained I was to be one of three interviewees, one from each Service. Also, that there had been a change to the plan and that the interview wasn't going to be conducted by the legendary Mr Baxter, but by a group of school children, with Raymond Baxter doing the voice-over. I felt somewhat out of place to be there, as my new associates had already been in and made the news. The Naval representative was the Sea King pilot who flew his helicopter into the acrid clouds engulfing *Sir Galahad*'s fo'c'sle, where he used the rotor downwash to blow the inflatable life rafts, so dangerously close alongside, away from the burning ship. The Royal Air Force's representative was the Harrier pilot who, during 2 Para's attack at Goose Green, was shot down and evaded capture, to return safe and well a few days later – and there was me representing the Army.

After lunch we were introduced to the group of children and the interviews began. The RN pilot was interviewed next to a number of model ships display boxes, as typically seen in maritime museums; the RAF Harrier pilot was filmed sat in a mobile Harrier mock-up cockpit and I was filmed on a 105mm Light Gun. It wasn't long before it was all over and we made our goodbyes. It was on the way out that I asked if there was any chance of getting two tickets to see the show. My host took me to the ticket office and asked the question on my behalf, with the secretary reluctantly asking when for. I explained that my fiancé was away during the week and that we were only available to go at the weekend. I was rather surprised at her attitude throughout, as it was somewhat aloof, standoffish and unwarranted. She took my name and gave me two tickets, saying 'black tie – don't be late'. Without looking I put the tickets into my pocket, said thank you and departed back to Aldershot.

Later that day I rang Jill and told her of my day in London. I told her I'd secured tickets and mentioned that it was black tie, which went without further comment. As we prepared ourselves, Jill asked where we were sitting to warrant 'black tie'? It was only then as I read the tickets that things fell into place, as we were to be sitting in the Royal Box! The icing on the cake was to happen about two weeks later, when a BBC-embossed envelope arrived for me at the mess; which contained a brief letter of thanks and a cheque for £50 Pounds, as an appearance fee! The Royal Tournament aired later in the summer and the interviews were well received all round.

The Gunner public relations set-up was soon keen to cash in, following on from my appearance at the Royal Tournament. I was sent to the Artillery's main Regimental Officers Mess, at the Depot Regiment in Woolwich, for an Artillery Young Officer's publicity photo shoot, with the intension of providing some 'glossy' pictures, to promote the social side, in a formal setting, of a young officer's life. The plan was for a group of some five or six subalterns, accompanied by some very attractive young ladies, in a staged mess kit dinner in the Officers Mess, with some of the Regiment's finest pieces of silver on display. The only reason I was there was because as a Second Lieutenant I had two medals and the Falklands Campaign medal was the shot that they were after. It was a tedious affair and I couldn't wait to get back to Aldershot. I never did see anything in print as a result of it.

The BC's Pistol

We soon settled back down into Regimental life, with the humdrum of barrack routine setting the pace. A few months later I was in the Battery lines and was asked to go to the Battery Office, to take a phone call from the RAF Police at Brize Norton.

Once we had established who we were, the RAF Police Corporal asked me if we had a 9mm pistol, serial number '123456'? I replied that we did and as to why was he asking, because our pistol was back in San Carlos Water, under many fathoms; having been in an underslung load of Battery stores and equipment, which was lost when jettisoned in an air attack during the landing phase. He told me that during a random search of bags of a returning soldier, who in fact was a Corporal in the Royal Engineers, that this pistol had come to light. The RAF Police Corporal then went on to say that this pistol had been traded for an Argentine folding-butt 7.62mm rifle, by a Gunner after the end of hostilities. The Corporal also went on to say that he'd traced the serial number through the MoD's 'master' ledger, which showed that we were its rightful keeper.

The pistol was in fact assigned to the BC; however, Tony Rice was adamant that he would not go to war armed with just a pistol and kept it with the BQMS, taking an SLR rifle in its place. This pistol, whilst in the care of the BQMS's party was kept in the 'Battery Box', which held small non-essential, but valuable items. Whilst taking this call from Brize Norton, the BSM was at hand and monitoring the conversation and immediately realised what was going and sent for both the BQMS, Staff Sergeant McQueenie and Gunner Brown, the latter being the only Gunner in the BQMS set up at that time. The BQMS denied all knowledge of the unfolding story of the BC's pistol, citing that Gunner Brown had told him that it was lost, along with other stores, when being jettisoned as part of an underslung load, when being flown ashore in an air attack, which matched Brown's story, with the burden of suspicion falling squarely at the feet of Gunner Brown.

Brown was marched in front of the BSM, who put quickly put the case against him and realising that his cover story was unraveling at an alarming rate came clean. Brown told of the time that he was at Goose Green, shortly after the battle and during the initial clean-up of the settlement, when he was 'wandering' about, aiming to bag an Upland Goose for the pot, chanced on the Royal Engineer Corporal in question, who had in his possession an Argentine folding-butt FN rifle. After a few failed attempts Brown gave up and approached the Corporal with a view to make an opportunistic trade. The deal was done and Brown went off with his new 'trophy'. The irony of the situation was that stories of returning soldiers being caught in possession of illegal firearms were filtering through and were being severely punished. Brown developed cold feet just before returning home and disposed of his 'trophy'. The Corporal however, chanced his arm and was caught red handed. Gunner Brown was subsequently charged and eventually placed in front of the Commanding Officer, who warned him off for Court Martial. With Bill Moore away and being the only junior officer in the Battery, I was detailed off to act as Gunner Brown's Defending Officer. With Gunner Brown pleading Guilty, my role as his Defending Officer was relatively straightforward, namely that of entering a Plea of Mitigation on his behalf.

The day of the Court Martial quickly came and all parties met at Aldershot's Courts Martial Centre. The role of the Prosecuting Officer defaulted to the Adjutant who, in the time that this had taken to come to Court had changed post. The incumbent was Captain Chris Brown, fresh from his exploits in the Falklands with 148 (Meiktila) Commando Forward Observation Battery Royal Artillery, who supported the special forces during the war. Chris Brown also had a law degree and was looking forward proceedings. The hearing was essentially rather straight forward, with the Adjutant and the then Army Legal Corps stating the case against Gunner Brown, who in turn was entering a guilty plea, with me following up with Brown's Plea of Mitigation. However, the presiding Judge quickly grew tired of the Army Legal Corps representative's style of delivery, with Chris Brown in tow, and called a halt to proceedings, citing that we weren't in America and reminded them that we were in a military court of law. It would be fair to say that having seen the Judge Advocate express his displeasure, I wasn't looking forward to my turn.

It was clear that the 'bench' was frustrated at the Prosecution by the time it came for me to speak on Brown's behalf, with my plea being well received. The Prosecution's call for Brown's Army discharge was successfully batted down to a £100 fine and 'soldier on', much to the disbelief of the opposition. Gunner Brown couldn't believe his luck and thanked me profusely.

The *Europic Ferry* Incident

Gunner Brown's Court Martial wasn't the only one on the books at the Garrison Courts Martial Centre, with another member of the Battery, Gunner Gowland, facing charges soon after; relating to unauthorised tampering of ammunition aboard the *Europic Ferry*, during the voyage south. One of the questions put to an accused soldier, is to ask if they have a defending officer in mind, to represent them throughout proceedings. No sooner had the question been put to Gowland, that he requested me to fulfil the role on his behalf. He told me in no uncertain terms that based on Gunner Brown's result, that I was his preferred option.

Gunner Gowland's story has its roots in the Battery's deployment at Salisbury Plain's Westdown Army Camp, in March-April. We were based there in support of the Royal School of Artillery, whilst the outgoing Support Regiment was being dismantled and 2nd Regiment Royal Artillery's moving to provide gunnery support at Larkhill. As part of the day-to-day support tasks, we also used the time to conduct the mandatory annual personal skills and weapons tests required of each of us. For one reason or another, Gunner Gowland missed the L2 Hand Grenade lesson, which went unnoticed. To recap for the journey south, the Battery was split into three groups: the BC's party flew out directly to Ascension on 22 April, as part of 2 Para's advance group.

The 26th, saw the bulk of the Battery under Captain Bob Ash embark and sail on *Norland*, with the guns, vehicles and technical stores under the BK, Captain David Gibbins, with a small maintenance party embarked on *Europic Ferry*. This relatively small container and roll-on-roll off ferry also had crammed on board the field ambulances as well as 1,000 tons of artillery ammunition, along with a variety of small arms munitions. One of the roles of the maintenance party was to provide a fire watch on the vehicle deck that contained the vast ammunition stocks.

Within a few days of leaving Ascension, it was the turn of Gunner Gowland to provide such a watch. Whilst walking around, Gowland came across a pallet of L2 Grenades and he elected to carry out a spot of 'on the job' personal training. Grenades in their transport packaging come in two parts, the detonator and the main body. To assemble a grenade, the detonator is screwed into the main body, with the grenade made safe by the spilt-pin holding the handle and firing mechanism in situ. Gowland found the two main component parts and opened each box. He examined each part in turn and assembled them a few times.

On the last disassembly, Gowland sought to further investigate the workings of the detonator, before placing the main body to one side. Gowland grasped the detonator in his right hand, placed his left index finger in the safety firing ring and pulled out the split-pin. Once the split pin was clear of the detonator's head, two things immediately happened. Firstly, the spring mechanism causes the handle to fly off, which in turn releases the firing pin into the head of the detonator and initiates the firing process. At this point, there are seven seconds before it explodes.

When he saw the handle fly away, Gowland realises that he's made an error and desperately tries to put things right, by attempting to put the safety pin back into the head, in the misguided hope that all will be well. When the detonator exploded, he was hunched over and holding it into his stomach, still trying to relocate the split-pin. The ensuing explosion blew him across the deck with considerable force. On regaining his senses, he saw that his cloths had been shredded and that he'd suffered significant blast injuries to his hands and was completely missing three fingers, the two middle from his right and the index finger on his left hand. There were also blast/flash burns to his hands and face, with multiple mini bits of the detonator's casing penetrating bare flesh. Gowland pick up at least one of his fingers and made his way to the BK's cabin. He knocked on the door and waited to be called in. David Gibbins recounts 'John the pilot was the first to the door, who when seeing Gowland standing in front of him, called out 'Doc, this one's for you.' Captain Mike von Bertele, one of the Parachute Field Ambulance's doctors, with whom I was also sharing the cabin with, shouted at Gowland in no uncertain terms to get out of the cabin, as he was dripping blood everywhere, before rushing over to help.'

Mike von Bertele patched Gunner Gowland up and he was cross-decked over to the hospital ship *Uganda* by Captain John Greenhalgh, one of the Army Air Corps Detachment's pilots, before being returned back to Ascension, for onward repatriation to the UK. It was only when David Gibbins went down to see the scene of the accident that the full magnitude to the situation unfold. The stark reality was that Gunner Gowland had, through a misguided desire to conduct some self-help grenade training, has caused an explosion among 1,000 tons of artillery ammunition; which could have catastrophic consequences, not only for those on board *Europic*, but for the entire planned forth-coming invasion.

The time came for Gowland's Court Martial and once again the main players reassembled. Remembering the chastening experience from Gunner Brown's hearing, the prosecution laid out their case, seeking his discharge, with me following on after Gowland's guilt plea, with his mitigating plea. Against all the odds, the board came down on our side and once again I'd secured a £100 fine and to 'soldier on'! Of course, Gowland was as thankful as Brown. Just before I left the Regiment, a Gunner from another Battery was warned off for Court Martial and immediately requested my services! Sadly for him I was to leave before proceedings began and was unable to help.

Appendix I

Letters

IN MARCH 2013, THE Falkland Islanders were deciding their fate in a sovereignty referendum, which was making the world news. It was during one of the numerous BBC television interviews that I saw Hattie Kilmartin. This initiated an internet search, which then prompted me to send a speculative email:

Dear Kevin and Hattie,
    I am writing to you, having recently seen Hattie on the BBC news here in the UK, speaking about the referendum on sovereignty and was spurred in to action. When I saw the name Kilmartin, I wondered if there was a connection to Bluff Cove and did a simple Google search, hence this email.
    By way of introduction, back in 1982 following the end of hostilities, I was a 'guest' at the settlement there at Bluff Cove, as a young Second Lieutenant with 29 Corunna Field Battery Royal Artillery, where I was put up in the space above the garage, before moving out into a caravan. I'm currently in the process of writing out my diaries from the build-up, the war and the journey home, which makes reference to Bluff Cove and made the link. We moved in on the 17 June 82 and I recall that there were 4 of you there at the time, Tim and Jean Dobbin, with you Kevin and at that time Diane. I also recall from my diary that on the 19th, 'Had a bath in the house (Kevin's and Diane's), that went down well, along with their stew, tea, coffee and gin & tonic'!
    I've never forgotten the warmth of the hospitality shown to us and if I didn't say so before leaving, I do so now.
    The farm's website made interesting reading and I spotted a photo of it showing the settlement and remembered that I have one taken from a similar vantage point, which I've attached.
    With best regards to you both,
    Tom
    PS: Excellent news on the ballot result.

Kevin Kilmartin responded:

Dear Tom,
    Many thanks for your kind words and the nostalgic photograph. Sorry it is taking so long to respond; life here is always hectic. Margaret Thatcher's death followed on from the referendum, and some of the same journalists came down to Stanley for that. It looks as though the new oil port, when it is built, might be called Port

Thatcher, although there is some talk of renaming the airport at Mount Pleasant … We are heading towards the 31st anniversary of 1982 events. I suspect that this Thursday will see a big and possibly violent demonstration in Buenos Aires on the anniversary of the sinking of the *Belgrano*. The target of the demonstrators might be the Lan Chile offices in order to protest about the weekly flight from the Falklands to Santiago.

I think I first met members of 29 battery on June 2, 1982. I think Tony Rice may have been on that first helicopter that landed on the ridge outside Bluff Cove settlement. Anyway, three guns were put in position about a mile to the southwest of the settlement, at Fitz Cove. I seem to remember Tony Rice telling me that the gunners weren't informed that the Scots Guards were going to land at Yellow Beach in Bluff Cove and for a time they considered swinging the guns around to fire at whatever it was that was coming towards Bluff Cove from East Island.

The battery then moved forward about 5 miles to just south of Mt Challenger where the dirt road from Stanley to Mount Pleasant has now been built. I can't remember whether the Battery moved forward again after that, but 97 battery which was established just east of Yellow Beach at Bluff Cove moved forward to Port Harriet.

After the surrender, all six guns of 29 Battery came back to the farm settlement and were put in a line on the green. There were the about 120 men around the settlement, the bulk of them in the shearing shed. A shower was made from a 40-gallon drum with a burner underneath in the shearing shed engine room. The cooks fired up to the peat fired bread oven in one of the sheds and produced a constant stream of bread, pizzas, and pies. The ingredients came from Sgt McQueen, who knew everything there was to know about razzing and seem to have his own personal helicopter on standby. I remember going with him to some of the large Argentine tents full of stores at Stanley airport. I tried to load an under slung net full of very large Parmesan cheeses.

I think that most of the battery left after a few days and perhaps went back on *Norland* but a dozen guys were left behind to look after the six guns. I seem to remember that every time it was their turn to leave something happened and they had to stay a few days longer. One of them was the infamous Jardine.

It was at about this time that Tony Rice or maybe it was Tony Holt sent me into Stanley to meet General Moore. Their concern was that the replacement battery that was due to arrive was to be stationed at Bluff Cove for a four-month tour of duty. The view from the gunners was that Fitzroy would be the better place as it had much bigger sheds and a lot of potential accommodation. My mission to talk to the general about this was successful and the next battery did go to Fitzroy.

When the missing Scots Guards turned up at Bluff Cove several weeks later, I contacted the battery at Fitzroy on the famous phone line as used by 2 Para. The major offered to send a bodybag round in the morning until I explained that the corpse had had a bath and was eating an enormous supper.

We used to give each battery at Fitzroy a piglet, which would be fattened up and then barbecued for their farewell feast. One young gunner named Ambrose was in charge of one of the piglets and became extremely distraught when his comrades killed and ate it.

I think that these six guns are still here at Mount Pleasant. The son of a friend of mine came down to work on the farm for a summer and took part in a lot of military activity. I seem to remember that he was present on the range when a shell went astray from one of the guns. Fortunately, I didn't have to explain to his parents that I had let him go out on exercise and that he had met with an accident. He joined the artillery and is now a brigadier.

Tim and Jean have both died and are buried out here overlooking the Fitzroy River. Diane lives in Australia.

We meet up with lot of Veterans each year. Have you been back? We hope to meet up with you one day and thank you personally.

Best wishes, Kevin

I replied:

Dear Kevin,

Thank you for taking the time to get back and I agree, life seems to gather pace at an alarming rate. Memories of our time in '82 seem like it was only yesterday. The strange thing was that after seeing you on the TV talking about the referendum, allowing for the fact that we're all 30+ years older, is that I felt that I could have been standing by watching it there from the side, hence the initial Google search.

Margaret Thatcher's death swept the nation and certainly divided opinion in the country as to her legacy, but what wasn't in question were her actions and resolve to returning the Falkland Islands to their rightful owners. I wouldn't be at all surprised to see something, such as the new oil port, named after her. There has been little news of disruptions in Argentina, although there has been a fair bit posturing on the political front, which has tailed off since MT's funeral. It seems that when the Argentine leadership comes in for a hard time at home, the one way that they try and deflect the political heat is to stir up the past, which just happens to be about this time of year! As an aside, my father's brother settled in Argentina in the late 50s, working his way up managing very larger estancias; before marrying a local girl and settling down to raise a family. His eldest, back in '82, was just too young for conscription, which raised the question from my family of what would I have done if he was playing for the other side? I simply replied – 'tell him to duck'! The only thing that seems to be reported on with any sort of regularity, is that of the disruptions/intimidation to the cruise ships, which appear to be every 2 weeks or so. It's a cheap shot in trying to hamper the cruise liners and doesn't do their cause any good at all. I know of a few here who have been on a South Atlantic cruise and who report that it was just the most amazing experience. I only hope that it's allowed to continue and that many more can share the secrets of 'Down South'.

As to our initial arrival at Bluff Cove, I have no record as to when Tony Rice first flew in, as he wasn't located with us on the gun position. My diary has it that I flew in on the 3rd June, from our location at Head of the Bay House, San Carlos Water, on the first wave to set up the position. We landed on the ridge just behind the settlement, in front of the trenches occupied by A Company of 2 PARA. During the initial phases of the set up, I was helping Bill Moore (Lieutenant, our Gun Position Officer) when a young paratrooper came over and asked what we were doing. I briefly explained and that I was actually quite busy, before asking if there was anything else. He replied in a dead pan manner, that his trench was the furthest forward trench in the Company and then pointed and said 'over that way is Stanley, and there's nothing between my trench and the Argies – but you'.

Somewhat taken back by this revelation, I called over to Bill and relayed the story. He sought clarification from on high, who agreed that it wasn't the best place to be and we moved back to the south west and away from the settlement. The gunners had to man-handle the first gun some 800m over the tussock grass, which was no mean feat in itself. Eventually all 6 guns were set up down near the water's edge.

Many thanks for clarifying the name of Fitz Cove, as I didn't note it down. You are absolutely correct about the tale of the Scots Guards. on the 6th June and of the 'landing craft in the bay', except that we weren't considering swinging the guns around, but that we had them firmly in our sights and were ready to fire!

We remained there at Fitz Cove until the 10th June, when I went forward with 3 guns to that dirt road position, to the south of Mt Challenger, leaving the other 3 guns behind. They followed on later the next day, where we remained until the 17th June, when we all returned to join you at Bluff Cove. I would be grateful if you would clarify a vague memory of during our time on the dirt track, which was rekindled by your story of the bread oven. I recall that the residents of Bluff Cove brought us up fresh rations, but "m not sure as to the dates. Firstly, was this a true recollection and secondly, was it during fighting or after the ceasefire?

When we came back we did indeed site the guns on the green and spread ourselves into whatever shelter we could find. The bulk of the Battery went into the shearing shed, with the officers and the sergeant majors taking up residence above the garage. The garage below was used to provide the radio link. I remember staying in the 'attic' until being turfed out into a caravan 'out the back'. I too remember SSgt McQueenie's uncanny ability to rustle up a helicopter and return with all sorts of 'booty'. You are not alone in your recollection of Gnr Jardine. He was McQueenie's side-kick, who also had his moments.

During this time, Tony Rice directed his efforts on securing our return home, which was far from clear cut. In fact, having been given the news that all those involved in the initial landings were to go home as soon as possible, we were told that as there were no other gunners available to replace us, that we could be there for up to a further 4 months! That led to Tony Rice stepping up his efforts and some progress was made. He had secured a number of berths on a soon-to-return auxiliary landing ship and I left Bluff Cove on the 29th June, with a party of 27 to sail back to the UK.

Plans were made for the balance of the Battery (less the rear party) to return home, with the eventual outcome of them returning back home by air. As for my voyage home, thankfully we only had to sail half way, before catching a flight from Ascension Island; however, the 14-day sea voyage gave one and all the chance to unwind after our adventures. The rear party followed on some time after the main body departed, but I'm not sure by how long. The ironic thing was that having been the first to leave Bluff Cove, my party was the last to get home.

I've since been in contact with Tony Rice regarding your visit to see General Moore, who has clarified that it was in fact Tony Holt, our Commanding Officer, who was the architect of the meeting.

I do remember the pigs (2 if correct), who as I recall, had a shelter on the side of the fence. My only memory of fresh meat on the Island was mutton, and that there was lots of it on the hoof. In fact, one abiding memory was the shock I felt when being present when you fed the pigs. I was brought up next to a farm who had pigs, that fed them various types of pig meal/nuts, along with the occasional swill, coupled by the fact that my father was a vet, so was comfortable with a pig's lot. That illusion was shattered when you threw into the sty a sheep's carcass, which was stripped to the bone in seconds with some relish!

I don't recall what happened to the guns and I've since asked the question. As for your friend's son joining the Artillery, I'm pretty confident that he will be known by the Corunna officers. I was one of the first to leave after 18 years, having trained as a helicopter pilot shortly after the war and continue to do so now, working with the emergency services. Bill Moore, as mentioned above, recently retired from the Gunners as a Major General and is co-working on my diaries, adding his recollections for completeness.

I recall that Tim and Jean made the trip up to England and joined us in a celebration in Aldershot sometime 'shortly' after the war. As to their final resting place, I'm sure it's a fitting spot and one that haS met with their approval. I read into the fact that you and Dianne had moved on, having visited your website, and seen that you are married to Hattie and have young Toby to keep you on your toes!

As for going back … no I haven't; however, it's on my list of things to do, but as to when is a different story. I think that having a beer would be rather good.

I've attached a few more pictures of the settlement, which does show the considerable garden redevelopment of the day, along with Fitz Cove and the track south of Mt Challenger.

Best regards,

Tom

Appendix II

D+12,646: Falklands Revisited 2017

AS A GROUP of six officers, there has always been a strong bond between us, forged by those testing days in 1982 and tempered by the fact that we were an independent battery keen to show our worth. In recent years, we have met up on a regular basis, maintaining that bond between us, with our gatherings triggered by a generic 'let's meet up' email. Busy lives and work schedules haven't always been kind and it has usually taken some time to sort out a suitable date but, nevertheless, sort it out we do. So, in late June 2016, it came as no surprise to get an email from Tony in my mailbox; however, I wasn't quite prepared for its content. Tony proposed that as 2017 was going be the 35th Anniversary the Battery officers reunion should be held down in the Falkland Islands, suggesting early January 2017 as a suitable date. Considering how long it normally takes us to sort out one of regular get-togethers, as well as the magnitude of the proposal, it was a surprise to see that we all signed up to the concept, effectively by return of post.

Proposing such a venture is one thing, putting it into action is something else. The concept of the trip was relatively simple – we fly there, have time on the islands and fly back. Life, of course, is never that simple. The Falklands are supported by an air bridge, flown by a regular scheduled RAF-sponsored MOD-contracted flight service and on the face of it, securing one's passage is done by applying for the flights. The bulk of passengers are made up of service personnel and contractors for the military garrisons, both in Ascension and in the Falklands; as well as a set number of seats for the Falkland Islands Government Office, which includes Falkland Islanders travelling to and from the UK. When all these 'seats' are accounted for, any spare capacity is given over to concession flights. These flights are effectively cut-priced fares, designed to fill empty seats, and are made available to both veterans and bereaved families from the war, as well as tourists. The matter of accommodation was also proving to be a difficult factor, as there is only a limited number of available beds and it being the summer in the South Atlantic, it was the height of their tourist season. With Tony taking the lead, applications for our concession flights were duly made via the South Atlantic Medal Association 1982 (SAMA82) within days, with early feedback suggesting that such early bids would help put us to the top of the list. Notwithstanding that, we would have to wait until mid-December to find out if our applications were successful.

Unbeknown to me in early November, was that three members of the battery: Joe Walker, Ernie Dobson, Steve Sprotson, along with a member from 43 Battery RA (Blowpipe Detachment), were to make their own trip back to the Falklands, which proved to be a most useful source of information. I'd met Joe Walker and Ernie Dobson at a battery reunion in June, where we talked through Tony's outline plan, which clearly had sown the seeds for their own visit. To learn of their visit and to pick up on such recent detail was very helpful, but the thing that stuck with me was the way Joe described the warmth and gratitude of the islanders towards them, wherever they went.

In mid-November, Tony received notification from SAMA82 of a change to the start date, which brought the flight forwards by two days, which was accepted by all. However, disaster struck on 1 December, when Tony received notification that not all our return flights were going to be met and put out an emergency email warning us to that effect. The RAF could get us there, but they couldn't get us all back, which was met with a collective cry of 'we've been there before'! I did offer that it wasn't something that we hadn't overcome previously. Sadly, this news was too much for David and Bill who had to withdraw from the trip.

At this point I was unaware that there was a safety net in place, in the form of the Falklands Veterans Foundation (FVF), which stepped in, with Karen Cole, the Operations Manager who effectively saved our reunion. Set up in 2002, the FVF is a charity set up in partnership with other service charities, to provide a network of support to veterans and their immediate families; as well as providing a permanent self-contained residence, called Liberty Lodge, in Stanley. The Lodge also provides those service personnel based in the Falklands a respite from garrison life. After a tense twenty-four hours, the FVF came through with four confirmed flights, as well as providing us with accommodation for our first three nights.

As part of travelling with the FVF, flight applications had to be resubmitted to the Falkland Islands Government Office, where seats not taken by their allocation are taken up by the FVF and the full cost fare is met by the charity. The FVF, along with other service charities, is the beneficiary of Government fines imposed on the banks, as a result of the LIBOR lending rate scandal. In turn, we were to donate towards the cost of the fare, to the sum of the concession flight. The scene was set for our departure on 2 January. Our start date couldn't have come quickly enough, albeit that we knew that we were in for a long and tiring journey ahead.

Having double-checked travel documents and bags, we individually set off for RAF Brize Norton. Knowing that the main arterial routes out of the south west would be very slow going, post the festive break, my route to 'Brize' took me up and over Salisbury Plain. It's a journey I've made countless times over the years; however, this one felt different in some way. By the time that I reached Tilshead and the centre of the Plain, it was cold, frosty and just getting dark. Low in the clear night sky was Venus, framed by a waxing crescent moon, and I could clearly see the black silhouette of Westdown Camp ahead.

As I drove past, my mind took me back to the time we spent there in early 1982, in particular 'running around' at the SMIGs course and appreciating just how important that period was for us all. By early evening Tony, Bob, James and myself had all mustered and began to be processed by the RAF

Movements. It had been a number of years since any of us had flown 'Crab Air' and we were unsure what to expect. Our collective experiences told of being messed around by the 'Movers' and then flown in cattle class in aged VC10s. This time Departures had a different feel, service personnel traveled in civilian clothing, albeit it with camouflaged day sacks, and there were numerous contractors and families; however, it still was a military contract flight and we knew it would take a long time to get through the system. We also knew that we would be flying in an Airbus A330 Voyager, but what I didn't expect was to see a civilian flight crew wait to board.

We finally departed around midnight on the first of our eight-hour legs, which was punctuated by a two-hour stop over at Ascension for both fuel and to replenish the aircraft for the final leg, as well as change flight crews. It was in the holding area on Ascension that the first part of our story was retold. The holding area is very close to the dispersal area where I flew ashore from the *Norland*, with the intension of bore-sighting the guns and took refuge from the blistering sun and heat of the tarmac under the wing of the Vulcan bomber. Despite the thirty-five-year gap, the geography looked familiar, it was a humid 28 degrees centigrade and Green Mountain was typically covered in thick cloud. Looking out over the bay I could picture the ships at anchor and *Norland* in particular. The last leg was as uneventful as the first and, so it was, after almost twenty-four hours (despite the time difference) that we arrived at the island's garrison at Mount Pleasant.

By this time, we were well into the afternoon of 3 January and D+12,646. Considering that this was now meant to be the height of their summer, we were cut no slack and, true to form, we disembarked into a cold 9 degrees and driving heavy rain! We were me by Kevin Kilmartin, who kindly picked us up at the airport and drove us into Stanley, on what we were to discover was one of the significant changes to the islands, namely the new road system. The wide cambered hardcore/loose chipping roads are generally well maintained, although there are short stretches of metalled road between Stanley and the garrison; however, the deep drainage gullies either side are unforgiving if you leave the road, and a 40mph speed limit is in place.

It was great to finally meet up with Kevin again after all these years and it was as if we'd not been long away. He brought us up to speed with the local politics, the change to island life, not just by the garrison at Mount Pleasant, or by Stanley's expansion, but to the booming tourist industry as well, all serviced by the island's new road network.

As such, island life and especially around Stanley, is experiencing an economic boom that the islanders are finding it difficult to keep pace with. Consequently, most have three or four jobs to cope with the level of tourism, which we witnessed at first hand when we saw the first of many cruise liners call in. It was, as on every occasion, all hands to the pumps to get passengers ashore, into their respective tour groups and off on their excursions. Kevin told of the main tourist 'attractions' as being: battlefield tours, visiting penguin colonies and for the less adventurous, group tours around Stanley.

Our route into Stanley took us through the location of our final gun position and once in Stanley, via 'suburbia' it's clearly evident that there had been a housing boom since we were last here. Our first stop was to briefly call into their 'town house' and meet Kevin's wife Hattie, by way of brief introductions, before we arrived at the welcome sight of Liberty Lodge and into the care of Ellen Davis, the Lodge's caretaker/manager. The Lodge was a revelation, it's fully self-contained, providing multi-occupancy en-suite accommodation in very comfortable surroundings. The one golden rule that was impressed upon us by Ellen, a full islander, was that there is a 'no outside boots/shoes inside', which was not only in force here, but in every islander's house we were sure to visit. Also residing at the Lodge, were three naval veterans, all of whom were Senior Rates on HMS *Illustrious*, one of the Task Force's two aircraft carriers. They proved excellent company and proved that inter-service rivalry was alive and in rude health! Collectively they had been down on a number of occasions between them and provided a good source of local intelligence, namely where to find our first beer.

Our first full day was one of orientation within Stanley and the immediate surrounding area, making use of one of the Lodge's 4x4 vehicles made available for our use, over our first three days. Looking out from the Lodge directly across the harbour, lay one of the many cruise ships we were to see call in, ferrying countless passengers ashore and with clear skies it looked most promising indeed. After a leisurely start, we ventured out to explore Stanley and thankfully we had the 4x4 to do it in. True to form the weather changed, as I noted in my little notebook 'RAIN, RAIN, RAIN!' and with a cool 9 degrees on a biting wind it felt bitter and this was summer! A local

Our party on the first day outside Liberty Lodge, 4 January 2017. Left to right are: Bob Ash, Tony Rice, James Watson and the author.

One of the large cruise ships just outside the harbour entrance, 5 January 2017. During the tourist season, Stanley can expect some three to five liners in per week, bringing many thousands of tourists each year.

tried to tell me that the Falklands actually had a lower annual rainfall than the UK, but I did point out that the seasonal variations between summer and winter weather was an abstract concept, as all weather types could probably happen on any given day, with the only true test of season being the length of daylight. It didn't take long for the rain to blow through, but it was to keep coming back in bands throughout the day.

One of my projects was to try and recreate a 'then and now' photographic challenge, depending on what lay ahead and we'd look to grab opportunities as they came along. First call was the racecourse and despite Stanley being relatively compact, as well as having both a map and knowing where the racecourse was, it was actually harder to find than it should have been. Further locations were taken in, as well as visiting the main Liberation Monument, citing every element of the Task Force, with the simple inscription 'IN MEMORY OF THOSE WHO LIBERATED US – 14 JUNE 1982. On the rear crescent wall, large plates listed the fallen: military, merchant seamen and civilian alike, which brought home the very real collective cost and true debt of gratitude.

As previously mentioned, the new road system has transformed travel both around Stanley, as well as the islands and being on the outskirts, we decided to drive up and onto Wireless Ridge and salvage something from the weather. The new road up from Moody Brook bisects 2 Paras' line of advance during this final battle and we drove up and onto the Argentine defensive positions there from the other side, which makes for a quick and easy visit. The first task was to orientate oneself to the battlefield's main features, so we went back to 2 Paras' start point, to retrace its first and subsequent objectives, before the final race into Stanley.

Aside the road, Argentine observation bunkers are easily accessible and parking up on the top of the ridge takes one amongst their defensive locations. Low dry stone walls mark firing points and the remains of heavy machine-gun mounts still lie in situ. Out in the open is also the remains of a rusting large recoilless rifle. Peppering the ridge line are numerous water-filled shell craters, their distinctive round shape clearly standing out within the natural peaty surface.

Along the ridge to Stanley, we saw a cross to one of 2 Para's fallen, with commanding views of the battlefield and the surrounding hills, as well as down across the bay to Stanley, some 5,000 metres away across the Sound. Seeing at first-hand and listening to Tony, Bob and James recall their experiences and their description of events, as if it was yesterday, was staggering. Their explanations to my numerous questions was captivating and what was warming to hear, was the black humour that they recalled from those dark times.

The weather was taking its toll and we agreed that we would return to Wireless Ridge on another day, so we headed back to the Lodge for some respite. Driving along the shore road we passed numerous groups of rain-soaked tour groups, most of whom were inadequately dressed for the prevailing conditions. One tourist in particular caught our eye, as the bedraggled individual was wearing an oversized thin drab green plastic poncho and trudged along miserably at the rear. James quick to spot the individual in question highlighted their plight by saying: 'this one looks as happy as an Argie prisoner walking along here thirty-five years ago!'

A lull in the weather was enough for us to get back out and explore our local surroundings. We decided to take in the old airport, as I had one of my 'then and now' pictures to recapture, as well as call into Surf Bay, having seen it signposted on the road out. Being the closest sandy beach to Stanley it's very popular; however, its curved, beautiful sandy beach hides its sinister past. As part of the Argentine defences, Surf Bay was heavily mined. One of the many information signs dotted around pointed out that the de-mining program surprisingly only began in 2010, with Surf Bay being one of the first sites to be cleared. Mine clearance contractors removed some 1,000 mines from January to June 2010, giving an insight into the scope and scale of the task ahead. Just around the bay, and only a few hundred meters away, we came across the grey granite memorial to HMS *Glamorgan*, looking out over the water behind. At the time, on 12 June, *Glamorgan* had been providing naval gunfire in support of 45 Commando's attack on Two Sisters and was on her way back to the safety of the naval air defence umbrella, when she was hit close to this spot, by a shore-based Exocet missile, killing fourteen of the ship's company.

Journeying back into Stanley we decided to visit the 1982 Memorial Wood, in an area which would have been located on Stanley's eastern edge, but with the new buildings expanding eastwards, now sits well within the built-up area. The concept is very simple, a tree or shrub has been planted for every serviceman lost during the war, each marked by a small plaque at the base, with a central map showing where each and every memorial is located. Their growth varies throughout, each one utterly dependent on where it was planted, with those on the rocky slopes having a harder time of it. The larger trees, planted on more fertile level ground, provide much needed shelter from the strong prevailing wind. We were a quite reflective group that followed the meandering path through the wood, as we searched for the 2 Para Officers' memorials, of those killed at the battle of Darwin and Goose Green and a quiet moment was spent at each. When we came across 'H' Jones' tree, Tony crawled under the low hanging branches to respectfully straighten a small wooden cross of remembrance, that had been blown over in the wind. It was easy to lose oneself to one's thoughts within the plantation, as the trees blocked out the surrounding area, which heightened the feeling of serenity. What we were surprised to see was a section had been set aside for those killed after the war. The tragic reality is that to date, forty-two 'new' trees have since been added.

Leaving the Memorial Wood, we ventured back through Stanley and chanced across Kevin by the quayside, fresh from taking a couple of hundred tourists on his own penguin tour, located on his farmland. We commentated on how the old Stanley from 1982 looked rather tired and how it contrasted with the new estates and buildings cocooning the old town. What we all agreed on, was there was little in the way of any visible landscape gardening and perhaps a missed job opportunity?

There is one thing that has clearly changed for the better, evident by little window signs simply stating 'wifi hotspot', is that Stanley has been brought into the world of global connectivity. Having said that, all is not good with the island's internet access. Connectivity comes at a price, made all the more expensive in that a cable connection to the mainland and Argentina is not forthcoming. Argentina has denied the islanders cable access, literally severing ties to the Falklands. The only option open is to use a satellite, which has driven prices far greater than they need be. This is compounded by the poor decision that telecommunication provision has been given to a single supplier, who has the monopoly for broadband internet access and mobile communications and nothing looks like it is going to change for some time to come. As a visitor, buying into the system is some ten times more expensive than that of the UK and the amount of data available is paltry. Having said that, the population has global connectivity and is no longer a sleepy backwater that was happy to see the world slip by. A radio service has always been present, which apart from the BBC's World Service, was rather parochial back in the day. One of the benefits of having a military garrison on one's doorstep is that it provides all the trappings for media services, in the form of the British Forces Broadcasting Services (BFBS). BFPS provides radio and television service to British servicemen and women, along with their families when garrisoned abroad. Television is an eclectic mix of what's on back in the UK, with popular programmes getting similar scheduling as back home, along with BBC, ITN and Sky news, which is time-shifted by the GMT differential to keep it 'timely'; importantly, this is made available to the islanders.

For our second day, we elected to have somewhat of a cultural experience, which started off with a visit to Stanley's Museum, which proved to be a revelation. The museum, whilst being the 'national' museum is compact in size, but is packed full of artefacts covering the diverse history of the Falklands, including the islands' natural resources, including both the fauna and flora, as well as focusing on the present, such as sheep farming and fishing. There was an area dedicated to the events of 1982, but it was only a small part of what is on display and we all commented that it thankfully didn't dominate the museum. Whilst of defining importance, those seventy or so days in 1982, are only a blink in the eye of the history of the Falklands. The islands have a rich maritime history, from exploration, the whaling industry to its position off the southern tip of South America and its strategic location. Stanley's natural deep water harbour was both a refuge and naval stronghold during both world wars.

After visiting the museum, it was time to make the short journey over to Government House and have afternoon tea with the Governor, Colin Roberts. Far from being singled out for special attention, the Governor makes a point of inviting as many veterans to tea as possible, which reinforces the debt of gratitude to those who liberated the Falklands. Whilst a small token, it was well received and he explained how life in the Falklands had changed since we were here last. Equally, he was keen to learn as to what part we had to play in proceedings.

We were to learn that, excluding the cost of the military garrison, the islands economy is very much in the black; with fishing taking top spot, closely followed by tourism, with sheep coming someway behind in third. There has been somewhat of a population explosion since 1982, where numbers have risen from some 1,800 to the current figure, based on the 2016 Census, of some 3,000; with those not full islanders being referred to as 'blow ins'. Of that number some 400 or so live out in the 'Camp', with the majority living in East Falkland. The surprising statistic was that the fishing industry has approximately 4,000 fishermen afloat around the islands at any one time, hence fishing taking top spot in the local economy. On the domestic front, free health care provision comes in the form of the rebuilt (1987) King Edward Memorial Hospital, which boasts twenty-seven beds, along with dental and pharmacy services, all to our own National Health Service standards. The biggest surprise was the subject of education. Whist the islands' primary schooling remains relatively unchanged, the co-educational Falkland Islands Community School was a revelation. Opened in 1992, it caters for children from 11-16, taking children to GCSE level, as well as being part of the community leisure centre and public library. Similarly to health, the education system is free to tertiary education, where those wishing to continue to A Levels are sponsored to continue their education in the UK. Last, but by no means least, are those who wish to continue onto university, where again their fees are met. Despite being

One of the many minefields that still litter the islands, 11 January 2017. This particular minefield lies on the beach approach to Yorke Bay and Gypsy Cove. The islanders themselves appear ambivalent to them, preferring them to remain in situ, many believing that clearing them could potentially destroy the penguin colonies and seriously damage the tourism industry. However, the UK Government has signed up to a mine clearance program which is slowly removing them.

exposed to the 'bright lights' and trappings of everything that the UK has to offer, there is a welcoming statistic that there is an eighty-five per cent return rate, of those who are schooled in the UK.

After leaving Government House we ventured over towards the airport and see the penguins at Gypsy Cove. On route we stopped off at one of the old coastal defence battery positions that cover the approaches into Stanley, again reinforcing the strategic importance of the Falklands. The later part of our short ride to the Cove took us past one of the many minefields that have still to be cleared. The small red and white minefield markers carry the simple warning: 'DANGER MINES' sandwiching a skull and cross bones. The short walk from the car park along a clearly defined track and pathway took us towards our first penguin encounter. The colony of Magellanic Penguins was, for the majority, down on the beach, but a number were around their nesting burrows on the steep banks leading down to the water. Any notion of wandering down to them is dispelled by the numerous warning signs placed on the edge of the path. The stark warning that the area is 'believed to be clear of mines' clearly suggests that this is not an option! Notwithstanding that, there were numerous burrows close by and most of the penguins were not put off by our proximity, affording us our first photo opportunity.

After three nights in Stanley, it was time for us to move out to our next planned location at San Carlos, but not before swapping 4x4s, staying at Kingsford Valley Farm (KVF), which is owned by Matthew McMullen and Andi Neate. Almost equidistant from Stanley, just off the ring road, the seventy-mile journey takes some two hours, with us choosing to go anticlockwise via the northern route. Shortly after leaving Stanley and just before we reached the Battery's final gun position, we turned right under the shadow of Mount Kent and into what was effectively for us, uncharted territory. As we rounded the base of Mount Kent, we stopped off at the roadside to look through the burnt-out helicopter wreckages of an Argentine Chinook and Puma. During the War, the Argentines sought to disperse their helicopters out of Stanley and into the surrounding area, as a way of not having all their eggs in one basket. The only flaw in their plan was that they didn't account for the SAS, who blew them up once their night-time pattern was established. It's still possible to see the helicopter's main components, namely: engines, gearboxes, main rotor blades and parts of the main frame.

Whilst our journey was done under leaden skies, the extensive views were fantastic. By the time we reached the turning off to San Carlos the skies had broken, which made cresting over the ridge opposite Sussex Mountains and looking down into San Carlos Water, with the sun shining brightly, truly spectacular. The panoramic views from our high vantage point swept around the mountains surrounding the Sound, up to Fanning Head and over to West Falkland. Looking down in front of us lay the tiny red and white farmstead that I knew so well – Head of the Bay House. Panning round and down to our right lay our destination at KVF, with Ajax Bay nestling into the hillside over the water. Arriving at the farm we were met by Matthew and Andi, who showed us to our self-catering accommodation. This was quite a moment for Tony, as after helping to take the surrender following the Battle of Darwin and Goose Green, he was present when the settlement's occupants were let out of their community hall, after being held there in captivity, and Matthew, a three-month-old baby, was also incarcerated at that time.

After quickly settling in, we made our way over to the settlement's small museum, which focuses on the landings and the early phases of the war. The museum sits just above Blue Beach and the exact spot where Tony, Bob and James landed. I asked if it looked familiar, only to be met by a collective: 'dunno, it was pitch black at the time … couldn't see a thing!'. The only thing Bob did recall was him telling of how he almost became one of the first casualties of the land war, as when he was making his way around the shoreline, en route to 2 Para's first locations on Sussex Mountains, that he almost stepped on a large seal, which had hauled out and took offence at being disturbed!

We continued around the very short walk and onto the military cemetery. The first thing you see is the Union Flag, which was flying in the strong breeze, followed by the circular stone surrounding wall which provides much-needed shelter. The wall stands around one meter high and is fittingly crafted to resemble one of the stone sheep corrals located around the islands. The cemetery is situated on a slight slope, which allows for views up and down San Carlos Water, just below. Along with the surrounding mountains it given a sense of inviolable tranquility. Two groups of seven graves, each of two ranks, four in the front and three behind, flank the main memorial on the rear wall. A further single grave lies near the entrance, but is not related to 1982. The large main memorial is carved with part of the inscription reading: '… to the abiding memory of the sailors, soldiers and airmen who gave their lives and who have no known grave but the sea here beside the graves of their comrades …', with their names carved into large stone panels which flank the main memorial.

We walked around in relative silence, pausing at each grave and being struck by the numbers of names on the wall. It felt so peaceful. After a while and moving to leave, I made my way down to the entrance gate and turned to see Tony and Bob were close behind, when I noticed James further back, making his way over to the grave of Chris Dent, 2 Para's A Company Second in Command. I stopped and turned to face the grave site, almost anticipating what James was about to do, who I sensed was unaware of our presence. I stood silently watching, as did James in front of the grave, when both Tony and Bob joined me and realising the solemnity of the occasion stood beside me, all without headdress. James lent over and tidied the grave of loose vegetation, before picking up a half-buried Parachute Regiment cap badge he spotted in the soil, which he cleaned and gently placed at the base of the grave stone.

Standing back up, James reached into his pocket and pulled out a small wooden cross of remembrance, which he also placed at the base. Standing back up again, James then took out a sheet of paper and silently read the passage, before replacing it and stood with his head bowed in a final mark of respect. I was later to find out that James had read the Parachute Regiment's Collect and was unaware that I was able to share in his very private moment. We made our way out of the cemetery leaving James and headed off back towards our accommodation, when I elected to go out onto the adjacent narrow headland that once doubled up as the settlement's airstrip, to reflect on what had just passed. I can't say if it was as a result of witnessing James's touching tribute, or the strong South Atlantic wind blowing directly into my face, but I shed a tear.

The lone walk over the headland allowed me to lose myself in my thoughts and take in my surroundings. The headland itself runs almost halfway across the Sound and on its tip, it feels as if one's right in the middle of the water. From there, there are unobstructed views from the bottom of the Sound at Head of the Bay House, up to Fanning Head, with a clear view over to Ajax Bay and the industrial refrigeration plant that became the field hospital. Walking back, I saw James leave the cemetery and make his way back to the settlement when I called him across. Making our way back we commented on just how peaceful San Carlos Water actually is, which was a far cry from our previous experiences. It's difficult to describe the hustle and bustle of the anchorage, which was continually buzzing with helicopter traffic, interspersed with Argentine air attacks and the ensuing melee. Armed with a small set of binoculars we tried to locate HMS *Antelope*'s marker buoy, marking the spot where she sank and is designated a War Grave, but were thwarted by the choppy seas. We also tried to picture where *Norland* was anchored when we disembarked on D Day and in real terms, just how short our respective journeys were. The one thing that did surprise James was seeing in daylight just how far that first night march up and on to Sussex Mountains actually was.

The next day, 7 January, was a big one for me, as it was my first real tangible experience of the trip and our visit to the first gun position. We had arranged to meet the owners – Ted and Sheila Jones, with the aim of trying to reconstruct the layout of how we were deployed. The farmstead had clearly been extended over the years, however a number of the original buildings and features were still evident. I explained how we came to be based at their farm, as well as describing how we came to utilise the then empty house. The house was fundamentally the same, but it was a strange feeling going inside, now full of the trappings of family life and into their living room that was once our Command Post; as it must have been for them to realise what we had got up to. We were all surprised to learn that Sheila had actually been brought up at Head of the Bay House and that her first childhood memories were of the farm.

After leaving school at fourteen, the family moved and relocated to the

Bluff Cove's sheep sheering shed today. On the far left is James Watson, with Kevin Kilmartin to his right, 10 January 2017.

During our tour inside the sheep sheering shed we came across one of our old command post chairs. As a CPO, it was only right that the author tried it out!

top of the Sound at Port San Carlos, with Ted and Sheila marrying a few years later, setting up home in San Carlos, before moving back to the farm of her childhood. We were equally surprised to learn that Sheila had only visited Stanley on three occasions, once to give birth, which gives some idea just how difficult getting around the Islands was before the road network was in place. Ted, who was originally from San Carlos, was able to point out where he thought we had been sited, based on what he assumed to be our trenches; which, when coupled with my photographs, we were able to accurately confirm the location of three gun platforms.

The trenches themselves were our local defence trenches, which marked the extremity of our footprint, which was greater than Tony, Bob or James realised. As I pointed out, Bill was faced with trying to deploy the guns to a generic template, but had limited options, as the deciding factor was the suitability of the ground. I also found the position of the alternate Command Post and 'my' hole in the ground, over by the now derelict corral. Using the photographs, we worked out the rough location of one of the forward platforms, but it was difficult to be specific due to farm machinery and it being a general storage area. The new large shed and yard complex by the farm's entrance, had by now obscured any trace of the two the platforms.

The author presenting a copy of a painting depicting the Battery's occupation of Head of the Bay House to the current owners, Ted and Shelia Jones, 7 January 2017. The picture was signed by our party and space has been left for other members of the Battery to sign it should they visit. On closer inspection it is really a picture within a picture, as the framing of the photograph is much the same as that of the painting.

At the start of our visit, I presented a framed copy of a painting I, along with Tony and David had commissioned in 1983, to Ted and Sheila, with the intent of having further Battery veterans signing it, should they visit them. After making our farewells, I set about with help from James, to reconstruct more then and now photographs for posterity.

It was between venues and back having lunch at KVF that I chanced upon one of the very few peat heating furnaces, situated in a shed adjacent to the main house. Almost every dwelling, or commercial premise, that we encountered now makes use of a combination of wind and/or solar energy, supplemented by a ubiquitous green poly tank of domestic heating oil/kerosine, so finding such furnace was relatively uncommon. It was when Matthew stoked the embers to rejuvenate the fire that the unmistakable smell of burning peat filled the air, causing the hairs on the back of my neck to stand on end. It flashed me straight back to memories of the Command Post and that little pot belly stove we resurrected.

After lunch, we made our way back around the sound and Head of the Bay House and on to Ajax Bay. Parking up at the lone farmhouse directly opposite San Carlos, we walked approximately1,500 meters to the industrial complex at Ajax Bay. Built in the 1950s, the refrigeration plant was conceived to process and freeze mutton for export, making use of the natural deep water harbour it sits beside. It soon became commercially unviable and was effectively just closed up and left unattended, before it was pressed into service as a field hospital, known as 'The Red and Green Life Machine'.

The deep water harbour provided the ideal location for the Commandos' logistical set up, which, apart from a sign, there's little else to show of it, with access denied to the buildings themselves. Poignantly, Ajax Bay also marks the location where Tony helped lay to rest those killed at Darwin and Goose Green, in a temporary mass grave. After the *Galahad* was hit at Bluff Cove, the bodies of those Welsh Guardsmen were also interred here, providing the temporary resting place for forty-four souls. A large white cairn stands beside a dotted line of while stones marking the edge of the grave site. Offering a complete contrast to proceedings, is a colony of Gentoo Penguins, whose nest sites lie adjacent to the derelict buildings and proved to be a welcome distraction. Seemingly oblivious of us humans, they continued to potter around and allowed us a close-up photo opportunity.

With it being just off the route back to San Carlos, we made use of the hour or so left in the day to have a quick look upon Sussex Mountains and at 2 Para's positions. What was hoping to be a relatively straightforward task, proved to be anything but. The top of the ridge has clearly been the subject of multi-occupancy and with fading memories and changes in the land, such as tracks and radio masts, what is there now wasn't there then. From my point of view, what I did see was the incredible view out to Darwin

This is the view from the rearward slope of 2 Paras' position on top of Sussex Mountain, looking north up 'Bomb Alley' to San Carlos Water, on 8 January 2017. On the near shoreline, the small cluster of white houses (dots) is Head of the Bay House. The cluster on the right shoreline, at the base of the thin promontory, is San Carlos settlement. Opposite, and in the last bay on the left, is Ajax Bay. At the end of the sound, by the hill of Fanning Head, lies the entrance.

and Goose Green, as well as to the south and Lafonia. Lafonia is sparsely populated, with its low-lying peninsular accounting for almost half the land mass of East Falkland. Equally, my high vantage point gave outstanding views back down into San Carlos Water, with the predominantly white red or green buildings easily standing out around the water's edge. With the air so clear it was a wonderful sight, the natural beauty of the islands in all their glory shone in the afternoon sun.

After a truly peaceful stay at KVF, we made our farewells and headed back up onto Sussex Mountains, having had an evening to work out where the Battery's observation parties had been located. Armed with this new information we quickly found Tony and Bob's observation positions, helped by the small dry stone walls that were built to conceal their presence. Concurrently, James had moved some distance along the slope, as the two forward companies would have been tactically separated, to find where he was sited. James returned to the vehicle with a satisfied smile, suggesting a degree of success. Whilst James couldn't specifically find his position, he did find pressed into the peat, an old plastic lighter with the words 'North Sea Ferries' on the side, proving that he'd found a 2 Para location and not a subsequent occupation.

Making our way down off the ridge line and its stunning views, we followed the line of the old 1982 track towards Camilla Creek House to meet the current owners – Albert and Sally Mcleod and their son John, who was fourteen at the time. In 1982, The McLeods had been living in Goose Green and like all the other residents were held in the community hall. Sally told of those very difficult days and of the three 'escape hatches' the occupants had cut into the hall's floor; allowing for them to seek refuge under the floor whenever they felt the need, which can still be seen in the planking of the wooden floor. Camilla Creek House was important for being the stop-off point, where the battalion orders were given, in readiness for the ensuing battle and Tony presented them with a photograph of the Orders Group. We continued down the track, with James' old battle map confirming our route, before we arrived at Darwin and began the first part of walking the battlefield. The 'map view' belies the difficulties faced on the ground. A central spine of higher ground effectively split 2 Para's A Company and James on the left and B Company with Bob on the right; with B Company fighting its way through Boca House and beyond. It wasn't before long that A Company's advance came under intense Argentine fire and the Battalion attack was stalling; when it was at this time that the Commanding Officer – H. Jones – sought to break that deadlock and charged off up a gully, followed closely behind by Tony. The battle itself is well documented and is not the subject of this book, save to say that a memorial cross can be found at the spot where 'H' fell, mortally wounded.

It was both truly staggering and humbling to listen to the three of them recount their stories and how the battle played out for them. Just as at Wireless Ridge, every question I asked was candidly answered and reinforced the small margins that they fought through. It was an emotional time, as the ground marked the spot where friends had fallen and each were given space to take it all in.

We continued up to the area known as the Gorse Line, which is basically on old dilapidated, overgrown dry stone wall and marks the boundary between the settlements, which marks the end of 2 Para's advance on day one of the battle. As events unfolded, it also marked the end of the fighting, when a Harrier was called in and bombed the outskirts of Goose Green, which completely broke the Argentines' fighting spirit.

After overnighting in Goose Green and before we left, Tony took us through the story of the Argentine surrender, which is a story in itself, suffice it to say that it is very impressive. We moved out of Goose Green and up to the 2 Para memorial that stands overlooking both communities, before continuing on to the Argentine War Cemetery around and on the other shore. The weather was dire, low misty cloud shrouded everything and the rain on the strong breeze dropped the temperature considerably, but we all felt it our duty to visit and pay our respects. At the islanders request, the Argentine Cemetery is not located on the Darwin and Goose Green isthmus, but on the opposite shore, the sighting of which was to ensure that the graves were out of direct view. What can be seen from the settlements is the top of the large white cross, which is in the centre of the main memorial wall. The cemetery is fenced off and open to the elements, with rows of white crosses marking each of the 237 graves, with a total of 412 commemorated within. A weathered granite memorial stone simply gives just a name, or the inscription: 'Soldado Argentino solo condocido por Dios' – 'Argentine Soldier known only by God'.

Our route took us on to Fitzroy, where 2 Para regrouped after the battle, in search of the memorials to both *Galahad* and *Tristram*. Seeking a helping hand, we parked up by the main shearing shed and chanced upon a local. Against the odds, we were to discover that the local we bumped into was George Butler, now eighty-four, who was working and staying at Bluff Cove when we first arrived there in 1982 and we couldn't tell who was more surprised! The memorials were only a few hundred meters around the shore line and we made our way around. The small almost circular shaped cove where the lifeboats came in is guarded by two promontories, approximately 100 metres apart, each with a memorial to those killed, looking out to sea.

Looking out from the land, the Welsh Guards War Memorial stands on the left, with the Merchant Navy's memorial to those killed on both ships to the right. I told of how the air raid developed and how it flew over our position at Bluff Cove and of our collective effort to halt it. I also impressed upon them of the fact that David Gibbins and John McQueenie were present and helped many of the injured ashore, before returning to the position very subdued. What we did clear up when we visited Fitzroy's small museum, was the *Galahad* Bluff Cove/Fitzroy misnomer. The reality was that the ships were attacked just outside Fitzroy's harbour, which as the crow flies, is not too far from Bluff Cove, with the inaccuracy perpetuated by Brian Hanrahan, a war reporter embedded with the Task Force who misidentified the location and it was never corrected.

The final short leg of our day's journey took us to Bluff Cove for our two-night stop over with the Kilmartins. After quickly settling in and eager to use the weather window, we jumped into Kevin's Land Rover and he drove us up onto the ridge line to the south where we parked, before descending down the other side and onto our second gun position at Fitz Cove. Just before we made our way down the slope, I pointed out that we were in the area that was initially designated as our intended location, as well as emphasising the folly of deploying us on such an exposed position and in full view of the enemy.

At the time of our deployment to Bluff Cove, the main defensive ring of mountains on the approach to Stanley was still very much in Argentine hands. Both Bob and James were quick to comment that the area was more suited as an observation point than a gun position. All three were equally surprised to learn that we had manhandled the first gun to be flown in down into the cove. Moving down into the slope, it was as if nothing had changed and it was exactly as I remembered it. Unlike at Head of the Bay House, I had the gun displacements, making swift work of identifying where each of our six guns were sited. The exact position of each being confirmed by the small amount of artillery 'waste' still laying on the surface. The majority of these confirmatory finds were related to the hard black plastic cartridge tube packing material, the shell's metal horseshoe fuse holders, as well as small cone proximity fuse covers. We were also able to pick out on the drier ground the local defence trenches.

The one find that surprised us all was the discovery of the southern Blowpipe firing trench, still sporting two empty missile tubes, almost certainly fired at the Argentine Skyhawks prior the air attack on *Galahad* and *Tristram*. There was no evidence of where the Command Post was sited, nor my little peat shelter; however I was able to describe the layout of the position and recounted the tale of how we came close to sinking the Scots Guards in their landing craft! Being so close to the main settlement, the military did not use the area surrounding at Fitz Cove for training, hence the site had almost certainly remained untouched since we left it. Kevin pointed out that he couldn't remember the last time that he ventured over the ridge into the cove, as he had no specific need to, along with the fact that he only thought we had three guns deployed here. Rather than travel back in the Land Rover, James and I elected to walk back along the ridge, in order to identify the area of James's observation position, as well as where we first disembarked from the Chinook.

We had a much-needed break from being battlefield detectives on 10 January, with Kevin taking us on our own private tour to see his penguins at Bluff Cove Lagoon. The tour is a major attraction for visiting cruise ships and its proximity to Stanley allows for a short journey, which can't be said for others. Also located at the site is the Sea Cabbage Cafe, which serves quintessential English tea and cakes, as well as a gift shop and small museum, completing the tourist experience. The penguin colony is well-used to seeing visitors and were probably thankful that we were small in

Our party at the Kilmartins' private penguin colony at Bluff Cove Lagoon. Left to right are Tony Rice, Bob Ash, James Watson and the author, 10 January 2017. (Courtesy of Tony Rice)

number. Whilst there were some small penguin chicks present, there were still adult males incubating eggs on their feet, under a belly flap, to keep them safe and calm; nevertheless, they all duly obliged for the mandatory photoshoot.

Bluff Cove Lagoon is a truly idyllic setting and leaving the others I ventured out onto the windswept and un-spoilt sandy beach. Apart from the relatively small footprint of the cafe tucked into the shoreline, there is no other evidence of human activity and I found the peace and solitude up-lifting. After rejoining the group, we made our way back to Bluff Cove, where Kevin continued our tour of the settlement, including the shearing shed. Surprisingly, sat in the middle of the floor inside the shed, was what looked like one of our old Command Post chairs, which I duly tried out for size. Apart from the living room at Head of the Bay House, it was the only real tangible connection with the Command Post and it felt reassuringly familiar sitting back in it. We were also to come across a number of our old artillery ammunition boxes, now being recycled to store tools and other small items.

For my final night at Bluff Cove, I elected to spend it in the garage, just as I'd done thirty-five years ago. The big difference now was that it had been turned into a workshop and storage facility for the gift shop, as well as being fully weather-proofed and centrally heated. By the standards of yesteryear, it was comparative luxury.

The following morning, after making our farewells and thanking both Kevin and Hattie for hosting us, we made our way back to Stanley and the last gun position at Wether Ground. From the settlement the location is easily identified some six kilometres away, by the scar in the landscape where the road's short incline comes down off the ridge. From my photographs, we could pick out where the position was, but unfortunately the much-widened road, coupled with the wide drainage ditches, meant that part of the position had been lost to development. We were able to identify one gun platform, with another as a strong contender, but the general lack of physical evidence, as found at Fitz Cove, made for a frustrating time. Considering just how much ammunition we had fired, it was surprising to see such little evidence on the ground, but the finds we did come across were very similar to those previously discovered. It was disappointing to find that the area by the small stream where the Command Post was sited on the roadside, has now been dug out to become a large culvert and, like other areas, has been lost. Given more time to explore and walk the ground, we may have discovered more further down the slope, but that was not to be.

Moving back into Stanley, we made our way to our last accommodation stop and two nights at Bennet House B&B, which proved on arrival to be a surreal experience. I had taken a number of photographs with me on the trip, including one of the house thirty-five years ago, which was of an Argentine officer posing outside, taken by a colleague. As was par for the course, James and I set about recreating the scene. After settling in, we each had something to do and I set off into Stanley, with the sole intention of visiting one of the many souvenir shops and perhaps do a bit of classic sightseeing on the way.

As I passed the iconic whalebone arches of Stanley Cathedral, I stopped and looked over and felt an urge to go inside. We'd been in there to look around when we first arrived, but this was different. I walked in and sat down, alone and in total silence and my mind took be back to the brief service we had on the *Norland*, on the eve of the landings, when the Padre, David Cooper, invited us to make our peace. It was now that I felt the need to say thank you for looking after me and I did just that. I sat there for a further short period before getting up and quietly going on my way. Looking back now, I can't explain why I felt the way I did, save that it felt the right thing to do.

For our last full day, we split along party lines, with Tony, Bob and James revisiting Wireless Ridge, whilst I set about recapturing those outstanding then and now photographs. Along with my own photographs, there were a number of ones taken from the set of that Argentine officer still to be completed. My biggest challenge was that Stanley has almost tripled in size and that the new building developments were in the main, going up from where those pictures were taken. Having said that, I was able to use the landscape's hard evidence and the aspects within the photographs to get most done. Finally satisfied with what I had captured for my photographic challenge, I wandered along the seafront and towards the souvenir shops, to pick up the few gifts left to procure. Mission accomplished, I ventured down to the quayside, purchased a hot chocolate and sat watching the hive

One of the smaller cruise ships is seen here inside the inner harbour. Those with a passenger capacity of under 500 are allowed in. On the quayside, sits a static Red Routemaster London bus, which is one of the last places you would expect to see one, 12 January 2017.

of activity that was getting passengers to and from their cruise ship, with a feeling of true contentment.

The journey home was as uneventful as the one down and as we parted company at Brize Norton, we left each having had an amazing time. There was plenty of laughter and yes there were a few hard moments, but on balance we came away with having had a thoroughly positive experience.

Despite their ruggedness, the Falklands are truly beautiful. My memories of the events of thirty-five years ago are more greyscale than colourful, as then we made every effort to blend into the landscape and not be seen;. However, now the natural hues appear more vibrant and welcoming, leaving memories that will last a lifetime. The islanders themselves are naturally self-reliant and form a rightly proud community who look out for each other. As I reflect back on all that we went through, and the sacrifices made, I asked myself two simple questions: was it worth it and would I do it again? The simple answer to both is – yes.

Bibliography

Anderson, D., *The Falklands War 1982* (Osprey Publishing Ltd., 2002).

Anonymous, *Introduction to Blowpipe*, (Royal School of Artillery, 1983).

Bolia, R. S., *The Bluff Cove Disaster – Small Wars Journal*, 2004. www.smallwarsjournal.com/documents/bolia1.pdf (Accessed 12 April 2015).

Brown, D., *The Royal Navy and the Falklands War* (Arrow Books Ltd., 1989).

Fox, R., *Eyewitness Falklands* (Methuen, London, 1982).

Goldstein, R.J., *The New York Times, Twentieth Century in Review - Political Censorship* (Fitzroy Dearborn Publishers, 2001).

Howe, J., 'Men from Corunna who put the Argies to flight', *Sunderland Echo*, 19 June 2002.

Seear, M., *With the Gurkhas in the Falklands – A War Journal* (BlueBeach Media, 2006).

4th Field Regiment Royal Artillery, After Action Report October 1982, *4 Field Regiment In The Falkland Islands April - July 1982*.

Map Talk: Falklands War/Archive 10.

Index